LAMENTATIONS
and EZEKIEL
for
EVERYONE

OLD TESTAMENT FOR EVERYONE
John Goldingay

LAMENTATIONS *and* EZEKIEL

for

EVERYONE

JOHN
GOLDINGAY

WESTMINSTER
JOHN KNOX PRESS
LOUISVILLE • KENTUCKY

First published in the United States of America in 2016
by Westminster John Knox Press
100 Witherspoon Street
Louisville, Kentucky

First published in Great Britain in 2016
by Society for Promoting Christian Knowledge
36 Causton Street
London SW1P 4ST

16 17 18 19 20 21 22 23 24 25—10 9 8 7 6 5 4 3 2 1

Cover design by Lisa Buckley
Cover photo: Sunset in the clear waters of Swat © Shahid Ali Khan /
www.shutterstock.com

Library of Congress Cataloging-in-Publication Data

Names: Goldingay, John, author.
Title: Lamentations and Ezekiel for everyone / John Goldingay.
Description: Louisville, KY : Westminster John Knox Press, 2016. | Series:
  Old Testament for everyone | Description based on print version record and
  CIP data provided by publisher; resource not viewed.
Identifiers: LCCN 2016019887 (print) | LCCN 2016018918 (ebook) | ISBN
  9781611647761 (ebk.) | ISBN 9780664233891 (pbk. : alk. paper)
Subjects: LCSH: Bible. Lamentations--Commentaries. | Bible.
  Ezekiel--Commentaries.
Classification: LCC BS1535.53 (print) | LCC BS1535.53 .G65 2016 (ebook) | DDC
  224/.3077--dc23
LC record available at https://lccn.loc.gov/2016019887

Most Westminster John Knox Press books are available at special quantity
discounts when purchased in bulk by corporations, organizations, and special-
interest groups. For more information, please e-mail SpecialSales@wjkbooks.com.

CONTENTS

ACKNOWLEDGMENTS

The translation at the beginning of each chapter (and in other biblical quotations) is my own. I have stuck closer to the Hebrew than modern translations often do when they are designed for reading in church so that you can see more precisely what the text says. Thus although I prefer to use gender-inclusive language, I have let the translation stay gendered if inclusivizing it would obscure whether the text was using singular or plural—in other words, the translation often uses "he" where in my own writing I would say "they" or "he or she." Sometimes I have added words to make the meaning clear, and I have put these words in square brackets. When the text uses the name of God, Yahweh, I have kept the name instead of replacing it with "the Lord" as translations usually do. And I've transliterated some other names in a way that's different from the way translations traditionally do, partly to make it easier to work out the pronunciation. At the end of the book is a glossary of some terms that recur in the text, such as geographical, historical, and theological expressions. In each chapter (though not in the introduction) these terms are highlighted in **bold** the first time they occur.

The stories that follow the translation often concern my friends or my family. While none are made up, they are sometimes heavily disguised in order to be fair to people. Sometimes I have disguised them so well that when I came to read the stories again, I was not sure at first whom I was describing. My first wife, Ann, appears in a number of them. A few months after I started writing The Old Testament for Everyone, she died after negotiating with multiple sclerosis for forty-three

ACKNOWLEDGMENTS

years. Our shared dealings with her illness and disability over these years contribute significantly to what I write in ways that you may be able to see but also in ways that are less obvious.

Then, a year or so before I started writing this particular volume, I fell in love with and married Kathleen Scott, and I'm grateful for my new life with her and for her insightful comments on the manuscript, which have been so careful and illuminating that she practically deserves to be credited as coauthor.

I'm also grateful to Matt Sousa for reading through the manuscript and pointing out things I needed to correct or clarify and to Tom Bennett for checking the proofs.

INTRODUCTION

As far as Jesus and the New Testament writers were concerned, the Jewish Scriptures that Christians call the "Old Testament" *were* the Scriptures. In saying that, I cut corners a bit, as the New Testament never gives us a list of these Scriptures, but the body of writings that the Jewish people accept is as near as we can get to identifying the collection that Jesus and the New Testament writers would have worked with. The church also came to accept some extra books such as Maccabees and Ecclesiasticus that were traditionally called the "Apocrypha," the books that were "hidden away"—a name that came to imply "spurious." They're now often known as the "Deuterocanonical Writings," which is more cumbersome but less pejorative; it simply indicates that these books have less authority than the Torah, the Prophets, and the Writings. The precise list of them varies among different churches. For the purposes of this series that seeks to expound the "Old Testament for Everyone," by the "Old Testament" we mean the Scriptures accepted by the Jewish community, though in the Jewish Bible they come in a different order, as the Torah, the Prophets, and the Writings.

They were not "old" in the sense of antiquated or out of date; I sometimes like to refer to them as the First Testament rather than the Old Testament to make that point. For Jesus and the New Testament writers, they were a living resource for understanding God, God's ways in the world, and God's ways with us. They were "useful for teaching, for reproof, for correction, and for training in righteousness, so that the person who belongs to God can be proficient, equipped for

1

every good work" (2 Timothy 3:16–17). They were for everyone, in fact. So it's strange that Christians don't read them very much. My aim in these volumes is to help you do so.

My hesitation is that you may read me instead of the Scriptures. Don't fall into that trap. I like the fact that this series includes much of the biblical text. Don't skip over it. In the end, that's the bit that matters.

An Outline of the Old Testament

The Christian Old Testament puts the books in the Jewish Bible in a distinctive order:

> Genesis to Kings: A story that runs from the creation of the world to the exile of Judahites to Babylon
> Chronicles to Esther: A second version of this story, continuing it into the years after the exile
> Job, Psalms, Proverbs, Ecclesiastes, Song of Songs: Some poetic books
> Isaiah to Malachi: The teaching of some prophets

Here is an outline of the history that lies at the books' background. (I give no dates for events in Genesis, which involves too much guesswork.)

1200s	Moses, the exodus, Joshua
1100s	The "judges"
1000s	King Saul, King David
900s	King Solomon; the nation splits into two, Ephraim and Judah
800s	Elijah, Elisha
700s	Amos, Hosea, Isaiah, Micah; Assyria the superpower; the fall of Ephraim
600s	Jeremiah, King Josiah; Babylon the superpower
500s	Ezekiel; the fall of Judah; Persia the superpower; Judahites free to return home

400s	Ezra, Nehemiah
300s	Greece the superpower
200s	Syria and Egypt the regional powers pulling Judah one way or the other
100s	Judah's rebellion against Syrian power and gain of independence
000s	Rome the superpower

Lamentations

Lamentations is a series of five psalm-like prayers that follow Jeremiah in the English Bible and grieve over the destruction of Jerusalem. As far as we know, they have nothing directly to do with Jeremiah, but he'd agree with their understanding of what has happened, particularly their understanding of the city's destruction. It's an act brought about by human enemies, but it comes as an act of divine punishment for the city's faithlessness over the years. In the Hebrew Bible the poems come elsewhere, not after Jeremiah. They're associated with four other short books (Song of Songs, Ruth, Ecclesiastes, and Esther) because each of the five was used at one festival every year. Lamentations belongs to Tisha B'av, an occasion in July or August when the Jewish community recalls the occasions when Jerusalem was destroyed, in 587 and in AD 70. This usage fits well the nature of the five prayers, which grieve over the first of those two destructions, express sorrow at the sins that led to it, and plead with God for mercy.

Ezekiel

Ezekiel would also agree with Lamentations' understanding of what has happened to Jerusalem. He was a younger contemporary of Jeremiah, but he'd been taken off to Babylon with the people who were transported there in 597, a decade before the city's final fall. For the last years before that event he was thus seeking to prepare Judahites in Babylon for it, at the same time as Jeremiah was seeking to prepare people in Jerusalem.

His book is neatly organized, as follows:

Chapters 1–3:	The vision in which Yahweh commissions him
Chapters 4–24:	His messages to the exiles before Jerusalem's final fall, dominated by warnings
Chapters 25–32:	His messages about other nations
Chapters 33–48:	His messages to the exiles after the city's fall, dominated by encouragements

Like Jeremiah, Ezekiel came from a priestly family, but he never functioned as a priest because he'd been transported from Jerusalem before he reached the right age. You could say that this event turned him into a priestly pastor or a priestly prophet. He has a priest's way of thinking, as emerges in the way he describes the people's waywardness, God's disciplining them, and the way God will restore them.

The book begins with an appearance by Yahweh in Babylon, which leads into Yahweh's commissioning Ezekiel to preach to his people there, though the young man is warned that they won't listen. All through reading his book, we have to bear in mind that he isn't in Jerusalem. He sees much of what is happening in the city, but he sees it by visionary means. He talks much about the city and about the clan area of Judah around it, but he does so for the sake of people from Jerusalem who have been taken into exile. He needs to get them to see that the continuing waywardness of the people left behind in the city makes its judgment and fall inevitable. Like Jeremiah in his ministry in Jerusalem itself, he has to get them to see that the fall of Jerusalem and their exile isn't the end of judgment, soon to be followed by restoration. They're only its beginning. He portrays the city's waywardness in a priest's terms. While he speaks of the faithlessness of its people to one another, he's more concerned about the faithlessness of their religious life. The form that judgment will take is thus Yahweh's departure from the temple.

Halfway through the book, at the end of chapter 24, Yahweh tells him that a fugitive from the city that has now fallen is about to arrive in Babylon to bring news of this event. This announcement prepares the way for good news, which occupies the second half of the book. One function of the messages about other nations is that they constitute a transition to the good news, because bad news for Judah's adversaries is good news for Judah itself, though in themselves they also function as warnings to Judah not to think that alliances with other nations might be their salvation.

News of the city's fall comes in chapter 33. It doesn't mean that Ezekiel's work as a prophet is over. Indeed, his mouth is opened in a new way. He now shares a series of positive visions of what Yahweh intends. This last section of the book is dominated by an account of his being taken on a visionary tour through a remodeled temple, though it lies at the center of a remodeled country. The fact that his vision of a new future takes this form is a further reflection of the fact that Yahweh chose a priest to be his prophet in Babylon, and by means of him Yahweh pictures the future in priestly terms. Ezekiel's vision was especially influential on John of Patmos in providing the imagery that appears in his visions in the book of Revelation.

LAMENTATIONS 1:1–22

The City Pours Out Its Heart

1   Oh! The city sits alone,
    that was great with a people.
  She became like a widow,
    she who was great among the nations.
  She who was a queen among states
    became a slave.

2   She weeps and weeps in the night;
    there are tears on her cheeks.
  She has no comforter
    from all her allies.
  All her friends broke faith with her;
    they became her enemies.

3   Judah went into exile after affliction
    and hard servitude.
  Even when she dwelt among the nations
    she didn't find a resting place.
  All her pursuers caught her
    amid her distresses.

4   The roads to Zion mourn,
    because of the lack of people coming for the
      set occasions.
  All her gateways are deserted,
    her priests are groaning.
  Her girls are suffering,
    and her—it's hard for her.

5   Her foes became her head,
    her enemies are at ease.
  Because Yahweh made her suffer
    on account of the great number of her rebellions.
  Her infants went into exile
    in front of the foe.

6   All her glory went away
    from Ms. Zion.
  Her officials became like deer
    that had found no pasture.

They walked without strength
  before the pursuer.
7 Jerusalem's been mindful,
    in her days of affliction and wandering,
  of all the delightful things she had,
    which there were from days before.
  When her people fell into the hand of the foe
    and there was no one helping her,
  as the foes saw her,
    they laughed at her coming to an end.
8 Jerusalem offended and offended;
    therefore she became taboo.
  All the people who honored her treated her as
      wretched
    because they saw her exposure.
  Yes, she groaned
    and turned away.
9 Though her uncleanness was in her skirts,
    she hadn't been mindful of her future.
  She went down astonishingly;
    she had no comforter.
  "Yahweh, look at my affliction,
    because the enemy's triumphed."
10 The foe laid his hand
    on all things in which she delighted.
  Because she saw the nations
    come to her sanctuary,
  who you commanded should not come
    into your congregation.
11 All her people are groaning,
    searching for bread.
  They gave the things in which they delighted
    for food to bring life back.
  "Look, Yahweh, pay heed,
    because I've become wretched."
12 It's nothing to you, all you who pass along the
      road;
    pay heed and look.

Is there any pain like my pain,
     which was dealt out to me,
when Yahweh made me suffer
     on the day of his angry blazing?
13 From above he sent fire,
     into my bones, and it overwhelmed them.
He spread a net for my feet;
     he turned me back.
He made me a desolation,
     faint all day long.
14 The yoke of my rebellions was bound on,
     they interweave by his hand.
They came up onto my neck;
     he made my strength fail.
The Lord gave me into the hands
     of people before whom I cannot stand.
15 The Lord in my midst threw aside
     all my strong men.
He proclaimed a date against me
     for breaking my young men.
The Lord trod in a press
     young Ms. Judah.
16 On account of these things I'm weeping;
     both my eyes are flowing with water.
Because a comforter is far from me,
     someone bringing my life back.
My children became desolate,
     because an enemy's prevailed.
17 Zion spread out her hands;
     there's no one comforting her.
Yahweh commanded against Jacob
     his foes all around him.
Jerusalem became
     something taboo among them.
18 Yahweh is in the right,
     because I rebelled against his word.
Do listen, all you peoples,
     see my pain.

8

My girls and my young men
went into captivity.
19 I called to my friends;
those people deceived me.
My priests and my elders
perished in the city,
when they searched for food for themselves
so that they might bring their life back.
20 See, Yahweh, how I had distress,
my insides churned.
My heart turned over within me,
because I rebelled and rebelled.
Outside, the sword destroyed;
at home, simply death.
21 Though people heard when I was groaning,
I had no comforter.
When all my enemies heard
of the evil that's happened to me, they rejoiced.
Because you yourself acted,
you brought about the day you proclaimed—they
should be like me.
22 All their evil should come before you—
deal with them,
as you dealt with me
on account of all my rebellions.
Because my groans are many,
and my heart is faint.

We've just returned from driving around cities in Turkey such as Ephesus and Laodicea to whose churches John writes in Revelation, some of which Paul also visited. Seeing them generated a twofold shock. First there's their size. I'd thought of them as something more like villages or small towns, but they're monumentally vast. They're the New York, Los Angeles, London, and Glasgow of their day. The second shock is then the fact that they're simply ruins. Ephesus, for instance, was destroyed by the Goths in AD 262 and again by an earthquake in 614. What was it like to go through that experience? How did people pray in light of the event? How do you pray in light of an earthquake or a tsunami or an event such as 9/11?

Lamentations tells us the answer from Jerusalem's angle, in light of the city's devastation by the **Babylonians** in 587. It begins with a bare exclamation, "Oh!"—a cry of pain. This word gives the book its title in Hebrew (the title "Lamentations" comes from the old Greek translation). It's also the first word in chapter 2 and in chapter 4. One reason for opening the book with this Hebrew word is that it begins with the first letter of the alphabet, *aleph*. The chapter has twenty-two verses; that number recurs in each chapter of the book. It's the number of letters in the Hebrew alphabet. In the first four chapters the verses begin with the successive letters of the alphabet. The poems give expression to grief and pain from A to Z. Linking with this fact, the word *all* comes sixteen times: all **Judah**'s allies fail it, all the people's pursuers catch them, all its enemies gloat, all passersby ignore it, though all peoples are urged to listen to its cry of pain, all **Zion**'s strong men are thrown aside, all its people are gone and all its gateways are deserted, all its glory, all its honor, and all its treasures are gone, all day Zion faints, all its rebellions have met with their punishment, and all their enemies' **evil** should come before **Yahweh** to the same end.

One should allow for hyperbole; the Old Testament makes clear that the Babylonians didn't transport the city's entire population (still less Judah as a whole), and many people who fled from the city and the country during the Babylonian invasion doubtless crept back when the Babylonian army was gone. Yet the contrast between past and present is horrifying. Jerusalem was not a great city like Ephesus, or Babylon. But with its temple and its palaces, for its people it was a great city. Further, it was a great city because of the great God worshiped there. The poem imagines it as a person

10

bewailing the loss of its people, a mother bewailing the loss of her children. The roads to Jerusalem mourn because they're not full of pilgrims coming to its festivals. Conversely, the sanctuary's been invaded by pagan feet (it would be no problem if these foreigners came to worship Yahweh, but they came to pillage).

Why did it happen? Whereas the Psalms protest about invasions that Jerusalem's done nothing to deserve, Lamentations knows that this time the city cannot claim innocence. It's been rebellious. It's offended against Yahweh's expectations, fallen short of them, missed the target because it hasn't even aimed at it. It resembles someone unclean because of an involvement in something carrying a **taboo** (for instance, contact with blood or death or false worship).

The reference to friends and allies offers a further hint about the nature of its waywardness. Several prophets berate Judah for assuming that alliances with nations such as Egypt or **Philistia** are the proper safeguard for its destiny, that these people would support Judah in a crisis. The prophets' assessment has been vindicated. The city is like a woman whose nakedness has been exposed.

The poem shows that knowing you got what you deserved doesn't mean you can't pray for mercy. The city does so. The poem describes Zion as spreading out her hands in the posture of appeal but finding no comforter. In what direction is she spreading them—toward Yahweh, or toward those other helpers in whom she has trusted?

The people who pray this poem don't know, but for later readers like us, its fivefold reference to there being no comforter offers paradoxical reassurance. During the decades when the poem is being used in Jerusalem, Yahweh will give the order, "Comfort, comfort my people" (Isaiah 40). "There's no comforter" is the truth about the situation at the moment, but things won't be that way forever.

LAMENTATIONS 2:1–22

I Don't Get Angry

¹ Oh! With his anger the Lord clouds over
Ms. Zion.
He threw down Israel's splendor
from the heavens to the earth.
He was not mindful of his footstool
on his day of anger.
² The Lord swallowed up all Jacob's pastures
and didn't spare.
In his fury he tore down
Ms. Judah's strongholds.
He brought to the earth, made ordinary,
the kingdom and its officials.
³ He cut off every horn of Israel
in his angry blazing.
He turned back his right hand
from before the enemy.
He burned against Jacob like a flaming fire
consuming all around.
⁴ He directed his bow like an enemy,
took his stand with his right hand like a foe.
He slew everyone
who delighted the eye.
In Ms. Zion's tent
he poured out his rage like fire.
⁵ The Lord became like an enemy;
he swallowed up Israel.
He swallowed up all her citadels,
destroyed her strongholds.
He made great in Ms. Judah
the mourning and moaning.
⁶ He violated his shelter like a garden,
destroyed his set place.
Yahweh caused set occasion and Sabbath
to be disregarded in Zion.

In his angry wrath he spurned
    king and priest.
7 The Lord rejected his altar,
    abandoned his sanctuary.
He gave over the walls of its citadels
    into the enemy's hand.
They gave voice in Yahweh's house
    as on the day of a set occasion.
8 Yahweh decided to destroy
    Ms. Zion's wall.
He stretched out a line,
    he didn't turn back his hand from swallowing up.
He made rampart and wall mourn;
    together they languished.
9 Her gateways sank into the earth;
    he destroyed, wiped out her bars.
Her king and her officials are among the nations;
    there's no teaching.
Her prophets, too,
    found no vision from Yahweh.
10 Ms. Zion's elders
    sit on the earth, they're silent.
They've taken up dirt onto their head,
    they've wound on sackcloth.
Jerusalem's girls
    have lowered their head to the earth.
11 My eyes are spent with tears,
    my insides churn.
My heart pours out to the earth
    on account of the shattering of my dear people,
while infant and suckling faint
    in the town's squares.
12 To their mothers they say,
    "Where are grain and wine?"
as they faint like someone wounded
    in the city's squares,
as their life pours out
    at their mothers' breast.

13 What can I testify, what can I liken to you,
    Ms. Jerusalem?
What can I compare with you so I may comfort you,
    fair Ms. Zion?
Because your shattering is as vast as the sea;
    who can heal you?
14 Your prophets saw for you
    things that were empty and arid.
They didn't reveal your waywardness
    so as to restore your fortunes.
They saw for you
    empty prophecies and seductions.
15 All the people who pass your way
    have clapped their hands at you.
They've whistled and shaken their head
    at Ms. Jerusalem:
"Is this the city of which they used to say,
    'Complete in beauty, a joy of the entire earth'?"
16 Against you all your enemies
    have opened their mouth wide.
They've whistled and ground their teeth,
    they've said, "We have swallowed her up.
Indeed this is the day that we've looked forward to;
    we've attained it, we've seen it."
17 Yahweh did what he schemed,
    he accomplished his word,
that which he'd commanded long ago;
    he tore down and didn't spare.
He let the enemy rejoice over you,
    exalted the horn of your foes.
18 Their soul cried out to the Lord;
    Ms. Zion's wall,
let tears go down like a torrent,
    day and night.
Don't give yourself respite;
    your dear eye must not stop.
19 Get up, resound at night,
    at the start of the watches.

Pour out your soul like water
    in the presence of the Lord.
Lift up your hands to him
    for the life of your infants,
who faint with hunger
    at every street corner.

20 Look, Yahweh, pay attention,
    to the one with whom you've dealt hard like this.
Do women eat their fruit,
    the babies they dandle?
Are priest and prophet slain
    in the Lord's sanctuary?

21 Young person and old
    lay on the ground in the streets.
My girls and my young men
    fell by the sword.
You slew them on your day of anger,
    you slaughtered them and didn't spare.

22 You summon (as on the day of a set occasion)
    terrors for me from all around.
On Yahweh's day of anger
    there was no one surviving or escaping.
Those whom I dandled and raised—
    my enemy finished them off.

A friend of mine told us a story about a church teaching event where people were invited to "draw their anger." He described his wife's mother, "a grand old Southern lady," grasping her pencil firmly and declaring, "I don't get angry." He was not implying she was always all sweetness and light. He reminded me of an occasion when I'd taken part in a teaching event on the Psalms for some pastors. I hadn't talked about the anger in the Psalms, and one of the pastors did so, with the evident assumption that it was a problem. I remember reflecting on how he seemed to be someone bound in on himself emotionally and I wondered whether his anger was turned in on himself. I don't get angry very often, but when I allow myself to do so, it's a bit scary for me, whatever effect it has on other people.

Lamentations is both scared and not scared of God's anger. It's an especially prominent theme in this chapter, which uses a range of words to describe these strong feelings of God's. The Hebrew word for "anger" is also the word for one's nose, which suggests it may link with the idea of snorting with anger. The word for "fury" comes from a verb that means "go over," which suggests feelings that burst out from someone and overwhelm the object of them. The background of the word for "blazing" lies in the idea of burning, so it suggests blazing anger that consumes the angry person and consumes the object of the anger. Indeed, Lamentations goes on from talk about angry blazing to speak of God burning against Jacob like a flaming fire consuming all around and pouring out rage like fire. The word for "rage" also means "heat." The word for "wrath" refers more to an attitude or to speech; in later Hebrew and in related languages it denotes threatening or scolding or cursing (or a camel's roar).

The poet and the people who used this prayer wouldn't be continually conscious of the different nuances of these words; part of their effect would be simply the piling up of different words with related meaning. They were certainly not afraid to talk of God's anger, as the Scriptures aren't afraid to talk of human anger, not merely as a sin but as a passion that can energize action. Whereas we're inclined to divide emotions into good and bad (mercy and compassion are good, anger and hatred are bad), the Scriptures see these emotions as neutral. The question is, in what context are you showing mercy or hatred? Sometimes mercy is wrong and hatred is right, for human beings, and for God. We have this range of emotions through being made in God's image. Conversely, God's having this range of emotions indicates that God is a real person, not a principle or an abstract idea or an essence underlying everything or a being without passions. Passion doesn't mean irrationality or arbitrariness but being involved and energized as a feeling being as well as a thinking being.

In principle, then, for God to be capable of blazing anger is good news. Of course, when you've become the object of that anger, the situation is scary. Judah has done so, and there's nothing to be gained by denying it. Human beings can be properly angry about situations but unable to do anything about them. When God sees things are wrong, he can do something about it. Often he declines to do so. He's "long-suffering"—literally, "long of anger" or "long-tempered." But sometimes he decides, "That's it—the time has come to stop being long-tempered." The length of the time God is prepared to be merciful may then be matched by the force of the anger.

You can tell by the results. A child may know when Mother has decided "That's it" because the child feels the force of Mother's hand. Over the centuries Jerusalem has usually deserved to feel the force of Yahweh's hand, but hasn't usually done so. Most generations lived in a century when long-tempered-ness was operating. This generation lived at the wrong moment. Like the first poem, this one offers a series of expressions of what the force of Yahweh's hand brought. One image it uses is an animal's horn, which embodies its strength. It pictures pagan voices shouting in the sanctuary as if it were a festival. It notes how children suffer in war; maybe the image of children asking for wine is a figure of speech based on wine's capacity to dull pain. It notes how Judah's spiritual leadership failed and how God has stopped speaking to the leaders who were supposed to guide the people. It urges the city's very walls to let tears flow; the image is the origin of the idea of the "Wailing Wall" in Jerusalem.

When you are the victims of God's anger and you know you deserved it, nevertheless you don't just have to lie down and put up with it. The poem both accepts what God has done and protests about it. As God is a real person and not just an abstract idea, so the relationship between God and Israel is a real relationship, forthright and frank, not a polite formality. When there's a real relationship, people can say anything to one another. No holds have to be barred on either side of the relationship between God and Israel.

LAMENTATIONS 3:1–66

Yahweh's Shadow Side

1 I'm the man who saw affliction,
  by his furious club.
2 He drove me and made me go
  in darkness, not light.
3 Yes, against me repeatedly
  he'd turn his hand all day long.
4 He wore away my flesh and skin,
  broke my bones.
5 He built up around me
  poison and weariness.
6 He made me live in darkness,
  like those long dead.
7 He walled me in and I couldn't get out,
  he made my chains heavy.
8 Even when I'd cry out and call for help,
  he shut out my plea.
9 He walled in my ways with stonework,
  twisted my paths.
10 He was a lurking bear to me,
  a lion in hiding.
11 He diverted my ways and mangled me,
  made me desolate.
12 He directed his bow and set me up
  as the target for his arrow.
13 He made the shafts from his quiver
  come into my heart.
14 I became a joke to all my people,
  their song all day long.

15 He filled me with bitter herbs,
   saturated me with vinegar.
16 He broke my teeth on the gravel,
   bent me down in the ashes.
17 My spirit gave up on well-being,
   I forgot good things.
18 I said, "My distinction has perished,
   and my hope from Yahweh."
19 To be mindful of my affliction and wandering
   was vinegar and poison.
20 My spirit is mindful, so mindful,
   and it bows down within me.

21 This I bring back to my mind;
   therefore I shall wait.
22 Yahweh's acts of commitment [mean] that
        we're not finished,
   that his compassion isn't spent.
23 They're new every morning;
   his steadfastness is great.
24 Yahweh is my share, my spirit said;
   therefore I shall wait for him.
25 Yahweh is good to people who look to him,
   to the spirit that seeks from him.
26 It's good that one waits and keeps still
   for Yahweh's deliverance.
27 It's good for a man
   that he carries a yoke in his youth.
28 He should sit alone and be still
   when he's put it on him.
29 He should put his mouth in the dirt;
   perhaps there's hope.
30 He should give his jaw to the one who hits him,
   become full of reviling.
31 Because the Lord
   doesn't reject forever.
32 Rather he brings suffering but has compassion,
   in the greatness of his acts of commitment.

³³ Because it's not from his heart that he afflicts,
and brings suffering to human beings.
³⁴ Crushing under his feet
all earth's prisoners,
³⁵ deflecting the decision for a man
before the presence of the One on High,
³⁶ turning someone aside in his case:
has the Lord not seen?
³⁷ Who's the person who's spoken and it's happened,
though the Lord hasn't commanded?
³⁸ Is it not from the mouth of the One on High
that evil things and good things issue?
³⁹ Of what should a living person complain,
a man in connection with his offenses?
⁴⁰ Let's search and examine our ways
and turn back to Yahweh.
⁴¹ Let's lift up our mind with our hands
to God in the heavens.
⁴² When we ourselves rebelled and defied,
you yourself didn't pardon.
⁴³ You wrapped yourself in anger and pursued us,
you slaughtered and didn't spare.
⁴⁴ You wrapped yourself in your cloud
so that a plea didn't pass through.
⁴⁵ You make us trash and refuse
amid the peoples.
⁴⁶ Against us all our enemies
have opened their mouth wide.
⁴⁷ Terror and trap have become ours,
ruin and shattering.
⁴⁸ My eye flows with streams of water
because of the shattering of my fair people.
⁴⁹ My eye has poured and won't stop,
without respite,
⁵⁰ until Yahweh looks down
and sees from the heavens.
⁵¹ My eye has dealt hard with my spirit
because of all the girls in my city.

⁵² My enemies hunted me relentlessly
   like a bird for no reason.
⁵³ They put an end to my life in a pit
   and threw stones at me.
⁵⁴ Water flowed over my head;
   I said, "I'm lost."
⁵⁵ I called on your name, Yahweh,
   from the deepest pit.
⁵⁶ You listened to my voice, "Don't close your ear
   concerning my relief, to my cry for help."
⁵⁷ You came near on the day when I'd call on you;
   you said, "Don't be afraid."
⁵⁸ You contended for my spirit's cause, Yahweh,
   you restored my life.

⁵⁹ You've seen the wrong done to me, Yahweh:
   decide my case.
⁶⁰ You've seen all their redress,
   all their intentions for me.
⁶¹ You've listened to their reviling, Yahweh,
   all their intentions against me,
⁶² the words of the people who stand up against me
   and their muttering against me all day long.
⁶³ Look at them sitting and standing up;
   I'm their song.
⁶⁴ Give them back what they deserve, Yahweh,
   in accordance with the action of their hands.
⁶⁵ May you give them a covering over their mind,
   your curse be on them.
⁶⁶ May you pursue them in anger and destroy them
   from under Yahweh's heavens.

This quarter I'm on sabbatical leave, so I can sit in my office on my own, writing about the Old Testament, and I love doing so. I also love standing in front of a class and "performing," though I find it more tiring. I think I'm probably more of an introvert than an extrovert. Yet my friends would laugh at that idea, precisely because I can switch into performance mode. To put it technically, my dominant side is introvert, but my shadow side is extrovert. Many people are the opposite. There's nothing right or wrong with either position. "Shadow side" doesn't imply something dark. It just means subordinate as opposed to dominant.

That image of a dominant and a shadow side helps us understand something about God that this chapter expresses when it says that God "doesn't afflict from his heart" (v. 33). The statement comes at the midpoint of Lamentations, at the center of the middle chapter. Whereas the personified city was prominent in the first two chapters, a male "I" now speaks, but we shouldn't try to identify the "I" with some individual. The poem's function is the same. The speaker represents the community, expresses what the community needs to express to God. The "I" is like the "I" of some psalms, which they intend other people to identify with. This poem has sixty-six instead of twenty-two verses, but it's the same length as the previous chapters. The verses are divided differently because there are three lines beginning with each letter of the alphabet.

Yahweh afflicts. The chapter starts with a reference to the club that Yahweh wields in his anger, then line after line has Yahweh as the subject of punitive action—drove, broke, walled in, shut out, mangled, and so on. You might have thought the speaker would turn away from Yahweh in disgust. Yet he knows that Yahweh's afflicting is only half the story. When we go through tough experiences, the challenge is to own two sets of facts, the facts about the hard things that have happened and the facts about God's love and compassion that are still facts. It's easier to deny one set of facts, either avoid facing the tough realities or abandon the truths about God. Lamentations insists on being real about both sets. It goes on from the facts about God's afflicting to the facts about God's **commitment**, compassion, and steadfastness, which are "new every morning." The verses have inspired several hymns and songs, but people who sing these may not realize the dynamic of the words' setting, as affirmations made in the context of the experience of affliction.

Both **evil** things and good things (that is, trouble and blessing) come from the one God (v. 38). Yet whereas people sometimes picture God as equally balanced between love and justice, Lamentations makes clear that God isn't balanced in that sense. God's heart, God's dominant or major side, is commitment, compassion, and steadfastness. But God has a shadow or minor side, the capacity to make himself act in judgment. It doesn't come from God's heart, from the center of God's being, but it does just as truly come from God, from somewhere nearer the edge of God's character that God is able to access and express (like introvert professors or pastors who can call on their shadow-side capacity to "perform").

The insistence on facing two sets of facts is another link with some psalms. These, too, can lament at suffering yet also grant that one may not be able to deny having deserved it. They can incorporate bold declarations of trust in God on the basis of facts other than one's current experience. They can also recollect how God has answered prayer in the past, and in the penultimate paragraph this poem does so. The poem in effect invites **Judahites** not to be so overwhelmed by God's recent abandonment that they forget another aspect of the dynamic of their past relationship with God. Enemies attacked; they prayed; God responded. It also invites God not to forget that dynamic. In the first two poems there isn't much prayer in the sense of urging God to act. This poem's last paragraph pleads with God to take action against the people's attackers so that their restoration may be possible. Like other prayers in both Old and New Testament, the poem is uninhibited in its appeals. Judah has no scope for taking action against its oppressors, and the poem shows no interest in doing so. It can only urge God to take action, and leave God to decide whether to do so. God's present declining to listen to the people's plea can't be the end of the story. It's possible to wait and hope and look for God to respond.

LAMENTATIONS 4:1–22

When Theology Shatters

1 Oh! Gold tarnishes,
  fine gold changes.
 Sacred stones pour out
  at every street corner.
2 Zion's precious children,
  worth their weight in pure gold—
 oh, they're reckoned as clay vessels,
  the work of a potter's hands.
3 Even jackals offer the breast,
  nurse their young.
 My dear people has become cruel,
  like ostriches in the wilderness.
4 The suckling's tongue sticks
  to the roof of its mouth for thirst.
 Infants ask for bread;
  there's no one offering it to them.
5 People who ate gourmet food
  are desolate in the streets.
 People brought up in purple
  cling to rubbish heaps.
6 The waywardness of my dear people had become greater
  than the offense of Sodom,
 which was overturned in a moment,
  though hands didn't whirl at it.
7 Her Nazirites were purer than snow,
  whiter than milk.
 Their frame was redder than coral,
  their body was sapphire.
8 Their appearance became blacker than soot;
  they weren't recognized in the streets.
 Their skin shriveled on their frame;
  it became dry like wood.
9 The people slain by the sword were better off
  than the people slain by famine,

those who slip away, wounded,
    without the produce of the field.
10 The hands of compassionate women
    cooked their children.
They became food for them
    in the course of the shattering of my dear
        people.
11 Yahweh spent his rage,
    poured out his angry blazing.
He kindled fire in Zion;
    it consumed its foundations.
12 The kings of the earth didn't believe,
    or all the world's inhabitants,
that foe or enemy would come
    through Jerusalem's gateways.
13 Because of her prophets' offenses,
    her priests' wayward acts,
who shed in her midst
    the blood of the faithful,
14 they wandered blind through the streets,
    they were defiled with blood,
without people being able
    to touch their clothes.
15 "Go away, polluted," people called to them,
    "Go away, go away, don't touch."
When they fled and wandered, people said among
        the nations,
    "They must stay no longer."
16 Yahweh's face divided them up,
    he no longer looks to them.
They didn't respect the priests,
    they didn't show favor to the elders.
17 Our eyes still spend themselves
    looking for help in vain.
On our watchtowers we watched
    for a nation that wouldn't deliver.
18 People hounded our steps
    so that we didn't walk in our squares.

Our end was near, our days were full,
    because our end had come.
19 Our pursuers became swifter
    than the eagles of the heavens.
They chased us on the mountains,
    they lay in wait for us in the wilderness.
20 The breath of our lungs, Yahweh's anointed,
    was captured in their traps,
the one of whom we had said, "In his shade
    we'll live among the nations."
21 Rejoice and celebrate, Ms. Edom,
    you who live in the country of Uz.
To you, too, the chalice will pass;
    you'll get drunk and will strip naked.
22 Your waywardness is complete, Ms. Zion;
    he will no longer exile you.
He's attending to your waywardness, Ms. Edom;
    he's exposing your offenses.

I have a new boss, who was appointed on the retirement of his predecessor a couple of years ago. His appointment was an answer to prayer. My wife was involved in encouraging people to pray for the right result, but she thought we were pressing our students too hard to be involved in this prayer. Theological study raises many questions. You thought you knew how to think about God, life, salvation, Scripture, and ethical questions, but you find yourself interacting with students and faculty who see them in different ways, and you have to read books that see them in more different ways. For a while, at least, you're not sure what to think about them, and you're not sure how to think about prayer.

Alongside the other afflictions brought by Jerusalem's conquerors was an undermining of some of people's faith assumptions. They had a basis for thinking Jerusalem would never fall. There's some hyperbole involved in declaring that the world's inhabitants and kings thought nobody would ever be able to take Jerusalem, but part of David's canniness in making Jerusalem his capital lay in its having a near-impregnable position in Judah's mountains. Further, the conviction that Jerusalem would never fall had a theological basis. Isaiah had encouraged people to believe it.

Lamentations 2:15 has already imagined people passing the devastated city asking rhetorically, "Is this the city of which they used to say, 'Complete in beauty, a joy of the entire earth'?" Not many people pass by Jerusalem. It's not on a main road; it became important because David made the city his capital, not because it was in a strategic position. The passersby asking this question are a projection of the Judahites themselves, like those kings and nations. The question is one the Jerusalemites are themselves asking, as is hinted by the fact that the phrases describing the city come virtually straight from Psalm 48. The basis for the songs people sang about Zion was more than its physical impressiveness. It was the joy of the entire earth in the sense that the whole world had reason for rejoicing in it because it was "Yahweh's city," "the Great King's city." Isaiah had given its people a basis for assuming Yahweh would never abandon it, but he's done so. No more could it be the place to which the nations would be drawn to acknowledge Yahweh. Jerusalem's fall has undercut something at the center of Judah's faith. The point is underscored by the horrifying picture of the depths to which people have been reduced, as loving mothers eat the flesh of their dead babies.

Lamentations 4:20 draws attention to another faith assumption that Jerusalem's fall has undercut. Alongside Yahweh's commitment to Jerusalem went Yahweh's commitment to Israel's anointed king: David would always have a successor on the throne in Jerusalem. Having such a leader is important to a people's sense of security. They'd wanted to have a king like other peoples, and God had granted it. But now the Babylonians have transported one king to Babylon (Jehoiakin), seared out the eyes of another (Zedekiah), and killed his sons to ensure they'll never take David's throne. What has happened to God's promise?

In due course the temple and the city itself were rebuilt and a descendant of David was governor in Jerusalem. But those events are decades away for the people who composed and first used this lament. The first three poems started as laments or protests but eventually became prayers. This poem never makes that transition. The only addressing it does is to tell Edom that its moment will come. Maybe that undercutting of faith has made prayer impossible. If so, Yahweh isn't too distraught. He was still willing to have this poem in his book. People have to speak and write from where they are. He doesn't cut them off because challenges to their faith have made it impossible to pray.

LAMENTATIONS 5:1–22

Unless You've Totally Rejected Us . . .

[1] Be mindful, Yahweh, of what happened to us;
    look, and see our reviling.
[2] Our own possession was turned over to strangers,
    our homes to foreigners.
[3] We became orphans with no father,
    our mothers actual widows.
[4] We drank our water—for money;
    our wood comes for payment.
[5] We were pursued, at our neck;
    we were weary, but there was no rest for us.
[6] We've held out our hand to Egypt,
    to Assyria to get a fill of bread.
[7] Our parents offended and are no more,
    and we were the ones who carried their wayward acts.
[8] Servants ruled over us;
    there's no one freeing us from their hand.
[9] It's at the risk of our lives that we get our bread,
    because of the sword in the wilderness.

10 Our skin was as hot as an oven,
      because of the fever of famine.
11 They raped women in Zion,
      girls in Judah's cities.
12 Officials were hung up by their hand;
      elders weren't respected.
13 Young men carried a millstone,
      youths collapsed because of [a load of] wood.
14 Elders were gone from the gateway,
      young men from their music.
15 The joy of our spirit was gone;
      our dancing was turned to mourning.
16 The crown on our head fell;
      oh, alas for us, because we offended.
17 Because of this, our spirit became sick,
      because of these things, our eyes become dark,
18 because of Mount Zion, which is desolate;
      jackals have walked about on it.
19 You, Yahweh, sit forever,
      your throne endures through the generations.
20 Why do you disregard us in perpetuity,
      abandon us for length of days?
21 Bring us back to yourself, Yahweh, so that we may
         come back;
      make our days new, as before.
22 Unless you've totally rejected us,
      raged against us utterly . . .

A man came to see me this week because of something I said in a class about divorce and remarriage. I never discovered exactly what it was, but it didn't matter. He came not because he was impersonally interested in an ethical question but because he was thinking about divorce and remarriage. He'd decided his marriage was a mistake, his wife didn't seem to satisfy his needs, he'd grown attracted to someone else, his wife had reacted by saying, "OK, you go. I'm not going to stop you, but it's you who must file the papers." In an ideal world

I'd like to get him to reaffirm his commitment. A bit of him knows he should do so, but more of him cannot imagine it and cannot work out how he could. The process whereby people make such a commitment is mysterious, and the process whereby they might remake it is even more mysterious.

The next to last line in Lamentations presupposes the equivalent mystery in people's relationship with God. The composer(s) of Lamentations know that the people need to turn to **Yahweh** in repentance. In effect they express that repentance on people's behalf, yet, like the Psalms, they say what they say in order that other people may join in. We don't know how far they did so. The authors are pastors who know they cannot force or manipulate people into that turning. Actually God cannot do so either.

Yet in human relationships we also know that sometimes an extraordinary gesture of love can win over a person. God presupposed this dynamic in sending Jesus. God had already presupposed it in an action such as restoring **Judah** a few years after Lamentations was written. But at this moment, it hasn't happened. Further, it looks as if it never will. Time is passing; Lamentations 5 seems to come from later than the preceding chapters. It feels that the **exile** will last forever. The Hebrew Bible repeats the next to last verse at the end, so that when the book is used in worship, the poems don't close in too dark a way. Although this poem, too, has twenty-two verses, they're shorter than those of the preceding poems, and it doesn't work alphabetically. It's as if it cannot affirm a hope in pattern or order, and its brevity expresses how the community is running out of the energy to hope.

This "couple," Yahweh and Judah, are far apart. There seems no way of bringing them together. The poems are designed to work on both parties: to get Jerusalem to pray them and get Yahweh to listen to them. Maybe it's the other way around: to get Yahweh to listen to them and take the action that will draw Jerusalem into praying them. Both parties need to move.

We often assume that we, the human parties in the relationship, need to take the initiative in reaching out to God. The poem assumes that God needs to take the initiative; after all, God is bigger. God needs to turn people so that they turn. Of course preaching and praying are different, and the "preachers" of the exile such as prophets and the authors of books such as Kings are urging the people to turn even while Lamentations is urging God to turn and to make turning possible.

Lamentations shares with Kings an awareness of another mystery. Whose fault was it that God finally acted in such rage against Jerusalem? Many of the generation that lived through that experience could say they were no wickeder than their parents, grandparents, or great grandparents back in Manasseh's time. Truly the parents' sins are visited on the next generation and the generation after it. It's not that the exilic generation comprises people whose **faithfulness** contrasts with the **faithlessness** of preceding generations. It's that the preceding generations set their descendants on a path that they never left. These descendants don't thus have an excuse. Every generation stands before God responsible for itself. But there's indeed a sense in which the exilic generation carries the burden of its ancestors' sins. Maybe that fact will add to the motivation to God to treat them with compassion. Maybe.

EZEKIEL 1:1–28

God Can Show Up Where You Don't Expect or Deserve

¹In the thirtieth year, in the fourth month, on the fifth of the month, when I was among the exile community by the river Kebar, the heavens opened and I saw a great appearance of God. ²On the fifth of the month (it was the fifth year of King Jehoiakin's exile), ³Yahweh's message came to Ezekiel son of Buzi, the priest, in the Kaldeans' country by the river Kebar. Yahweh's hand came on him there.

⁴I saw: there, a storm wind came from the north, a great cloud, fire consuming itself, its brightness all around, from inside it a very gleam of electrum, from inside the fire, ⁵and from inside it the forms of four creatures. This was their appearance. They had human form, ⁶but they had each four faces and four wings. ⁷Their feet: a straight foot, but the sole of their feet was like the sole of a calf's foot, and they were sparkling like the gleam of burnished bronze. ⁸Human hands were under their wings on their four quarters. Their faces and their wings, belonging to the four of them: ⁹their wings touched each other. They wouldn't turn as they went; they'd go, each in the direction of its face. ¹⁰The form of their faces: a human face, but the four of them had a lion's face on the right, and the four of them had an ox's face on the left, and the four of them had an eagle's face. ¹¹So their faces. Their wings were stretching upward, two belonging to each touching each, and two covering its body. ¹²They'd go each in the direction of its face; to wherever the wind was to go, they'd go. They wouldn't turn as they went. ¹³So the form of the creatures. Their appearance was very coals of fire burning, the very appearance of torches. It was going about between the creatures. The fire had a brightness, and from the fire lightning was coming out. ¹⁴The creatures were running and coming back, the very appearance of lightning flashes.

¹⁵I looked at the creatures. There: one wheel on the earth beside [each of] the creatures with its four faces. ¹⁶The wheels' appearance and their construction: the very gleam of topaz. The form of each of the four of them: their appearance and their construction were like a wheel inside a wheel. ¹⁷When they went, they'd go in the direction of their four quarters; they wouldn't turn as they went. ¹⁸Their rims were high and awe-inspiring. Their rims were full of eyes around, belonging to the four of them. ¹⁹When the creatures went, the wheels would go, beside them. When the creatures lifted above the earth from on the earth, the wheels lifted. ²⁰To wherever the wind was to go, they'd go there, with the wind going. The wheels would lift alongside them, because the creature's spirit was in the wheels. ²¹When they went, they'd go; when they

stopped, they'd stop; when they lifted from on the earth, the wheels would lift alongside them, because the creature's spirit was in the wheels. [22]A form was above the creature's heads, a platform, the very gleam of crystal, awe-inspiring, spread out over their heads, above. [23]Under the platform their wings were straight toward each other. Each had two covering their bodies on one side, and each had two covering on the other side. [24]I heard the sound of their wings, the very sound of many waters, the very sound of Shadday, when they went, the sound of a tumult, the very sound of an army. When they stopped, they'd relax their wings.

[25]There was a sound above the platform over their head (when they stopped, they'd relax their wings). [26]Above the platform that was over their head was the very appearance of sapphire, the form of a throne, and above the form of the throne a form that was a very human appearance on it, above. [27]I saw the very gleam of electrum, the very appearance of fire within it around about, from the appearance of his waist upward and from the appearance of his waist downward I saw the very appearance of fire. Its brightness was all around. [28]The very appearance of the bow that comes in the cloud on a rainy day, such was the appearance of the brightness all around. That was the appearance of the form of Yahweh's splendor. I saw it and fell on my face, and heard a voice speaking.

I've remembered why I had that visit from the man I mentioned in connection with Lamentations 5. I'd talked in class about a pastor who ignored a call from God to go and serve him abroad as a missionary. His subsequent ministry in England had been greatly blessed, even though he was not in the place where God had wanted him. One failure in obedience to God doesn't have to ruin your whole life. The man who came to see me had been told that persisting with his new relationship and divorcing his wife so he could marry this other woman would mean God would never bless his new marriage. I told him you could never make such predictions because God is always having to decide afresh whether to be merciful or disciplinary. Our calling is to do the right thing because it's the right thing, not because we might forfeit God's blessing.

Ezekiel's community is people who were transported to **Babylon** in 597; five years have now passed. Anyone with religious sensitivity or principle knew that they'd deserved this fate (even if there were individuals like Ezekiel who didn't deserve it) and would wonder whether they could ever expect **Yahweh** to reach out to them in Babylon. Their feelings might be similar to those expressed in Lamentations after the further fall of Jerusalem in 587. They've forfeited any right to expect God's blessing. (We don't know what "the thirtieth year" refers to. Maybe Ezekiel was thirty years old, the age when he might have taken up his ministry as a priest if he hadn't been transported to Babylon.)

Out of the blue, in a literal sense, Yahweh appears in Babylon. Maybe Ezekiel sees a literal storm approaching, with wind, cloud, and lightning. If so, Yahweh turns the literal storm into an appearance of his own cloud carriage. Yahweh is coming to his people in Babylon—Babylon of all places! Not that he's coming with a message of comfort; rather the opposite. It does mean he hasn't simply washed his hands of them. Perhaps the vision's significance is to show that Yahweh has already been present with his people in Babylon; he now enables this prophet to see behind the veil constituted by the heavens themselves, to see that Yahweh is present, and to report that fact to the people.

There are limits to what God dares let Ezekiel see. Too direct an appearance of God would simply blind a mere human being. Most of what God lets Ezekiel see is his carriage pulled by four creatures—not mere horses but combinations of human being, animal, and bird (so they can fly and transport God through the heavens). They're subsequently called **cherubs.** Their combined features give them great maneuverability, as do the crisscross wheels on the carriage that can go this way or that at will. But they're driven by one will.

The creatures support a platform on which there stands a throne; on the throne is a human-like figure. Ezekiel is looking from below, so he sees little of the figure. His experience parallels that of Isaiah, who sees only the hem of God's robe. While God can be pictured as lion-like or rock-like, more often God is described as human-like—it links with the fact that human beings are made in God's image to represent God in the world. Ezekiel's account also safeguards God's transcendence (it won't let us think of God in too human terms) by using the name Shadday. The traditional translation "Almighty" is a guess. The only other Hebrew word with which the Old Testament links the name is a verb meaning "destroy," so people might take "Shadday" to suggest "destroyer"; this understanding would suit Ezekiel. It's also a solemn fact that the storm comes from the north, the direction where people often located God's abode, but also the direction from which invaders came. But then it declares that there was something of a rainbow's appearance about this God, one who put his bow away and let it hang in the sky without string and without arrows (see Genesis 9).

God's appearing to Ezekiel is both good news and solemn news. For Ezekiel's audience and for people reading his messages in written form, it also indicates that we'd better take his words seriously.

EZEKIEL 2:1–3:21

Panic and Nonchalance

[1]He said to me, Young man, stand on your feet, so I may speak with you. [2]A wind came into me as he spoke to me. It stood me on my feet and I listened to him speaking to me. [3]He said to me, Young man, I'm sending you to the Israelites, nations that rebel, who've rebelled against me. They and their ancestors have defied me right up to this day. [4]The descendants are hard-faced and tough-minded. I'm sending you to them, and

you're to say to them, "The Lord Yahweh has said this." [5]Whether they listen or refuse (because they're a rebellious household), they will acknowledge that a prophet's been among them. [6]So you, young man, don't be afraid of them and don't be afraid of their words, when thistles and thorns are with you and you're living with scorpions. Don't be afraid of their words, don't be shattered by them, because they're a rebellious household. [7]You're to speak my words to them whether they listen, or whether they refuse because they're rebellious. [8]You, young man, listen to what I'm speaking to you. Don't become rebellious like the rebellious household. Open your mouth and eat what I'm going to give you. [9]I saw: there, a hand extended to me, and there, in it a written scroll. [10]He spread it out in front of me. It was written on front and back. Laments, muttering, and groaning were written on it.

[3:1]He said to me, Young man, eat what you find. Eat this scroll, and go speak to Israel's household. [2]I opened my mouth and he fed me this scroll. [3]He said to me, Young man, feed your stomach, fill your insides with this scroll that I'm giving you. I ate, and in my mouth it became like honey for sweetness. [4]He said to me, Young man, get yourself, come to Israel's household and speak with my words to you. [5]Because not to a people unfathomable of speech and difficult of language—you're sent to Israel's household, [6]not to many peoples unfathomable of speech and difficult of language whose words you cannot listen to. If I sent you to them, those people would listen to you. [7]But Israel's household won't be willing to listen to you, because they're not willing to listen to me, because Israel's entire household are hard-headed and tough-minded. [8]There: I'm making your face hard over against their face and your head hard over against their head. [9]Like adamant harder than flint I'm making your head. You shall not be afraid of them, you shall not be shattered by them, because they're a rebellious household. [10]Then he said to me, Young man, accept with your mind all my words that I speak to you. Listen with your ears [11]and get yourself, come to the exile community, to the members of your people, and speak to them. Say to them, "The Lord Yahweh has said this," whether they listen or refuse.

¹²Then a wind lifted me, and I heard behind me a great quaking sound (Yahweh's splendor be worshiped from his place)—¹³the sound of the creatures' wings beating against each other and the sound of the wheels alongside them and a great quaking sound. ¹⁴So a wind lifted me and took me, and I went, fierce and in rage of spirit, with Yahweh's hand hard on me. ¹⁵I came to the exile community at Tel Abib living by the river Kebar. I lived where they were living, lived there desolate for seven days, ¹⁶and at the end of the seven days Yahweh's message came to me: ¹⁷Young man, I'm giving you as a lookout for Israel's household. You're to listen to the message from my mouth and warn them from me. ¹⁸When I say about the faithless person, "You'll definitely die," but you don't warn him and don't speak to warn the faithless person from his faithless way, to keep him alive: he, the faithless person, will die for his waywardness, but I shall look for his blood from your hand. ¹⁹But you—when you warn the faithless person and he doesn't turn back from his faithlessness, from his faithless way: he'll die for his waywardness, but you'll have saved your life. ²⁰And when a faithful person turns back from his faithfulness and does wrong and I put an obstacle in front of him, he'll die. Because you didn't warn him, for his offense he'll die, and his faithful acts that he's done won't be borne in mind. But I shall look for his blood from your hand. ²¹But you, when you warn him (the faithful person) that the faithful person shouldn't offend, and he doesn't offend, he'll definitely live because he let himself be warned, and you yourself will have saved your life.

The northeast of the United States is characterized today by a mixture of panic and nonchalance in light of warnings concerning the threat of a monumental storm which has issued in evacuation and the closing down of transport systems. It's hard for forecasters to know how pointedly to warn people about dangers that they think are imminent. A storm last year was milder than had been warned. On the other hand, last week some Italian scientists were sentenced to six years in prison for manslaughter for failing to give adequate warning of an earthquake in which three hundred people died.

Ezekiel is warned that he'll be held responsible in this way if he fails to warn people of the fate hanging over them. The fate isn't inevitable. While in a sense God's intentions are fixed (if people carry on as they are, the trouble will come), in another sense they're flexible (their implementation depends on people's response). Ezekiel's task is to work himself out of a job, to prove himself wrong.

God has a way of addressing Ezekiel that's distinctive to him. The Hebrew expression for "young man" is literally "son of man," a way of designating someone as "human being," with a hint of "mere human being." Ezekiel also has a distinctive way of speaking of God, as "Lord **Yahweh**." Yahweh is God's personal **name**; knowing that name is a precious privilege. Combining it with the word "Lord" reminds people that Yahweh isn't someone you can mess with. It's the message this exilic community needs to hear. The problem is that **Israel's** household is rebellious and defiant. Calling the household "Israel" suggests that this little group of **Judahites** represents the ancient people of God, which is good news. But calling them a household suggests they're like rebellious sons and daughters about whom their parents have said, "That's it—get out of this house."

Ezekiel is sent to the people in **exile** with his message, even though much of his critique will relate to what's still going on in Jerusalem. While Jeremiah is warning Judahites in Judah that their waywardness means there's worse trouble to come, Ezekiel is giving the same message to the Judahites in exile. He needs to do so because the Judahites in Jerusalem continue to be a rebellious household, and the exiles need to steel themselves for more bad news to come from there, and because the Judahites in **Babylon** haven't learned any lessons yet.

Ezekiel is given a nasty message to declare, but it tastes good because it's Yahweh's message. He's going to meet with opposition because it's a message of judgment. But there's an ironic sense in which he might look on the bright side. At least his audience doesn't speak a foreign language! Sometimes God's people think they have a prophetic message to give the world, but prophets aren't usually sent to the world. They're sent to their own people, and their own people reject them (which is more humiliating than the world's doing so). Ezekiel has to be prepared to be as tough as they are.

Yahweh isn't explicit about how he'll seek from Ezekiel's hand the blood of someone whom he has failed to warn, but it sounds like something to keep one awake at night. For people hearing Ezekiel or reading his prophecies, the warning's point is that there's no doubt Ezekiel fulfilled his commission, so that question didn't arise. The audience is responsible for its destiny. They have no one to blame but themselves.

EZEKIEL 3:22–4:17

The Power of an Image

²²Yahweh's hand came on me there and he said to me, Get up, go out to the vale, and I shall speak with you there. ²³So I got up and went out to the vale, and there—Yahweh's splendor was standing there, like the splendor I saw at the river Kebar. I fell on my face. ²⁴A wind came into me and stood me up on my feet. He spoke with me and said to me, Come, shut yourself up inside your house. ²⁵You, young man, there—they're putting ropes on you and tying you up with them. You're not to go out among them. ²⁶I shall make your tongue stick to your palate and you'll be dumb. To them, you won't be someone who reproves, because they're a rebellious household. ²⁷But when I speak with you, I shall open your mouth and you'll say to them, "The Lord Yahweh has said this." The person who listens may listen and the person who refuses may refuse, because they're a rebellious household.

⁴:¹You, young man, get yourself a brick and put it in front of you and engrave a city on it: Jerusalem. ²Prepare a siege against

it. Build a tower against it. Construct a ramp against it. Make a camp against it. Set up battering rams against it all around. [3]And you, get yourself an iron plate and put it as an iron wall between you and the city and set your face toward it. It will be under siege; you'll lay siege against it. It will be a sign for Israel's household.

[4]You yourself, lie on your left side and put the waywardness of Israel's household on [your side]. The number of the days that you lie on it, you'll carry their waywardness. [5]I myself am giving you the years of their waywardness, in number 390 days; you'll carry the waywardness of Israel's household. [6]When you complete these, you'll lie on your right side, a second time, and carry the waywardness of Judah's household. Forty days, a day for each year, I'm giving you.

[7]And toward Jerusalem's siege you're to set your face and your bared arm, and prophesy against it. [8]There: I'm putting ropes on you, and you aren't to turn from side to side until you've completed your days of siege. [9]You're to get yourself wheat, barley, beans, lentils, millet, and spelt, put them into a jar, and make them into bread for yourself. For the number of days that you're lying on your side, 390 days, you're to eat it. [10]The food that you eat, by weight, twenty shekels a day, you're to eat at the regular times, [11]and water by measure you're to drink, a sixth of a gallon you're to drink at the regular times. [12]You're to eat it as a barley cake. Cook it on human excrement in their sight. [13]Yahweh said, In this way the Israelites will eat their bread, defiled, among the nations where I'm banishing them. [14]I said, Oh no, Lord Yahweh, there, my person's not been defiled. I haven't eaten anything found dead or torn by an animal, from my youth until now. Impure meat hasn't come into my mouth. [15]So he said to me, See, I'm giving you animal dung instead of human excrement. You can make your bread on that. [16]He said to me, Young man, here am I, I'm going to break the bread supply in Jerusalem. They will eat bread by weight in anxiety, and drink water by measure in desolation, [17]so that they run out of bread and water and are desolate in relation to one another, and waste away because of their waywardness.

Almost my wife's first words as we woke up this morning were, "Oh, I had terrible dreams. I need to stop watching the news before we go to bed." There had been images of the storm to which I referred in connection with Ezekiel 2, which has been overwhelming New York. There had been pictures of the aftermath of an attack on a Sudanese weaponry factory, with the guess that it was undertaken by Israel and that it could be another step toward a Middle East war. Her dreams were perhaps not enhanced by the movie we had been watching that involved the threat of an asteroid striking the earth, or by the news item about snakes taking over the world (or perhaps just the Florida Everglades).

The power of images lies at the background of Ezekiel's ministry, both frightening and encouraging. Performance art can impact people powerfully. In the written form of Ezekiel's prophecies, the images appeal directly to the imagination; for the people among whom he lived, they're embodied before their eyes and symbolically enacted. First there's the image of a prophet who stays home and never speaks. It doesn't make sense. A prophet needs to be out among people and speaking. To stay home (perhaps he has accomplices who tie him up) and remain speechless is an expression of **Yahweh's** judgment on them. Yahweh doesn't wish to speak to them, because they've shown themselves to be people who don't wish to listen. Only on special occasions will Yahweh give him permission to open his mouth in Yahweh's **name**. The first symbolic action manifests a feature that will characterize others. The action isn't merely an image for Yahweh's not speaking to them. It puts into effect Yahweh's not speaking to them.

A symbolic enactment of the siege of Jerusalem follows. Although he ministers among the exiles in **Babylon**, Ezekiel's ministry focuses on Jerusalem. The exiles think their stay in the foreign city will be short, that Yahweh has surely made his point and will soon let them go home. There were prophets in Babylon telling them so. Ezekiel's task is to make people see that actually things have to get worse before they get better.

His bodily action explicates the point. Yahweh is taking into account a long history of rebellion and waywardness on Israel's part. It would be a mistake to press the numbers. Something like 390 years have passed since the building of the temple or since Ephraim split from Judah, but forty looks more like a symbolic number, and putting these two figures together generates 430 years, the length that Exodus 12 gives for Israel's oppression in Egypt. One way or another, Ezekiel's point is that there are centuries of waywardness to pay for. Perhaps Ezekiel actually lay there for that many days, but the symbolic action could work another way. Perhaps he lay there for fifteen minutes each day with a calendar, or lay there for one day with a calendar from which he kept tearing pages (to picture it in our terms). One way or another, he's embodying the penalty they're paying for their waywardness.

Subsequently, he enacts the implications of Jerusalem's coming fall in another way. There's to be a more terrible siege and exile than the one his audience has already experienced. There'll be a shortage of food, water, and fuel (presumably he's to make his bread before his enactment starts). The use of animal dung as fuel is an established practice, though not the use of human excrement. The point here is to provide an extreme illustration of the straits to which the city will be reduced. The Torah doesn't say anything about impurity associated with this use of human excrement, but you wouldn't need to be a priest to find it repulsive.

EZEKIEL 5:1–17

Amid the Nations

¹You, young man, get yourself a sharp sword, get it for yourself as a barber's razor, pass it over your head and over your beard.

Get yourself weighing scales and divide [the hair]. ²You're to burn a third in fire within the city when the days of the siege are fulfilled. Take a third and strike all around it with the sword. Scatter a third to the wind; I shall draw a sword after them. ³But get from there a few and bind them into the folds [of your clothes]. ⁴Get some of them again and throw them into the middle of the fire. Burn them in the fire. From this a fire will go out against the entire household of Israel.

⁵The Lord Yahweh said this: I put this Jerusalem amid the nations, with countries around it. ⁶But it rebelled against my decisions with more faithlessness than the nations, and against my laws more than the countries around it. Because people rejected my decisions, and my laws—they didn't walk by them. ⁷Therefore the Lord Yahweh said this: Because you've been more turbulent than the nations that are around you—you haven't walked by my laws, you haven't enacted my decisions, and you haven't acted in accordance with the decisions of the nations that are around you; ⁸therefore the Lord Yahweh said this: Here am I [acting] toward you, yes, I myself. I shall enact decisions among you in the sight of the nations. ⁹I shall do to you what I haven't done and the like of which I won't do again, on account of all your outrageous acts. ¹⁰Therefore in your midst [Jerusalem], parents will eat children and children will eat their parents. I shall enact decisions against you and scatter your remains to every wind.

¹¹Therefore as I live (the Lord Yahweh's declaration), if I don't, because you defiled my sanctuary with all your abominations and all your outrages . . .—yes, I myself will shave you, my eye won't spare you, and I myself won't pity you. ¹²One third of you will die in an epidemic or come to an end through famine in your midst. One third will fall by the sword around you. I shall scatter one third to every wind and draw a sword after them. ¹³My anger will spend itself and I shall give rest to my rage on them, and I shall find relief, and they will acknowledge that I, Yahweh, have spoken in my passion, when I've spent my rage against them. ¹⁴I shall make you a ruin and an object of reviling among the nations that are around you, in the sight of everyone passing by. ¹⁵It will be a reason for

reviling and ridicule, for discipline and desolation, to the nations that are around you, when I enact decisions against you in anger, rage, and furious reproofs. I, Yahweh, have spoken. [16]When I send off the evil arrows of famine on the people who were for destroying, which I shall send off to destroy you, I shall add famine upon you and break the bread supply for you. [17]I shall send off against you famine and evil creatures, and they will bereave you; epidemic and bloodshed will pass through you and I shall bring the sword against you. I, Yahweh, have spoken.

I went back to England for a visit a while ago and took the train from the West Country to London. I found myself admiring the countryside with its lush green meadows and pretty villages. I felt like an American tourist. I was especially struck by the spires or towers of churches that rose from villages. In times when you might have assumed that the villages were Christian, the spires or towers stood for the place of God and of worship at the center of the village's life. In an age when you can't assume that Christian faith is real to many people, they act as a reminder of God's reality. The church, and the congregation that worships there, is set amid the nation around it.

It's the position in which **Yahweh** put **Israel**. Its capital doesn't physically tower above the region around; it's not even the highest peak in its region. But Israel does stand at the center of the world. It does so physically, at the meeting point of Asia, Africa, and Europe (sorry, Americas), part of the explanation for its importance in political history. It wouldn't be surprising if its geographical location was a reason for God's choosing it as the place for implementing his purpose to redeem the world.

It links with this fact that Yahweh emphasizes Jerusalem's position amid the nations, with countries around it. Yahweh didn't send Israelites out to the nations to tell them about himself. This idea of mission is foreign to the Old Testament. God did intend Israel to be the means of the nations coming to acknowledge him. Genesis speaks of that result coming through his blessing of Israel. Ezekiel presupposes that it involves Israel living by God's **decisions** and laws. The trouble is that Israel assimilated to the nations around rather than modeling a different way. In Luke 12 Jesus commented that much is required of people to whom much is given; Israel was the original referent of that declaration. The Israelites didn't even live up to the nations' own standards, Yahweh shockingly asserts (maybe he has in mind their inclination to break treaties and rebel, which issued in the **Babylonians'** destruction of the city).

There's no neutrality for Jerusalem, no evading of its position amid the nations as a city with which Yahweh is especially involved. If it's not to be an embodiment of **faithfulness** and blessing, it will be an embodiment not only of **faithlessness** but of the calamity that follows, "in the sight of the nations." It will still be an object lesson, something from which the nations will learn of Yahweh's ways, even if it's by embodying how faithlessness gets its reward. Readers of the Old Testament sometimes worry about its speaking of God destroying nations and/or telling Israel to do so. At least God is even-handed. Nothing tougher is prescribed for other nations or done to them than is prescribed for Israel or done to them. We're then right to be worried about this dynamic. The Church, after all, constitutes a kind of extension of Israel. We, too, are set amid the nations to be a light on a hill. So if we turn out to be indistinguishable from the nations or even more unreliable than they are . . .

Ezekiel's action with the hair represents the fate that will come over the city's residents. The picture embodies Yahweh's devastating warning. There's no hint of the survival of anyone. Fortunately, these aren't Yahweh's last words on the subject.

EZEKIEL 6:1–14

About Intolerance

¹Yahweh's message came to me: ²Young man, set your face toward Israel's mountains and prophesy toward them. ³You're to say, Israel's mountains, listen to the Lord Yahweh's message. The Lord Yahweh said this about the mountains and hills, the ravines and canyons: Here am I, I'm going to bring the sword against you, and I shall wipe out your shrines. ⁴Your altars will be desolate, your incense stands broken. I shall make your slain fall in front of their lumps. ⁵I shall put the Israelites' corpses in front of their lumps and scatter your bones around your altars ⁶in all your settlements. The cities will be demolished and the shrines laid waste, so that when your altars are demolished and thus punished, when your lumps are broken and put an end to, when your incense stands are cut down and what you've made is wiped out, ⁷and when the slain person falls in your midst, you will acknowledge that I am Yahweh. ⁸But I shall let some remain over. When you have survivors of the sword among the nations, when you're scattered among the countries, ⁹your survivors will be mindful of me among the nations where they've been taken captive, that I've been broken with their immoral mind that turned away from me and with their immoral eyes after their lumps. They'll feel a loathing toward their own selves concerning the evils that they've done, for all their outrageous acts. ¹⁰They will acknowledge that I am Yahweh. Not for nothing did I speak about doing all this evil to them.

¹¹The Lord Yahweh said this: Clap your hands, stamp with your feet. Say, "Aaaagh!" about all the evil, outrageous acts of Israel's household, who will fall by sword, famine, and epidemic. ¹²The person who's far away will die by the epidemic, the one who's near will die by the sword, and the one who remains and is preserved will die by the famine. I shall spend my rage on them. ¹³You will acknowledge that I am Yahweh when their slain are among their lumps around their altars toward every high hill, on all the tops of the mountains, under every verdant tree and under every leafy oak, the place where

they presented a pleasing fragrance to all their lumps. [14]I shall stretch out my hand against them and make the country desolation and devastation, from the wilderness to Diblah, in all their settlements. And they will acknowledge that I am Yahweh.

In a bed and breakfast on a Turkish island last month, we were surprised to be woken up by church bells instead of the call of the minaret. After the First World War, as part of a peace deal between Turkey and Greece, hundreds of thousands of Christians in Turkey had to change places with hundreds of thousands of Muslims in Greece, but (we discovered) on this island a handful of Coptic monks had managed to hold on in what had once been the Greek/Christian Quarter. In some periods Christians and Muslims have been able to live together in religious tolerance, convinced of their beliefs yet able to live alongside the other. In other periods, this has been impossible. In the United States, it becomes harder and harder for believers and unbelievers to live together politically.

Evidently people in **Judah** had a hard time maintaining their faith and resisting the temptations of the country's traditional religion, and **Yahweh** is here confronting them. Addressing the mountains and valleys is a way of addressing the country as a whole, which is dominated by mountains and valleys. The shrines are the "high places." Any town or substantial village would have such a shrine, usually on some elevated location, and it was quite possible for these shrines to be places where Yahweh was worshiped in accordance with the **Torah**, but it was easy for the worship there to be more like worship of Canaanite gods in the assumptions it made about Yahweh (and Yahweh's wife!), or overtly to involve worship of those gods. That influence is implied by the reference to verdant trees and leafy oaks, the common context of the Canaanite rites. Likewise there was nothing wrong with the **altars**, incense stands, and pleasingly fragrant offerings. But they're rendered abhorrent by their association with **lumps**.

The objective of the action is that people "may acknowledge that I am Yahweh." It's a key phrase in Ezekiel. In a sense it's an odd expression—there's no argument over whether he is Yahweh. But the implications of the phrase are broader. The expression presupposes that Yahweh alone is really God, so it implies acknowledging God. And it implies acknowledging Yahweh in the sense of submitting to Yahweh.

Yahweh is "broken" by the people's turning away from him in their thinking and looking to other gods. The fury he feels goes along with deep pain. You could say that his threats are pain talking. He refers to the time when the Judahites will come to loathe themselves for what they've done. You could say that they'll be broken, too. But Yahweh presupposes that self-loathing can be a positive emotion, if it accompanies turning from **faithlessness** and acknowledgment of the truth.

Diblah is otherwise unknown; the name looks like a slip for Riblah (the difference is a "tittle" or serif, the tiniest part of a letter). "From the wilderness to Riblah" then means from the far south to the far north, in Syria. Unbeknown to Ezekiel, Riblah will be the location of some chilling scenes related in 2 Kings 25 after the final fall of Jerusalem.

EZEKIEL 7:1–27

You Vipers' Brood

¹Yahweh's message came to me: ²You, young man—the Lord Yahweh has said this to Israel's land: An end! The end is coming on the four corners of the country. ³The end is now upon you. I've sent off my anger against you, and I shall decide about you in accordance with your ways. I shall bring all your outrageous acts upon you. ⁴My eye won't spare you, I shall not have pity, because I shall bring upon you your ways and your outrageous acts that are in your midst. And you will acknowledge that I am Yahweh.

⁵The Lord Yahweh said this: A singular evil! Evil—there, it's coming. ⁶An end is coming! It's coming! The end is rousing itself against you! There, it's coming! ⁷The doom is coming upon you, you who inhabit the country. The time is coming. The day is near, tumult not cheering on the mountains. ⁸Now it's near. I shall pour out my rage on you and spend my anger against you. I shall decide about you in accordance with your ways and bring all your outrageous acts upon you. ⁹My eye won't spare, I shall not have pity. When in accordance with your ways I bring your acts upon you, your outrageous acts that are in your midst, you will acknowledge that I am Yahweh, the one who strikes down. ¹⁰There, the day! There, it's coming. The doom is coming out. The club has blossomed, pride has flourished, ¹¹violence has arisen, a faithless club. Nothing comes from them, not from the horde of them, not from anything of theirs; there's no distinction in them. ¹²The time is coming, the day is arriving. The buyer shouldn't celebrate, the seller shouldn't mourn, because wrath is upon its entire horde. ¹³Because the seller won't turn back to what he sold, even though their life is still among the living, because the vision about the entire horde won't turn back. Each with his waywardness—they won't hold onto their life.

¹⁴They've sounded the horn and made everything ready, but there's no one going to the battle, because my wrath is against its entire horde. ¹⁵The sword is in the street, epidemic and famine in the house. The person who's in the countryside will die by the sword, and the person who's in the city—famine or epidemic will consume him. ¹⁶Their survivors—they'll survive but be in the mountains like pigeons in the canyons, all of them moaning, each with his waywardness. ¹⁷All the hands will go limp, water will go down all the knees. ¹⁸They'll wrap on sackcloth, and shuddering will cover them, with disgrace on all faces and shornness on all their heads. ¹⁹They'll throw their silver into the streets; their gold will become taboo. Their silver and their gold won't be able to rescue them on the day of Yahweh's wrath, they won't satisfy people's desire or fill their stomachs, because their waywardness has become their downfall. ²⁰The jeweled attractiveness

[of the silver and gold], which they made into an object of pride—with it they made their outrageous images, their abominations. Therefore I'm making it taboo for them. [21]I shall give it into the hand of strangers as spoil, as plunder to the faithless of the earth, and they'll treat it as ordinary. [22]I shall turn away my face from them, and people will treat my treasured place as ordinary—intruders will come into it and treat it as ordinary. [23]Make a chain, because the country is full of bloody judgments, the city is full of violence. [24]I shall bring the most evil of the nations and they'll take possession of their houses. I shall put a stop to the majesty of the powerful. Their sanctuaries will be made ordinary. [25]Calamity is coming. People will seek peace but there'll be none. [26]Disaster will come upon disaster, report will follow upon report. They'll seek a vision from a prophet, but teaching will perish from priest and plans from elders. [27]The king will mourn, the ruler will put on desolation as clothing, the hands of the country's people will tremble. On the basis of their way I shall deal with them, and by their decisions I shall decide about them, and they will acknowledge that I am Yahweh.

I've been arranging with a member of our congregation to preach in our church this coming December 15th, and a day or two ago she sent me a message noting that the Gospel passage for the day included Jesus addressing people as a brood of vipers ("on which I always used to think it would be fun to preach, until now that it's mine"), and that furthermore "this will be the last sermon before the world is supposed to end on the 21st. Any suggestions?" Mayan scholars and astronomers pooh-pooh the idea that there's any basis for saying that the world will end on this date, and if you're reading this book, they'll have been proved right. Predictions of the end of the world have been falsified so often that people who are inclined to be skeptical have been bolstered in their skepticism.

We'll discover in Ezekiel 12 that people were skeptical about Ezekiel's declarations that "the end" is imminent. The end he's referring to is the end of **Judah's** independent life, the end of the time when Jerusalem is its capital and is a functioning city. In speaking of the end, he's taking up a declaration from Amos 8. Amos lived more than a century earlier; he was referring to the end coming on **Ephraim**. He'd been proved right. Ephraim existed no longer. It ought therefore to be frightening to have the words reapplied to Judah, which might have been inclined to feel rather superior to that renegade northern people who got their comeuppance. Ezekiel even picks up Amos's threatening trick of putting similar-sounding words together for effect, when he speaks of the end "rousing itself"—that Hebrew verb is similar to the Hebrew word for *the end*. Ezekiel also follows Amos in speaking of "the day." "The day of **Yahweh**" was supposed to be a day of joy, but Amos warned Ephraim that it would be a dark not a joyful day (see Amos 5). Ezekiel likewise declares that it will be "the day of Yahweh's wrath," not of Yahweh's blessing. It won't be a festival day when people are cheering but a day of turmoil and confusion.

Part of the basis for Ezekiel's certainty that this end will come is that (to use Jesus' expression) his people are a vipers' brood. God must surely therefore act in judgment. When Jesus speaks in these terms, he's following in the footsteps of prophets such as Amos and Ezekiel. Much of this chapter is jerky and much of the detail is puzzling, and I haven't tried to clean it up. I imagine his original audience found it jerky and puzzling, which meant they had to take the risk of thinking hard about it if they were to make sense of it. Yet the drift of it is clear.

Ezekiel is again addressing the situation back home, which is so important to people in **Babylon** who hope they'll be returning there soon. The country's life is characterized by violence and yet by confidence about the future; the people who'd escaped the **exile** that took Ezekiel and company to Babylon assume they dodged the bullet. They think they can defend themselves, but they won't be able to do so. They're on their way to catastrophe. Silver and gold will be of no use, whether they've been used to make images of people's deities (who will turn out to be useless) or whether they're thought of as financial resources (money is of no use in a siege). The silver and gold will just end up as loot for the invaders.

The most frightening declaration is that Yahweh has turned away from his people in Judah. He's walked out on his own house, and is happy for alien feet to invade it. When they turn to their prophets, priests, and elders, they'll find that they have nothing to say. When they turn to their leaders, they'll find them bemused.

As in Amos, the "end" or "Yahweh's day" isn't the end of the world after which there's nothing, or after which there's resurrection or life in heaven. It's an event in history where God shatters all the structures and order of his people's life in a fashion that might make them face the waywardness of their life and at least "acknowledge that he is Yahweh."

EZEKIEL 8:1–18

About Not Being at Home

¹In the sixth year, in the sixth month, on the fifth of the month, I was sitting in my house and the Judahite elders were sitting in front of me, and the hand of the Lord Yahweh fell on me there. ²I looked, and there—a form with a fiery appearance. From the appearance of his waist and downward there was fire, and from his waist and upward, a gold appearance, like the gleam of electrum. ³He put out the form of a hand and took me by the hair of my head, and a wind lifted me between the earth and the heavens and brought me to Jerusalem with a great appearance of God, to the door in the gateway to the inner courtyard that faces north, where was the seat of the provocative image, which provokes. ⁴There—the splendor of Israel's God appeared there, like the appearance that I saw in the vale.

⁵He said to me, "Young man, will you raise your eyes north-ward." I raised my eyes northward, and there, north of the

altar gateway, was this provocative image, at the entrance. ⁶He said to me, "Young man, do you see what they're doing, great outrages that Israel's household are doing here, so that I'd go far from my sanctuary? You'll see further great outrages." ⁷He brought me to the entrance of the courtyard. I looked, and there—a hole in the wall. ⁸He said to me, "Young man, will you break through the wall." I broke through the wall, and there—a door. ⁹He said to me, "Come in, look at the evil outrages that they're performing here." ¹⁰I came and looked, and there, every form of abominable reptile and animal and all the lumps of Israel's household, carved on the wall all the way around. ¹¹Seventy individuals of the elders of Israel's household, with Ja'azaniah son of Shaphan standing among them, were standing in front of them, each with his censer in his hand. The richness of the incense cloud was going up. ¹²He said to me, "Young man, have you seen what the elders of Israel's household are doing in the dark, each in his image-covered rooms? Because they're saying, 'Yahweh isn't looking at us. Yahweh's abandoned the country.'" ¹³He said to me, "You'll again see further great outrages that they're performing." ¹⁴He brought me to the door of the gateway of Yahweh's house that's to the north. There—the women were sitting there, bewailing Tammuz. ¹⁵He said to me, "Young man, have you seen? You'll again see further greater outrages than these." ¹⁶He brought me to the inner courtyard of Yahweh's house. There—at the gateway of Yahweh's palace, between the portico and the altar, some twenty-five men, their backs to Yahweh's palace and their faces to the east, and they were bowing low to the east, to the sun.

¹⁷He said to me, "Young man, have you seen? Is it too slight for Judah's household to perform the outrages that they've performed here? Because they've filled the country with violence and again vexed me. There they are, putting the branch to their nose. ¹⁸Yes, I myself will act in rage. My eye won't spare and I shall not pity. They'll call in my ears in a loud voice but I shall not listen to them."

Reentering the United States two weeks ago, I was grilled by the immigration officer (I think he was just trying to spice up a boring evening) about why I remain a resident alien and am not a citizen. My first answer is that I could never feel an American; I've been British for too long. I'm totally at home in the United States, and yet I know it's not my real home. On the other hand, I also know when I visit England that neither am I totally at home there any longer. I've been absent for too long. It's changed, and I've changed.

The **Israelites** were expected to be at home in Canaan, yet not to be at home in Canaan. They were expected to keep remembering how God had acted in their life before they arrived there and to keep remembering the revelation God had given them before they arrived there, and to live their lives there in a way that took those realities into account. It's a hard thing to do, and they weren't very good at doing it.

That dynamic is one factor underlying the phenomena that Ezekiel here critiques. A year after appearing to him and commissioning him, **Yahweh** appears to Ezekiel again. Yahweh does something that's spectacular in a different way. In a visionary sense, Yahweh takes Ezekiel back to Jerusalem to see what's happening in the temple. The taking is more forceful than that verb might imply; it's more like a parent hauling a child forcibly to bed. Ezekiel perhaps sees nothing he hadn't directly seen before being taken to **Babylon** six years previously. First there's the image that provokes Yahweh's anger and hostility. This language elsewhere suggests an image that allegedly represents Yahweh's wife, a goddess of love and marriage. Now Yahweh is the transcendent, heavenly, awe-inspiring God who had appeared to Ezekiel in that overpowering way, not a God with a wife and a sex life, but human beings feel more at home with a more everyday, mundane god who shares that experience and priority in human relationships. The image doesn't correspond to anything real, but people ascribe reality to it, so it does provoke Yahweh. It's not just a dead thing that makes no difference.

Second, there are representations of animals and snakes, more images of deities, which Ezekiel knows are mere **lumps**, but which people see as other ways of making deities more accessible and mundane. Breaking through a wall to see what people were doing in the dark, in private, suggests that the scene represents aspects of people's personal religious observance in their homes. What happens in private won't stay private. There's some sadness about the elders and Ja'azaniah being involved. The elders and Ja'azaniah's father had been part of a reform movement that had sought to abolish this kind of observance in Jerusalem (see 2 Kings 22–23). Their comments about Yahweh's forgetting them indicates how there would be contradictory understandings of the situation within the community. There was the possibility that Yahweh was chastising them but would soon restore them; there was the possibility that Yahweh had abandoned them; there was the possibility that the ideas about Yahweh expressed in the Torah and by prophets such as Jeremiah and Ezekiel were simply wrong.

Then there are the women mourning the death of the Babylonian god Tammuz, symbolized by the advent of the summer heat in the Middle East that seems to make everything die; the mourning rites will perhaps have involved praying for Tammuz's return to life, which would be symbolized by the arrival of the rains and the reviving of nature. Alongside them are the men turning their back on Yahweh and bowing down to the sun. The sun's heat is a danger, but without the sun there's no new morning each day, and the sun is the senior figure in the army of planets and stars that govern events on earth. All these observances promise to make people more at home in the world, more in control of **ordinary** life.

While we don't know what lies behind putting a branch to one's nose, it's apparently some form of insult, like giving someone the finger in the United States or the V-sign in Britain. Ezekiel's final words indicate that Yahweh takes just as much offense at the violence whereby the strong oppress the weak.

EZEKIEL 9:1–11

Who Are the People Who Groan and Moan?

[1]He called in my ears, "Come near, you who deal with the city, each of you with his implement of destruction in his hand." [2]And there—six men coming by way of the upper gateway that faces north, each with his implement of demolition in his hand, and a man among them dressed in linen, with a writing case at his waist. They came and stood beside the bronze altar. [3]Now the splendor of Israel's God had gone up from on the cherub on which it had been, to the house's terrace. He called to the man dressed in linen, at whose waist was the writing case. [4]Yahweh said to him, "Pass through the midst of the city, through Jerusalem's midst, and put an X on the foreheads of the people who are groaning and moaning over the outrages that are performed in its midst." [5]To these [other men] he said in my ears, "Pass through the city after him and attack. Your eye must not spare. You must not pity. [6]Slay elder, young man, girl, little one, women, outright. But any person on whom is the X—don't touch. Start from my sanctuary." So they started with the men who were the elders who were in front of the house. [7]He said to them, "Defile the house. Fill the courtyards with the slain. Go out." They went out and attacked in the city. [8]While they were attacking, I myself remained alone. I fell on my face and cried out and said, "Aaaagh! Lord Yahweh! Are you going to destroy all that remains of Israel by pouring out your rage on Jerusalem?" [9]He said to me, "The waywardness of the household of Israel and Judah is very, very great. The country is full of bloodshed. The city is full of injustice. Because they've said, 'Yahweh's abandoned the country. Yahweh isn't looking.' [10]I, too—my eye won't spare and I won't pity. I'm bringing their way on their head." [11]And there—the man clothed in linen, at whose waist was the writing case, was bringing back word: "I've acted in accordance with all that you commanded me."

My wife and I are on our way back from a meeting where we've been talking about genocide. My job was to talk about genocide in the Old Testament; Kathleen's was to talk about genocide in our contemporary world. She expressed her grieved passion about the situation of Darfuri refugees in Chad, forced to flee from their homes in Sudan nine years ago as an alternative to being killed or raped in their homeland, her grieved passion about the world's ignoring of their plight, and her grieved frustration that she couldn't succeed in her efforts to get just one girl out of the camps to go to college in a country such as Uganda. It makes Kathleen moan and groan at what she sees with the help of video from Chad.

Yahweh wants to know who in Jerusalem feels such passionate grief at what's going on there. The man with the writing case reminds me of the person from the taxation authorities who arrives at your door in a suit, carrying his laptop, coming to audit you. His task is to identify people who are grieving, moaning, and groaning. They're the people who will escape the disaster coming on the city. Ezekiel says nothing about their being people seeking to bring about change or reform. There are situations when you can do nothing about what's wrong in your community or church, except cry out to God about it. But you'd better be dissociating yourself from it. The Hebrew word for X is the name of the letter T, which in Ezekiel's time would look like an X, which makes a Christian think of the challenge to be people who take up the cross.

The vision seems unrealistic. When disasters happen, they affect the faithful as well as the faithless. Ezekiel knew it was so. Realistically, he notes that the calamity will fall on young men, girls, and children, as well as the men who'd be the main decision makers in a patriarchal society, and the elders and the women whose faithless worship Ezekiel has already witnessed. Everyone gains when the decision makers make faithful **decisions**, and everyone pays the price when they make faithless decisions. Further, Ezekiel himself was in **exile** even though he didn't identify with the practices in Jerusalem that led to the city's first fall in 597 and the first exile that followed. The vision's agenda lies elsewhere than in assuring individuals that they'll be OK. It doesn't say that the recorder finds anyone who's moaning and groaning. The vision's focus lies on how wide Yahweh's judgment will be. If the recorder finds people to mark, the implication is that there are few, and certainly that people who lack this mark will be treated mercilessly. The vision again rubs the exiles' noses in the fact that their home city isn't going to escape a terrible judgment. As usual Yahweh talks tougher than he means. Not everyone will be killed. He'll ensure that a remnant remains.

EZEKIEL 10:1–22

God Is Leaving

[1]I looked, and there—on the platform that was over the head of the cherubs was a very sapphire stone; the appearance of the form of a throne appeared on it. [2][Yahweh] said to the man clothed in linen, "Come in between the whirling, underneath the cherub, fill your hands with burning coals from between the cherubs, and scatter them over the city." He came in before my eyes. [3]The cherubs were standing at the right of the house when the man came in and the cloud was filling the inner courtyard. [4]Yahweh's splendor lifted from above the cherub above the house's terrace, the house was filled with the cloud, and the courtyard was full of the brightness of Yahweh's splendor. [5]The sound of the cherubs' wings made itself heard as far as the outer courtyard, like the voice of El Shadday when he speaks. [6]When he commanded the man dressed in linen, "Take fire from between the whirling, from between the cherubs," [the man] came in and stood beside the wheel. [7]A cherub put out its hand from between the cherubs to the fire that was between the cherubs, took it up, and put it into the hands of the one dressed in linen. He took it and went out. [8](The form of a human hand belonging to the cherubs was visible under their wings.)

⁹I looked, and there—four wheels beside the cherubs, one wheel beside one cherub, one wheel beside another cherub. The appearance of the wheels: the very gleam of beryl stone. ¹⁰Their appearance: the four of them had one form, as if one wheel were inside another wheel. ¹¹When they went, they'd go in the direction of their four quarters. They wouldn't turn as they went, because the place that the head faced, they'd follow it. They wouldn't turn as they went. ¹²Their entire body—their backs, their hands, and their wings—and the wheels were full of eyes all around (the wheels belonging to the four of them; ¹³these wheels had been called "the whirling," in my ears). ¹⁴Each had four faces. The face of one was a cherub's face. The face of the second was a human face. The third was a lion's face. The fourth was an eagle's face. ¹⁵The cherubs lifted; it was the creature that I'd seen by the river Kebar. ¹⁶When the cherubs went, the wheels would go beside them. When the cherubs raised their wings to lift from on the earth, the wheels wouldn't turn from beside them, too. ¹⁷When [the cherubs] stopped, they'd stop. When the cherubs lifted, they'd lift with them, because the spirit of life was in them.

¹⁸Yahweh's splendor went out from on the house's terrace and stood above the cherubs. ¹⁹The cherubs raised their wings and lifted from the earth before my eyes as they went out, with the wheels alongside them. It stood at the door of the east gateway of Yahweh's house, with the splendor of Israel's God over them, above. ²⁰It was the creature that I saw below Israel's God at the river Kebar. So I recognized that they were cherubs. ²¹Each had four faces and each had four wings, with the form of human hands under their wings. ²²The form of their faces—they were the faces that I saw by the river Kebar, their appearance and themselves. They'd each go in the direction of its face.

Yesterday we visited a church whose pastor described it as built in "1970s Safeway" style, a bare hall with rows of pews and a cross with a drum kit located in the front of it. Outside the building was a neat notice announcing that "the church meets here." The church is the people, not the building. The building is purely an enclosure for the people. The building made for a contrast with the Monastery of Hosios Loukas (Holy Luke, its founding prophet) in Greece and the Holy Wisdom Mosque in Turkey (originally a church), which we visited last month. There the soaring height of the ceilings with their paintings draws attention away from the congregation (there aren't any pews) to the glory of God.

The Jerusalem temple was a little like that, though not built on the scale of Holy Wisdom. God's glory, God's splendor, resided in it, and therefore people didn't go in. They knew God's intimate presence in other ways, not least by spending time in the temple courtyards, but the temple building reminded them of the awe-inspiring, transcendent aspect to God's presence. The horror of the vision in Ezekiel 10 is that God's presence is pulling out from the temple and the city. The appalling process began in the previous chapter, where **Yahweh**'s splendor, that glorious presence, moved to the temple threshold. Now the creatures take off from the threshold and hover over the city, to the east. The scribe now has another role, which again suggests that the main point about his earlier task was to prepare the way for Yahweh's act of judgment upon the entire city. It's he who initiates the fiery judgment with the fire from between the wheels.

Ezekiel continues to be in the midst of an experience of God appearing to him in a way that takes up the appearing associated with his commission as prophet, which suggests some good news. While the appalling news is that Yahweh is abandoning the temple in Jerusalem, Yahweh isn't simply going off no one knows where, but moving eastward. It fits with the way he's already appeared in **Babylon**. Ezekiel notes that the "creature[s]" in that earlier chapter can now be identified as **cherub[s]**, but they're not "cherubic." A few months ago, one of my key mentors and inspirations died. In his last sermon he reflected on his thinking and feelings as he drew near to death. "Away with all the pre-Raphaelite angels with their gaudy robes and rebuking haloes!" he said. "Away with all those babyish cherubs with their well-sculpted buttocks! Away with clouds and harps and all the medieval religious clutter that goes with them!"

EZEKIEL 11:1–25

A Small Sanctuary

¹A wind lifted me and brought me to the east gateway of Yahweh's house. There, at the door in the gateway, were twenty-five men. I saw among them Ja'azaniah son of Azzur and Pelatiah son of Benaiah, officials of the people. ²[Yahweh] said to me, "Young man, these are the men who plan wickedness and formulate evil counsel in this city, ³who say, 'The building of houses isn't at hand. It's the pot, and we're the meat.' ⁴Therefore prophesy against them. Prophesy, young man." ⁵Yahweh's spirit fell on me, and he said to me, "Say: Yahweh has said this: So you've said, Israel's household; I myself know what's come up into your spirit. ⁶You've made many people your slain in this city. You've filled its streets with the slain. ⁷Therefore the Lord Yahweh has said this: Your slain whom you've put in your midst: they're the meat. It's the pot, but he's making you go out from it. ⁸You're afraid of a sword, but I shall bring a sword upon you. ⁹I shall make you go out from its midst and give you into the hand of strangers. I shall implement decisions against you. ¹⁰By the sword you'll fall. At Israel's border I shall decide about you, and you will acknowledge that I am Yahweh. ¹¹It won't be a pot for you nor will you be the meat in it. At Israel's border I shall decide about you, ¹²and you will acknowledge that I am Yahweh, whose laws you didn't follow and whose decisions you didn't enact, but acted in accordance with the decisions of the nations that are around you." ¹³As I prophesied, Pelatiah son of Benaiah died. I fell on my face and cried out in a loud voice, "Aaaagh, Lord Yahweh, you're making an end of the remains of Israel!"

¹⁴Yahweh's message came to me: ¹⁵Young man, your relatives, your relatives who are the people in your extended family, all Israel's household, all of it, are the people of whom Jerusalem's residents have said, "Stay far away from Yahweh. It's being given to us, the country, as a possession." ¹⁶Therefore say, The Lord Yahweh has said this: Because I've moved them far away among the nations and because I've scattered them among the countries and become a small sanctuary for them in the countries where they've come, ¹⁷therefore say, The Lord Yahweh has said this: I shall collect you from the peoples, gather you from the countries where I scattered them, and I shall give you Israel's land. ¹⁸They'll come there and put away all their abominations and their outrages from them, ¹⁹and I shall give them one mind. I shall put a new spirit within you. I shall put away the mind of stone from their flesh and give them a mind of flesh, ²⁰so that they'll follow my laws, and keep my decisions and implement them. They'll be a people for me and I shall be God for them. ²¹But to the people whose mind is walking after the mind of their abominations and their outrages, I'm going to bring their way on their head (a declaration of the Lord Yahweh).

²²The cherubs lifted up their wings, with the wheels alongside them and the splendor of Israel's God over them, above. ²³Yahweh's splendor went up from over the midst of the city and stopped over the mountain that's on the east of the city. ²⁴A wind lifted me up and brought me to Kaldea to the exilic community with the appearance by God's spirit, and the appearance that I'd seen went up from over me. ²⁵I spoke to the exilic community all Yahweh's words that he'd shown me.

Our church building is a small sanctuary, and the congregation that meets there is a small church. When there are forty people there, it looks reasonably full. Yet a few years ago we used to have to put out extra chairs for people; we don't have to do so now. How shall we think about the future? Is it inevitable that we continue shrinking as older people pass on? A few new people have started coming in the past year or two. Might the congregation grow? What basis for hope do we have?

The departure of **Yahweh**'s splendor is a horrifying event that hangs over Jerusalem, which (we know with hindsight) will become a reality in four or five years' time. The city will fall; the temple will be destroyed. People in Jerusalem and people already in **Babylon** need to face the fact and prepare for it in their thinking. The encouragement to **Judahites** in Babylon is the fact that Yahweh isn't merely moving away from Jerusalem to reside somewhere inaccessible and unidentifiable in the wilderness. In the second paragraph he declares that he's already become a small-scale sanctuary for these Judahites. The exiles may have thought about building a sanctuary in Babylon, and may have done so, but Yahweh speaks not of dwelling in a sanctuary there but of *being* a sanctuary there. He is present there, even though there's no building. There's nothing revolutionary here. **Israelites** never assumed that Yahweh was only present in the temple, which would mean most of them could hardly ever be in his presence. There was a special guarantee of his presence there, but he was present throughout the country. He's also present in Babylon. Being in Jerusalem doesn't guarantee you're in Yahweh's presence, and being in Babylon doesn't rule out being in Yahweh's presence.

The people left in Jerusalem have excuses for thinking that the people taken into **exile** have been cast off by Yahweh and for telling them to stay well away from Yahweh and from Jerusalem. Some of them could be people who'd been cheated out of their land by people now in exile. They could claim that the exiles deserved their fate, and could reasonably rejoice that the country was given back to the people who'd previously been in proper possession of it. Others of them could be people glad to have a chance to appropriate land that properly belonged to people who'd been exiled.

Ezekiel hears the city's leaders talking in realistically gloomier terms. A positive future, the chance to build new homes, looks far away. The community is like the meat being cooked in a stewpot. The fire is getting hotter and hotter. Yet they won't draw the right inferences. Instead of encouraging the city to turn to Yahweh, they're trying to solve their problems by taking practical political decisions. But these decisions count as wicked, **evil** counsel. They're responsible for many deaths in the city through their misguided leadership and/or their involvement in the wrongdoing practiced by other people that Ezekiel and Jeremiah attack, such as the sacrifice of children, or in violence for the sake of gain. Typically, Ezekiel reworks their image against them. It was the people who've been killed who were like the meat in a pot, which these leaders were putting on the fire. If the city's the pot, these leaders won't remain in it, but will be thrown out to be slain another way. The reference to Israel's border again suggests how Judahite leaders were brought before the Babylonian authorities at Riblah (see the comment on chapter 6).

Within the vision, the prophecy starts getting implemented immediately. When one of the leaders drops dead (there's no indication that he died in real life), we might be surprised that Ezekiel protests. The protest again reflects the two sides to what Yahweh must do. On one hand, there's need for judgment; on the other, there's need to keep Israel in being. There was need for a prophet to declare judgment, but also to cry out for mercy on the guilty. There was need to scatter the people; there's need to gather them. There was need to be a small sanctuary to them in their scattering; there's need to be God for the people as a whole again. This promise and the associated promises about a new spirit and mind will be taken further in chapters 36–37.

In the vision, Yahweh's splendor stops moving as it passes the Mount of Olives, east of Jerusalem. It's as if it's hesitating to leave. There's still the possibility of its not doing so, if the city turns back to Yahweh.

EZEKIEL 12:1–28

God Won't Let Things Drag On

[1]Yahweh's message came to me: [2]Young man, you're living among a rebellious household, who have eyes for seeing but don't see, ears for hearing but don't hear, because they're a rebellious household. [3]You, young man, prepare things for exile for yourself and go into exile by day before their eyes. Go into exile from your place to another place before their eyes. Perhaps they'll see that they're a rebellious household. [4]You're to take your things out like things for exile by day, before their eyes, and you yourself are to go out in the evening, before their eyes, like people going out into exile. [5]Before their eyes, break through the wall for yourself and take it out through it. [6]Before their eyes, you're to lift it onto your shoulder. You're to take it out in the dark. You're to cover your face and not look at the country, because I'm making you a sign to Israel's household.

[7]I did just as I was commanded. I took my things out by day, like things for exile, and in the evening broke through the wall for myself with my hand. In the dark I took it out. I lifted it on my shoulder before their eyes.

[8]Yahweh's message came to me in the morning: [9]Young man, didn't Israel's household (a rebellious household) say to you, "What are you doing?" [10]Say to them, "The Lord Yahweh has said this: This prophecy [is about] the ruler in Jerusalem and all Israel's household that are among them." [11]Say, "I'm a sign for you. As I've done, so it will be done to them. They'll go into exile, into captivity." [12]The ruler who's among them will lift it onto his shoulder in the dark. He'll go out through the wall. They'll break through in order to take it out through it. He'll cover his face, because he won't look at the country with his eye. [13]I shall spread my net over him, and he'll be caught in my trap. I shall bring him to Babylon, to the Kaldeans' country, but he won't see it, and he'll die there. [14]Everyone who's around him, his support staff and all his legions, I shall scatter to every wind, and draw a sword after them. [15]They will acknowledge that I am Yahweh when I scatter

them among the nations and disperse them among the countries. [16]But I shall leave a few people from them from sword, famine, and epidemic, so that they may recount all their outrages among the nations where they come, and they will acknowledge that I am Yahweh.

[17]Yahweh's message came to me: [18]Young man, you're to eat your food with trembling and drink your water with shuddering and anxiety, [19]and say to the country's people, The Lord Yahweh has said this concerning Jerusalem's residents in the land of Israel: They'll eat their bread with anxiety and drink their water in desolation, so that their country may be desolate of what fills it because of the violence of all the people who live in it. [20]The inhabited cities will be wasted and the country will become a desolation, and you will acknowledge that I am Yahweh.

[21]Yahweh's message came to me: [22]Young man, what's this saying that you have in the land of Israel, Days grow long and every vision perishes? [23]Therefore say to them, "The Lord Yahweh has said this: I shall make this saying stop. They won't say it anymore in Israel." Rather, speak to them: The days are drawing near, and the message in every vision. [24]Because there won't anymore be empty vision or deceptive divination amid Israel's household. [25]Because I Yahweh shall speak the word that I speak and it will be done. It won't drag out anymore. Because in your days, rebellious household, I shall speak a word and do it (a declaration of the Lord Yahweh).

[26]Yahweh's message came to me: [27]Young man, there—Israel's household are saying, The vision that he sees is for many days and he prophesies for far-off times. [28]Therefore say to them: The Lord Yahweh has said this: All the words that I speak won't drag on anymore. The word that I speak will be done (a declaration of the Lord Yahweh).

During my teenage years the president of Egypt nationalized the Suez Canal, which had been owned by British and French stockholders. The action led to attempts by Britain, France, and Israel to take over the canal by military means. I was afraid that this event during the Cold War would push the United States (which backed Israel) and the Soviet Union (which backed Egypt) into starting the Third World War. And I recall a sermon in which the preacher declared that the Egyptian president's action fulfilled a prophecy in Ezekiel 29 in which the pharaoh declares (in the King James translation), "My river is mine own, and I have made it for myself."

It's one of a number of passages in Ezekiel that have been seen as anticipations of recent events in the Middle East. There are a number of bases on which one might question whether Ezekiel is prophesying political events 2,500 years after his day. They don't include that such prophecy is impossible. God surely could foresee events and reveal them to a prophet. This chapter provides an example in its statements about King Zedekiah. Covering the eyes and not looking at the country might suggest a grief that cannot take one last look. But people reading Ezekiel's prophecies in light of events four years later would inevitably think of the chilling happenings at Riblah to which we referred in connection with chapter 6, when the **Babylonians** capture and blind King Zedekiah after he breaks out of Jerusalem. The comment about going to Babylon but not seeing Babylon is even more explicit, though it would be a puzzling comment until its terrible fulfillment.

God is again getting Ezekiel to dramatize coming events, to try to break through to people. Again the drama does more than dramatize them. It initiates them. God can declare what's going to happen because he intends to make it happen. Another aspect of the chilling nature of the prophecy of **exile** happening to people's relatives and fellow **Judahites** back in Jerusalem is that it's not merely the Babylonians who capture Zedekiah. It's **Yahweh**. Yahweh has a sardonic note to add. An advantage of not simply killing off all the Judahites will be that people in the countries where the survivors go will naturally ask them how they came to be in exile, and they'll have to explain why

Yahweh brought about this catastrophe and thus offer a form of recognition of Yahweh.

Ezekiel does talk about the future, but he suggests one reason for questioning whether he talks about events in 2,500 years' time. His prophecies don't relate to far-off times, he says. God speaks to people in the present. When God talks about the future, it's the future that will affect the people to whom the prophet speaks. That may mean talking about a future that will turn out to be far off, as is the case when the New Testament talks about Jesus' second coming, but even then it's a future that's important to people in the present. Ezekiel's contemporaries were inclined to sardonic declarations about his prophecies relating to the distant future. You couldn't blame them. Jeremiah has been telling people for years that judgment is coming, but it doesn't come; Ezekiel is now imitating him. Doubters in Jerusalem who dodged the bullet a few years ago are fooling themselves that they'll do so again. They think they can afford to be laid back about Ezekiel's exotic prophecies. His point is then that Yahweh's message is one that doesn't presage events coming in a decade or century or millennium. The message will come true now. And it did.

The people mentioned in the previous chapter could have a contrasting reason for skepticism. They can't see when they'll be able to rebuild their city and they're tempted to see themselves as meat sitting in a pot and about to be cooked. Other prophets in Jerusalem and Babylon whose message contrasts with that of Jeremiah and Ezekiel are promising that restoration will soon come. But it fails to do so. People could understandably become skeptical about all prophecy. It's all pie in the sky. It never has relevance for the day we live in, only for some far future day when it might be fulfilled. That kind of prophecy raises problems for a prophet such as Ezekiel as he seeks to get his message heeded. But his prophecy will shortly be vindicated, and the empty vision and deceptive divination expressed in those promises come to an end, falsified. One can imagine that Ezekiel's prophetic contemporaries would have been as offended at being called diviners (the word is hardly ever used in a good sense) as they'd be offended at being called deceptive.

For people living 2,500 years later, the implication isn't that Ezekiel's warnings have no significance for this later day. When people made a point of preserving his messages, they did so in the conviction that their fulfillment didn't mean they had no relevance for the future. On the contrary, they'd been proved to be words from God, and they therefore deserved to be heeded by future generations, too. They don't directly refer to far-future events in veiled hints, but God's words uttered in a particular context aren't random. They express something of God's consistent concerns. The chapter reminds readers in every century of how easy it is to have eyes and ears that we don't use, the reason being that we don't want to see or hear what they could make known. We're rebels by nature.

EZEKIEL 13:1–23

About Building a Wall

¹Yahweh's message came to me: ²Young man, prophesy against Israel's prophets, who are prophesying. Say to the prophets [who speak] from their own mind, Listen to Yahweh's message. ³The Lord Yahweh has said this: Hey, against the mindless prophets who follow their own spirits and have seen nothing. ⁴Your prophets have been like jackals among ruins, Israel. ⁵You didn't go up into the breaks and build up the barrier around Israel's household so it would stand in the battle on Yahweh's day. ⁶They saw emptiness and lying divination, those who say "Yahweh's declaration" when Yahweh hadn't sent them, and expected the establishing of their message. ⁷Was it not an empty vision that you saw and lying divination that you uttered, saying "Yahweh's declaration" when I myself hadn't spoken? ⁸Therefore the Lord Yahweh has said this: Because you spoke emptiness and saw lies, here am I [acting]

toward you (a declaration of the Lord Yahweh). [9]My hand will be against the prophets who see emptiness and who divine lies. They won't be in my people's council. They won't be recorded in the record of Israel's household. They won't come into Israel's land. And you will acknowledge that I am the Lord Yahweh.

[10]Because, yes because they've misled my people, saying "Things will be well," when things won't be well, and "He's building a divider," but there—they're coating it with paint: [11]say to the people coating it with paint, It will fall. Pouring rain is coming and I shall send hailstones that will fall, and a storm wind will break it up. [12]There, the wall is falling. Will it not be said to you, "Where is the coating that you put on?"

[13]Therefore the Lord Yahweh has said this: I shall make a storm wind break out in my rage, and pouring rain will come in my anger and hailstones in my rage, to a complete end. [14]I shall tear down the wall that you've coated with paint, bring it to the earth, and its foundation will become visible. When it falls, you'll come to an end in its midst, and you will acknowledge that I am Yahweh. [15]I shall spend my rage on the wall and the people who coat it with paint, and say to you, There's no wall and there are no painters of it, [16]Israel's prophets who prophesy to Jerusalem and see a vision of things being well for it when things aren't going to be well (a declaration of the Lord Yahweh).

[17]And you, young man, set your face against your people's women, who prophesy out of their own minds. Prophesy against them. [18]You shall say: The Lord Yahweh has said this: Hey, to the people who sew bands on any wrists and make veils for the head of someone of any height, to trap their lives. Should you trap my people's lives but for yourselves keep yourselves alive? [19]You've treated me as ordinary to my people for handfuls of barley and crumbs of bread, to put to death people who shouldn't die and keep alive people who shouldn't live, with your lying to my people who listen to lying. [20]Therefore the Lord Yahweh has said this: Here am I, against your bands, where you're hunting the lives of beings that fly. I shall tear them off from on your arms and release the lives that

you're hunting of beings that fly. ²¹I shall tear off your veils and save my people from your hand. They'll no longer be prey in your hand, and you will acknowledge that I am Yahweh. ²²Because of your saddening the spirit of the faithful person with falsehood when I myself hadn't hurt him, and for your strengthening the hands of the faithless person so that he wouldn't turn back from his evil way so as to stay alive, ²³therefore you won't see emptiness and you won't practice divination anymore. I shall save my people from your hand, and you will acknowledge that I am Yahweh.

Most Sundays I stand in front of our congregation and preach, saying things that I believe express what God is saying to us. It's a frightening undertaking. I'm sincere as a preacher, but being sincere doesn't mean being right. I don't get the impression that people in the congregation disagree with me, but this fact might indicate only that they and I are colluding in my saying things they like. Every Sunday preachers in other churches are saying things that conflict with things that I might say. Some people at the meeting about genocide at which I spoke the other day, which I mentioned in connection with Ezekiel 9, certainly thought that some things that I said were dangerously wrong. I sometimes tell students, "Ten percent of what I say is wrong—the trouble is, I don't know which ten percent."

So I'm hesitant to assume I can simply identify with Ezekiel rather than with the "false prophets." They were quite sincere, wanting to bring Yahweh's message to people, and believing they were doing so. As a Judahite, it wouldn't have been immediately obvious to you who were true prophets and who were false ones. These other prophets spoke in Yahweh's name, said what Yahweh was intending to do in people's lives, and (to judge from the picture we get elsewhere) performed actions that embodied their message.

Ezekiel knows that actually their message comes from inside them, not from Yahweh. Maybe he implies that in their heart

71

of hearts they know it's so. Yet his comment about their expecting the fulfillment of their promises implies that they were indeed sincere, though self-deceived. They did see a vision, even though it was a self-generated one. Whether or not they realized it, they ought to be able to do so (he implies) because a moment's reflection on their message shows it to be irresponsible. Ezekiel again makes use of the similarity between words of different meaning. The prophet (*nabi*) is mindless, morally stupid (*nabal*).

The evidence is that they're failing to contribute to the city's protection at its moment of danger. The king was seeking to strengthen its physical defenses; maybe that's the "divider" Ezekiel refers to (and maybe he uses this word in order to disparage it). Whatever the divider is, it's something feeble that the prophets are making impressive by giving it a coat of paint. Being used to proper British houses made of brick, I'm regularly horrified when I see houses being built in California, all chicken wire and particle board. They look nice when they've been covered in stucco and paint, but they're so flimsy (earthquakes are part of the reason they're that way, though my wife the architect says it's also because it's cheap).

The painter-prophets' action will turn out to be futile if nothing is done about the city's moral and religious defenses. After all (chapter 12 reminded us), the king of **Babylon** is simply the person Yahweh uses to fulfill his intentions. Yahweh is the person Jerusalem needs to defend itself against. It's Yahweh's day that's coming, and Ezekiel 7 has already declared that it's to be a day of Yahweh's wrath, not of his blessing. The city can dodge the bullet, but the key to doing so is moral and religious. If it sorts itself out in that sense, it has nothing to fear on the day Yahweh acts in wrath. But the prophets are doing nothing to contribute to the construction of this kind of protection. They're assuring people that things will go well again, that they'll experience **well-being**, but their message is a bundle of empty lies. It doesn't correspond to any reality.

The frightening destiny of the prophets is that they'll even lose their place within Israel. Their names will disappear from its register. They'll forfeit their share in the land.

The women prophets also preach messages they've made up, whether consciously or not. Ezekiel is more explicit about how the religious observances they encourage threaten the community's destiny. The bands and veils are amulets, objects to protect the wearer and/or harm other people. They'd thus trap people like birds in a net instead of letting them fly free. The prophets believed that they'd protect people's lives and enhance their own, but the people they're protecting are people who ought not to be protected, and the people they're seeking to imperil are innocent people. In reality they're imperiling the people they claim to help because they're encouraging them to persist in their faithless ways. There's nothing wrong in principle with their getting paid for their ministry, but they're getting paid trivial amounts for what will turn out to be a very costly ministry—it costs other people their lives and it will cost them their own lives. The question the prophet or preacher has to ask isn't "Am I sincere?" but "Am I building the wall by encouraging **faithfulness** and confronting **faithlessness?**"

EZEKIEL 14:1–23

Noah, Danel, and Job

[1]People from among Israel's elders came to me and sat in front of me, [2]and Yahweh's message came to me: [3]Young man, these people have taken their lumps into their mind and placed their waywardness as an obstacle in front of their face. Shall I really let myself be inquired of by them? [4]Therefore speak to them and say to them, The Lord Yahweh has said this: Any individual from Israel's household who takes his lumps into his mind and sets his waywardness as an obstacle in front of his face, and comes to the prophet, I make answer to him with

it (with the great number of his lumps), [5]so as to lay hold of Israel's household with its mind, because they've become estranged from me with their lumps, all of them. [6]Therefore say to Israel's household, The Lord Yahweh has said this: Turn, turn yourselves back from your lumps, turn away your face from your outrages. [7]Because any individual from Israel's household or from the aliens residing in Israel who becomes estranged from following me and takes his lumps into his mind and sets his waywardness as an obstacle in front of his face, and comes to the prophet to inquire of him with me—I Yahweh make answer to him by myself. [8]I shall set my face against that person and make him a sign and a saying. I shall cut him off from among my people. And you will acknowledge that I am Yahweh. [9]When the prophet is trapped and speaks a message, I Yahweh will have trapped that prophet. I shall stretch out my hand against him and destroy him from among my people Israel. [10]They'll carry their waywardness. The inquirer's waywardness and the prophet's waywardness will be the same, [11]so that Israel's household may not wander again from following me and may not defile itself again with all its rebellions. They'll be a people for me and I shall be God for them (a declaration of the Lord Yahweh).

[12]Yahweh's message came to me: [13]Young man, when a country offends against me by committing a trespass, and I extend my hand against it, and break its bread supply and send famine against it and cut off from it human beings and animals, [14]and these three people were in its midst, Noah, Danel, and Job, they by their faithfulness would save their own lives (a declaration of the Lord Yahweh). [15]If I let evil creatures pass through the country, and they leave it childless and it becomes a desolation without anyone passing through in face of the beasts, [16]were these three people in its midst, as I live (a declaration of the Lord Yahweh), neither sons nor daughters would they save. They'd save themselves alone. The country would become a desolation. [17]Or I might bring a sword against that country and say, "A sword is to pass through the country, and I shall cut off from it human beings and animals"; [18]these three people in its midst (as I live—a declaration of the Lord Yahweh)

wouldn't save sons or daughters, but would save themselves alone. [19]Or I might send off an epidemic to that country and pour out my rage on it in bloodshed by cutting off from it human beings and animals; [20]Noah, Danel, and Job in its midst (as I live—a declaration of the Lord Yahweh) wouldn't save a son or a daughter. These people would save themselves alone by their faithfulness. [21]Because the Lord Yahweh has said this: How much more when I've sent off my four evil judgments—sword, famine, evil beasts, and epidemic—against Jerusalem, to cut off from it human beings and animals. [22]But there—survivors are being left in it, they're taking out sons and daughters. There they are, coming out to you. You'll see their way and their deeds, and be comforted about the evil that I shall have brought upon Jerusalem, all that I've brought upon it. [23]They'll comfort you because you'll see their way and their deeds and you will acknowledge that it was not for no reason that I did all that I did against it (a declaration of the Lord Yahweh).

At the top of each of the two columns of the prayer list that I use are the names of our children and our grandchildren. Except when something odd happens, I pray for them all every couple of days. There's nothing more important to many parents than what happens to their children. In the monumental storm that hit New York last weekend, the worst story related how a mother was trying to escape the storm with her two tiny children, and they got swept away. If you could fix things so that everything went well for your children, there's probably nothing you'd rather do. Yet when your children are grown up, you have to recognize that you can no longer fix things for them.

Ezekiel imagines three fathers concerned about their children. All are figures from the past, from before **Israel** existed or from outside Israel, all of them famously righteous and/or wise. The righteous Noah made sure that his children were in the boat in which the family escaped the flood. Job's story begins with declarations of his righteousness and his offering sacrifice for his children and thus praying for them, and it ends with his sharing his estate with them—the daughters as well as the sons. Danel isn't Daniel, the Old Testament figure, but a just judge in an ancient story from Syria who prays for a son and gets one. In all three cases the story is a tough one—Noah ends up cursing one of his sons, Job's first group of children die, and Danel's son dies. None of the three is able to fix things for their children.

The point of the appeal to their stories is to underline in yet another way the magnitude of the calamity that hangs over **Judah**. Even the presence of three famously upright fathers wouldn't save their children independently of the children's own **faithfulness**, let alone the community as a whole. It has to take responsibility for itself. It cannot hide behind anyone. The close of the section then makes the point about God's mercy that has to be set alongside the challenge. The logic of the warning is that God will destroy the whole community unless its members are faithful like the three heroes. But grace commonly means that logic breaks down. Children can't expect to escape calamity through a parent's faithfulness. Yet **Yahweh** will see that some people and their children survive to leave Jerusalem's ruins and join the people already in **exile**. The closing verse makes explicit that they don't survive because they deserve to. One look at their lives, which are typical of the Judahites', will show how the entire community will have deserved its fate. In an odd way it will be a comfort to the community already in exile, because it will indicate that events aren't morally meaningless and Yahweh isn't just arbitrary. Yahweh's drastic action was justified. Yet some people's children do survive, because of Yahweh's commitment to the community, not because of what they or their parents deserve.

Maybe Ezekiel's prophecy responds to a question the exiles were asking, but the first half of the chapter warns them not to expect too much by way of answers to their questions. As their representatives, the elders have apparently gathered to ask one. But they're people who "have taken their **lumps** into their mind and set their waywardness as an obstacle in front of their faces." That is, in their thinking and in their religious practice they're attached to images of Yahweh or images of other gods, images that are really just lumps of wood or, worse, are offensive to Yahweh, and are thus going to be their downfall. So how can they possibly expect to be able to come to inquire of Yahweh? OK, says Yahweh, I shall answer their questions, but I shall do so as a way of catching them out.

Yahweh may use a prophet to do so. It adds another peril to a prophet's position. Perhaps Ezekiel sees a danger to be wary of. More likely he has in mind the other prophets who easily bring people a message that comes from their own spirits. God declares the intention even to work through that process. If you're a prophet and people ask you a question and you think you have the answer, think three times before you give it, because God has said he's not keen on answering the questions of a community like this one. God may simply be using your capacity to find answers or to be imaginative as a means of bringing judgment on them and on you. It's a predicament for a prophet, though maybe an artificial one, because the point about the prophecy is again to try to get through to the community itself, this time by underlining the fact that it can expect no real response from Yahweh until it changes its ways. But yet again, the actual threat and also the possible action ultimately relate to a gracious purpose. Everything serves the aim of turning Israel into a people that doesn't wander from Yahweh, so that they're a people that belongs to Yahweh and Yahweh is a God who belongs to them.

EZEKIEL 15:1–8

They're Toast

¹Yahweh's message came to me: ²Young man, how will the grapevine's wood be better than the wood of any branch that's among the trees of the forest? ³Will wood be taken from it to

use for any work? Will they take a peg from it to hang an object on? ⁴There, it's put in the fire to be consumed. If the fire consumes the two ends of it and the middle of it's burned, is it useful for any work? ⁵There, when it was whole, it couldn't be used for any work. How much less when it consumes it and burns it can it be used for any work. ⁶Therefore the Lord Yahweh says this: As the wood of the grapevine among the trees of the forest that I gave to the fire for consuming, so I'm giving Jerusalem's residents. ⁷I'm setting my face against them. They got out from the fire, but the fire will consume them, and you will acknowledge that I'm Yahweh when I set my face against them. ⁸I shall make the country a desolation because they committed trespass (a declaration of the Lord Yahweh).

My wife asked me, out of the blue, whether I like olives, and I said I like them in a Bloody Mary (but that didn't count because that means green olives) and in tapenade, and I don't mind them in pasta sauce or casserole, and I like dipping bread in olive oil. But my olive consumption would nowhere near explain the acres and acres of olive trees that we saw in Turkey and Greece a few weeks ago (that's what she was recalling when she asked the question). Yet many of those acres seemed neglected or abandoned, and on one occasion we saw olive branches being burned. You can't do much with olive wood except make kitchen tools and tableware. You can't make furniture or build with it.

The same is even truer of the wood of a grapevine. Olive wood or grapevine wood isn't much use for anything except firewood. It's then convenient for Ezekiel that the olive tree and the grapevine are standard images for Israel. Isaiah 5 relates how Yahweh had carefully and painstakingly prepared a vineyard and planted a vine there. Psalm 80 presupposes that Yahweh had then neglected and abandoned this vine, and let it be burned. It can't see any reason for Yahweh's doing so, and it appeals for Yahweh to restore it. But Isaiah had declared that in his context there was good reason for this action on Yahweh's part. The vine hadn't produced any decent fruit. Jerusalem and **Judah** were characterized by bloodshed and cries of distress instead of the exercise of **authority** in a faithful way. Jeremiah 2 speaks in similar terms nearer Ezekiel's day. Ezekiel's way of making the point is to talk in terms of "trespass." The idea of trespass is that a person has rights and property that other people ought to respect. Judah has ignored Yahweh's rights as God. The exiles might think that the ends of the vine prunings have been burned (through the first fall of Jerusalem in 597) but that the main part of the vine is still intact. They got out of the fire. But it will turn out to have been only a temporary escape. The main part of the vine will get burned up, too.

EZEKIEL 16:1–34

You're Just a Whore

¹Yahweh's message came to me: ²Young man, get Jerusalem to acknowledge its outrages. ³You're to say, The Lord Yahweh has said this to Jerusalem: Your origin and birth were from the Canaanites' country; your father was an Amorite and your mother a Hittite. ⁴Your birth: on the day you were born, no one cut your cord and you weren't washed in water for cleansing. You weren't rubbed with salt at all or wrapped up at all. ⁵No eye cared about you so as to do one of these things for you to express compassion for you. You were thrown onto the surface of the countryside in loathing for you on the day you were born. ⁶But I passed by you and looked at you kicking about in your bloodiness. I said to you in your bloodiness, "Live." Yes, I said to you in your bloodiness, "Live, ⁷grow big." I made you like a plant in the countryside, and you grew big. You grew up and came to full loveliness; your breasts formed, your hair flourished. But you were naked, bare, ⁸and I passed by you and looked—there, your time was time for love. I spread my robe over you and covered your nakedness. I took an oath to you and came into covenant with you (a declaration of the

Lord Yahweh) and you became mine. ⁹I washed you in water and sluiced off the blood from on you and poured oil over you. ¹⁰I clothed you with embroidery and gave you leather footwear. I wrapped you around in fine linen and covered you in silk. ¹¹I adorned you with jewelry and put bracelets on your hands and a necklace on your neck. ¹²I put a ring on your nose, earrings on your ears, and a splendid tiara on your head. ¹³So you adorned yourself with gold and silver, and your clothing was of fine linen, silk, and embroidery, your food was choice flour, honey, and oil, and you became more and more beautiful, and attained a royal position. ¹⁴Your fame went out among the nations for your beauty, because it was complete through the splendor that I put on you (a declaration of the Lord Yahweh).

¹⁵But you trusted in your beauty and became immoral on the basis of your fame. You poured your immoralities on every passerby. It could become his. ¹⁶You took some of your clothes and made yourself colorful shrines, and engaged in immorality at them (not coming ones, and they shouldn't exist). ¹⁷You took your splendid things of gold and silver that I gave you and made yourself male images and acted immorally with them. ¹⁸You took your embroidered clothes and covered them and offered my oil and incense before them. ¹⁹My food that I gave you, fine flour, oil, and honey that I enabled you to eat, you offered before them as a pleasing fragrance, and so it became (a declaration of the Lord Yahweh). ²⁰You took your sons and your daughters whom you bore to me and sacrificed them to them as food: were your immoralities trivial? ²¹You slaughtered my children and gave them to them by making them pass through [fire]. ²²With all your abominations and your immoralities, you weren't mindful of your young days when you were naked and bare, kicking about in your bloodiness.

²³After all your evil, hey, hey, to you (a declaration of the Lord Yahweh)! ²⁴You built yourself an enclosure and made yourself a platform in every square. ²⁵At every crossroad you built your platform and made your beauty an outrage. You spread your legs to every passerby and multiplied your immoralities. ²⁶You were immoral with the Egyptians, your

neighbors with their big members. You multiplied your immorality to provoke me. [27]There—I'm stretching out my hand to you and cutting your allowance. I'm giving you over to the will of people who repudiate you, the Philistine women, who are ashamed of your scheming way.

[28]You were immoral with the Assyrians because you weren't sated. You were immoral with them, but you were still not satiated. [29]You multiplied your immorality with the trader country, Kaldea, but you were still not satiated by this. [30]How feeble was your mind (a declaration of the Lord Yahweh) when you did all these things, the action of an immoral, powerful woman. [31]When you built your enclosure at every crossroad and made your platform in every square, you were not like an immoral woman, in scorning a gift, [32]you adulterous wife who accepts strangers instead of her husband. [33]To all immoral women, men give a fee, but you—you've given a fee to all your lovers, and paid them to come to you for your immoralities from all around. [34]With you it was the opposite from [other] women in your immoralities. Immorality was not committed by following after you but through your giving a gift. A gift was not given to you. You were the opposite.

A little while ago a young woman who lived near us was put in jail after her baby was found dead in a trash bin behind a bar-restaurant, where she'd apparently put the unwanted child, to be found dead by a homeless man foraging in the trash bin for food. It's not the first such story; a little further away a little more recently, a woman was sent to prison after suffocating her baby, putting the body in a plastic bag, and leaving it in a dumpster. In Europe and in the United States, "Safe Haven" provisions have been developed in places near hospitals or police stations to make it possible for parents to leave an unwanted baby rather than abandon it to death. It's difficult to imagine the pain that might be involved for mother, father, and baby.

Yahweh describes Jerusalem as that kind of baby. Yahweh was the kind of person who then has the compassion to become the baby's adoptive father. But adopting a child is often a challenging business, especially as the child grows up. So it has been in this case. The grown-up girl is promiscuous. In the allegory, her immorality has two significances. It makes the same points that Ezekiel and other prophets make elsewhere, about religious unfaithfulness and political unfaithfulness. The religious unfaithfulness means going after other deities to try to ensure that the crops grow and the animals and people are fertile. The political unfaithfulness means looking to other nations such as Egypt, **Assyria**, and **Babylon**, to get their support to enable Jerusalem to retain the appearance of freedom.

At least half the responsibility would lie with the men in the community, who wielded at least half the power in Jerusalem's life. Part of the allegory's point is thus its potential impact on the male-dominated community. "You're just an immoral woman, an adulteress, a whore." The men would have pretty strong opinions about such women. Maybe they've never met one, and would be prepared to revile rather than ask what drove a woman into such a life choice. Maybe they've been involved with such a woman, which can make men even more condemnatory. It's customary for society to be extreme in its condemnation of women who are believed to live a life that doesn't match the sexual behavior that the society nominally accepts (though its actual life may be more complicated than the disapproval implies). Proclaiming to these men "YOU'RE JUST A WHORE" is designed as one more impassioned, extreme, and radical attempt to break through to them.

Attributing their parenthood to Canaanites, Amorites, and Hittites wouldn't be a compliment, either. None of these peoples are around in Ezekiel's day. They have in common that they feature in the lists of peoples that Yahweh undertook to displace to give Israel a home. In books such as Exodus, they're often the first peoples to be mentioned in these lists. The basis for their displacement isn't merely that they were in the way but that they were due for Yahweh's punishment for wrongdoing such as their practice of sacrificing children. But Israel's lifestyle has matched theirs instead of modeling an alternative. Ezekiel implies that this phenomenon isn't surprising. Like mother or father, like daughter.

Most of us coming across the cry of a baby in a dumpster would be moved with compassion. We'd have to pick up the baby. Yahweh is such a person. He couldn't resist the temptation to adopt the baby, clean her up, clothe her, and give her a home (rubbing with salt is a traditional practice with cleansing and antiseptic aims). He sees she has a chance to grow into a fine young woman. Then the allegory takes over. The **Torah** doesn't say that a father can't marry an adoptive daughter, but this relationship wouldn't be in keeping with other aspects of its concern to safeguard the family. Yahweh, however, takes this "daughter" in marriage—that is, enters into a covenant relationship with Jerusalem. The further washing suggests that Yahweh is getting the young woman ready for her wedding; the blood is perhaps menstrual blood, the sign that she's grown-up, and the oil is makeup. Her husband, the king, is able to provide her with adornment fit for a queen. But this attention turned her head. Her sexual unfaithfulness becomes the metaphor for religious and political unfaithfulness on Jerusalem's part. Even **Philistines** would be able to see how scandalously she'd behaved, like an independent woman who had no husband to whom she was supposed to be committed. In reality, she's feeble-minded.

EZEKIEL 16:35–63

Jerusalem, Her Mother, and Her Sisters

[35]Therefore, you whore, listen to Yahweh's message. [36]The Lord Yahweh has said this: Because your juice poured out and your nakedness exposed itself in your immoralities with your lovers and with all your outrageous lumps, and in accordance with the bloodshed of your children whom you gave to them,

[37]therefore here am I, I'm going to assemble all your lovers to whom you were nice, every one whom you loved as well as every one whom you repudiated. I shall assemble them against you from all around and expose your nakedness to them. They'll see all your nakedness [38]and I shall make for you the judgments appropriate for women who commit adultery or pour out blood. I shall make you into blood, rage, and passion. [39]I shall give you into their hand and they'll tear down your enclosure and break down your platforms. They'll strip you of your clothes, take your splendid things, and leave you naked and bare. [40]They'll bring up an assembly against you, pelt you with stones, and cut you down with their swords. [41]They'll burn your houses with fire and perform judgments against you before the eyes of many women. I shall make your immorality stop. You'll no more give gifts. [42]I shall lay to rest my rage with you and turn away my passion from you, and be quiet and not vexed anymore. [43]Because you weren't mindful of your young days and you infuriated me with all these things, I myself shall indeed—yes, I shall bring your way on your head (a declaration of the Lord Yahweh).

Have you not implemented your scheming with your outrages? [44]There, everyone who quotes sayings will quote this saying with regard to you: "Like mother, like daughter." [45]You're your mother's daughter, loathing her husband and her children. You're the sister of your sisters, who loathed their husbands and their children. Your mother was a Hittite, your father an Amorite. [46]Your big sister was Samaria, she and her daughters who were living to the north of you. Your little sister who was living to the south of you was Sodom and her daughters. [47]Did you not walk in their ways and act with their outrages? In a very short while you became more ruinous than them in all your ways. [48]As I live (a declaration of the Lord Yahweh), if Sodom your sister, she and her daughters, had acted as you and your daughters acted . . . [49]There, this was the waywardness of Sodom your sister: she and her daughters had dignity, plenty of food, quiet prosperity, but they didn't take the hand of the weak and needy. [50]They were lofty and they performed outrage before me. So I removed them, as I saw it. [51]Samaria didn't commit half your offenses; you've multiplied your offenses more than her. You made your sisters seem faithful with all your outrages that you committed.

[52]Yes, you—carry your shame, you who've pleaded for your sisters with your offenses with which you've acted more outrageously than them. They're more faithful than you. Yes, you—be disgraced. Carry your shame by your making your sisters seem faithful. [53]I shall restore their fortunes, the fortunes of Sodom and her daughters and the fortunes of Samaria and her daughters, and the fortunes of your captivity among them, [54]so that you'll carry your disgrace and be disgraced for all that you've done in enabling them to take comfort. [55]Your sister Sodom and her daughters will go back to what they were before, Samaria and her daughters will go back to what they were before, and you and your daughters will go back to what you were before. [56]Sodom your sister was not heard of in your mouth in the day of your dignity, [57]before your evil became open, the very time of the reviling of the daughters of Syria and all the peoples around her, the daughters of the Philistines, who jeer at you from all around. [58]Your scheming and your outrages—you yourself are bearing them (Yahweh's declaration).

[59]Because the Lord Yahweh has said this: Yes, I shall act with you as you've acted, in that you've despised the oath in contravening the covenant. [60]But I—I shall be mindful of my covenant with you in your young days. I shall establish for you a lasting covenant. [61]You'll be mindful of your ways and be ashamed, when you receive your sisters, the ones who are bigger than you and the ones who are younger than you. I shall give them to you as daughters, though not on the basis of your covenant. [62]I—I shall establish my covenant with you, and you will acknowledge that I am Yahweh, [63]so that you may be mindful and be disgraced. It won't be for you to open your mouth again in the face of your shame, when I make expiation for you for all that you've done (a declaration of the Lord Yahweh).

A friend was telling me today about an occasion in the country where she used to live, when a woman with a baby arrived at the front door to ask for help. She'd been the victim of bride kidnapping or marriage by abduction, which was the background to the majority of marriages in their culture. "It's their tradition." But more than half of the wives then get beaten by their husbands, and such treatment had finally become too much for this woman. We may not have bride kidnapping in the West, but we certainly have the abuse. I recently had a student come to talk to me because she was being assaulted by her husband, who played in a Christian rock band, and she wasn't sure whether or how she could or should get out of the marriage. She was wearing sunglasses because, she said, she'd fallen out of bed and had hit her face on the bedside table. I never got to talk to the husband, but I can imagine that he'd have had ways of trying to defend himself.

The abuse of wives in the Christian community makes Ezekiel's allegory dangerous. It could validate this abuse. There certainly was such abuse in Israel, as in other societies; Judges 19 is the most horrific story along those lines. Yet the Old Testament tells more stories about wives who hold their own in the marital relationship (women such as Sarah, Rebekah, Abigail, and Bathsheba) and doesn't require wives to obey or submit to their husbands. Perhaps that fact is part of the background for **Yahweh**'s risking Ezekiel's using this allegory out of his ongoing concern somehow to break through to the community—not least the men, who are required to identify with the wife in the allegory, not with the husband.

A prominent atheist has described the Old Testament's God as a jealous, unforgiving, vindictive, bloodthirsty, misogynistic, sadomasochistic, malevolent bully. In this allegory Yahweh is risking at least as much in connection with his revelation of himself as he is in connection with the possibility that men might take him as their model. Here, too, it is important to see this revelation of Yahweh as only part of the story. In the New Testament, too, it's easy to compile evidence for Jesus' being a nasty, unforgiving person. The judgmental side to Jesus has to be seen in connection with the compassionate, merciful side. Jesus shows himself to be the Son of his Father in his combining mercy and toughness.

In this second half of the chapter, Ezekiel first slates **Judah** for its appetite for unfaithfulness to Yahweh in politics and in religion. Without any concern for tastefulness he portrays this as analogous to a promiscuous woman's enthusiasm for sex without love. Yahweh will make Judah into blood, rage, and passion—that is, in furious rage he'll shed its blood as it has shed its own people's blood. He'll assemble a company to bring judgment on it, armed with stones, as in the story of the woman caught committing adultery (John 8). In real life this "assembly" will be a gathering of sword-carrying foreign forces attacking the city.

The Old Testament story talks of Israel bringing God's judgment on the Canaanites, but even before it had been written it became a story filled with irony because Israel had assimilated to the Canaanites rather than modeling an alternative way. In terms of the allegory, like mother, like daughter. The chapter underlines the vilification in two directions. It compares Jerusalem, Judah's capital, with Samaria, **Ephraim**'s capital. Samaria had fallen to the **Assyrians**, and it wouldn't be surprising if Jerusalem was unworried at the fate of its big sister, which was perhaps proud of its bigger place in the world. The comparison with Sodom and Gomorrah was even more of an insult. While Judah told a story about abusive same-sex relationships in Sodom (see Genesis 19), Ezekiel's critique focuses on the city's failure to care about the weak and needy in its midst or in the area around, who are often the victims of the big city's economic policies. Samaria and Sodom look like embodiments of **faithfulness** alongside Judah! Judah's life constitutes an appeal to God for mercy on those other cities! It's only fair that Jerusalem should experience the treatment envisaged for the Canaanites and enacted on Sodom and Samaria. Ezekiel adds the jeering of Syria (Ephraim's ally in interfering in Judah during Isaiah's day) and **Philistia** (Judah's traditional rival for control of the territory to Judah's west).

The combining of fury and mercy in Yahweh eventually surfaces in the chapter. Judgment won't be the end for Samaria, Sodom, or Jerusalem. Yahweh will restore the fortunes of all three. Jerusalem's giving up on its covenant relationship doesn't mean Yahweh will do so. Yahweh will keep working at the relationship. Ezekiel speaks of the covenant of Jerusalem's young days, making it easy to see here another reference to the marriage relationship between Yahweh and Jerusalem. His wife's unfaithfulness doesn't make Yahweh give up on the marriage. Samaria and Sodom aren't part of this covenant and couldn't be in the terms of the metaphor, but there can still be genuine faithful dealings between these cities and Yahweh. Typically, Ezekiel adds that even the covenant's restoration will underline the shame of its violation. Yet he ends with a final extraordinary allusion to Yahweh's mercy. Expiation is usually an action undertaken by human beings in acting to cleanse themselves of their defilement. Here Yahweh is the person who does the cleansing, to make it possible for the relationship to continue—like a mother cleaning up her baby so she isn't put off by the smell.

EZEKIEL 17:1–24

A Tale of Two Eagles

[1]Yahweh's message came to me: [2]Young man, unveil a puzzle, tell Israel's household a parable. [3]Say: The Lord Yahweh has said this: A big eagle, big-winged, long-feathered, full-plumaged, with coloring, came to Lebanon and took the top of a cedar. [4]He broke off the highest of its shoots, brought it to the merchant country, and put it in the traders' city. [5]He took some of the country's seed and put it in a seed plot; he placed it as a shoot by plentiful water, a willow. [6]It grew and became

a spreading vine, low in height, its branches turning to him, its roots being beneath it. So it became a vine, produced limbs, and sent out shoots. [7]But there was another big eagle, big-winged, much-plumaged. There—this vine turned its roots towards it and sent out its branches to it for it to water it, away from the beds where it was sown, [8]though it had been planted in a good plot by plentiful water so as to produce boughs, bear fruit, and become an impressive vine. [9]Say: The Lord Yahweh has said this: It may flourish, but will [the first eagle] not tear up its roots and strip off its fruit so that it withers? All the leaves of its growth will wither (not by means of a strong arm or by means of a large company) to destroy it from its roots. [10]There: though planted, will it flourish? Will it not totally wither when the east wind touches it? It will wither on the beds where it grew.

[11]Yahweh's message came to me: [12]Will you say to the rebellious household: Do you not acknowledge what these things are? Say: There: the king of Babylon came to Jerusalem, took its king and its officials, and brought them to him, to Babylon. [13]He took someone from the royal offspring and sealed a covenant with him and put him under oath, but took the important people in the country [14]so that it might be a lowly kingdom and not exalt itself, keeping his covenant so as to stand. [15]But [the king] rebelled against him by sending his aides to Egypt so it would give him horses and a large company. Will he flourish? Will the one who does these things escape? Will he contravene a covenant and escape? [16]As I live (a declaration of the Lord Yahweh), if he doesn't die in the place belonging to the king who made him king, whose oath he despised and whose covenant he contravened, in the middle of Babylon . . . [17]Pharaoh won't act toward him with a great force, a numerous assembly, with battle, with the constructing of a ramp and the building of a tower, to cut down many lives. [18][The king] despised an oath by contravening a covenant. There—he gave his hand, but did all these things. He won't escape. [19]Therefore the Lord Yahweh has said this: As I live, if I don't bring on his head my oath that he despised and my covenant that he contravened . . . [20]I shall spread my

net over him, and he'll be caught in my trap. I shall bring him to Babylon and enter into judgment with him there for the trespass that he committed against me. [21]All the fugitives in all his legions will fall by the sword and the rest will scatter to every wind, and you will acknowledge that I Yahweh have spoken.

[22]Yahweh has said this: And I myself shall take from the top of a tall cedar, and put from the highest of its shoots a tender one that I shall break off and myself plant on a lofty, tall mountain. [23]On Israel's high mountains I shall plant it. It will bear boughs and produce fruit, and become an impressive cedar. Every bird of every wing will dwell beneath it; in the shade of its branches they'll dwell. [24]All the trees in the countryside will acknowledge that I am Yahweh. I shall have brought low the exalted tree, exalted the lowly tree, withered the green tree, and made the withered tree flourish. I am Yahweh. I've spoken and I shall act.

Last night I watched the crime thriller or film noir *Stormy Monday*, for the fourth time, wondering whether this time I'd "get it." I think this time I more or less did. In one sense it's a simple story, about corruption and a wise-guy finally getting his comeuppance and a couple of lonely people finding each other and tragedy striking another couple. The points are simple ones. You don't need such a complicated film to make them. You know those facts about life (well, in some cases what you hope are facts). Yet needing to wrestle with the plot sequences and having the chance to rejoice in the light and the color in the movie gives bare facts an impact they wouldn't otherwise have.

Ezekiel knows that fact about communication. He tells another story that initially looks as if it has nothing to do with anything, though, like his other stories, it's the kind of allegory that works simply when you have the key. It makes one of his basic points again. He doesn't have many points to make. He needs to try every means to drive people to get his one or two basic ones. The first eagle is the **Babylonian** king, Nebuchadnezzar, Lebanon is **Israel**, the cedar is the Davidic line, the shoot is King Jehoiakin whom Nebuchadnezzar uprooted from being king and took off to Babylon, the merchant city, the traders' city. It's a telling description of Babylon. Describing it as a superpower points to its military strength, but much of the drive in creating an empire comes from economic ambition—from greed, you might say.

The seed Nebuchadnezzar took and planted was Zedekiah, the current ruler in Jerusalem. Ezekiel portrays him as having everything to play for. Cooperate with Nebuchadnezzar; things will go well. Just don't be ambitious; accept your subordinate position as a colonial entity within the empire. But south of **Judah** is that other near-imperial power, Egypt, the other big eagle, which was always Judah's temptation. Maybe a relationship with Egypt is key to flourishing, with greater independence? Not so much, Ezekiel warns. Nebuchadnezzar won't stand for it. The strengthening of Judah's position that Zedekiah thinks will issue from allying with Egypt will turn out illusory. Nebuchadnezzar will have no trouble dealing with Zedekiah and his people. Pharaoh may make promises, but when the chips are down, he won't deliver the goods. Zedekiah, too, will end up in Babylon, dead.

Ezekiel's interpretation of his allegory adds the terms covenant, oath, contravention, and rebellion. Zedekiah had "given his hand" to Nebuchadnezzar—shaken hands to seal the agreement. Zedekiah will pay the price for failing to kowtow to Nebuchadnezzar and thus fulfill the role for which Nebuchadnezzar appointed him. He's making a political error and will pay a political price. There'll be further levels to Ezekiel's allegory. Prophets think that kings should keep their word, and that political relationships involve trustworthiness. Despising an oath and contravening a covenant aren't merely bad choices or unwise decisions, to use our culture's customary language when someone does something wrong. They involve doing something wrong.

The allegory has another level. The previous chapter spoke of despising an oath and contravening a covenant, in describing Jerusalem's action in relation to Yahweh. The theological overtones of this language carry over here. Zedekiah's action raises questions about his relationship with Yahweh. Thus it is Yahweh who will bring Zedekiah to Babylon, because it's Yahweh's oath that he has despised and Yahweh's covenant he has contravened. Zedekiah is involved in trespass against Yahweh as well as rebellion against Nebuchadnezzar. Taking the oath and sealing the covenant would involve invoking Yahweh's **name**.

His rebellion involved yet another deeper issue. Jeremiah describes Nebuchadnezzar as Yahweh's servant. Ezekiel's understanding of the Babylonian king's significance is similar. Nebuchadnezzar is interested in Judah because he's the king of a great trading nation and Judah can help him with his economic ventures. But Yahweh is making use of Nebuchadnezzar's self-centered imperial aims to implement his will for Judah, which Zedekiah is resisting. It's Yahweh who'll capture Zedekiah in a trap and bring him to Babylon, by means of Nebuchadnezzar's doing so.

Once more, that's not the end of the story. Yahweh isn't finished with the Davidic line. In due course, he'll personally take action to put someone from that line on the throne in Jerusalem again. In a small way it came about with Zerubbabel's governorship in Jerusalem, described in the book of Ezra. But Ezekiel's more far-reaching vision feeds Israel's hope of the Messiah, who will be the means of bringing blessing to all the nations. We have to keep remembering that Ezekiel talks *about* Zedekiah, but he isn't in Jerusalem, where Zedekiah was. He's preaching to Zedekiah's subjects in Babylon, seeking to get them to look at the situation in Jerusalem in the right way and to prepare themselves for the trouble that must come.

EZEKIEL 18:1–32

Get Yourselves a New Mind and a New Spirit

[1]Yahweh's message came to me: [2]What is it to you people, using this saying on Israel's land, "Parents eat sour grapes, but children's teeth feel rough"? [3]As I live (a declaration of the Lord Yahweh), if you have any more using of this saying in Israel . . . [4]There: all lives are mine. As the parent's life, so the child's life, they're mine. The person who sins, he'll die. [5]When a person is faithful and makes decisions with faithfulness [6](he's not eaten on the mountains, nor raised his eyes to the lumps of Israel's household, nor defiled his neighbor's wife, nor does he approach a woman who's taboo, [7]nor does he wrong anyone, he gives back the pledge given him for a debt, he doesn't commit robbery, he gives his food to the hungry person, he covers the naked with clothes, [8]he doesn't give on the basis of earning interest nor take a profit, he turns his hand back from wrong, he makes truthful decisions between one person and another, [9]he walks by my laws and has kept my decisions by exercising truthfulness): he's faithful. He'll definitely live (a declaration of the Lord Yahweh).

[10]But he begets a violent son, a shedder of blood, who does each one of these things, [11]when he himself did none of these things: he's eaten on the mountains, defiled his neighbor's wife, wronged the weak and needy, committed robbery, doesn't return a pledge, has raised his eyes to the lumps, committed outrage, [13]given on the basis of earning interest and taken a profit, and is he to live? He won't live. One who has committed all these outrages will certainly die. His bloodshed will be against him.

[14]But now. He begets a son, and he sees all his father's offenses that he committed. He sees, and doesn't act in accordance with them. [15]He's not eaten on the mountains, raised his eyes to the lumps of Israel's household, defiled his neighbor's wife, [16]wronged anyone, exacted a pledge, or committed robbery, he's given his bread to a hungry person, covered the naked with clothes, [17]turned his hand back from wrong, not taken interest or profit, put my decisions into effect, walked by

93

my laws. He won't die through his father's waywardness. He'll definitely live. [18]His father, because he practiced fraud, committed robbery against his brother, and did what was not good among his people: there, he'll definitely die for his waywardness.

[19]You say, "Why has the son not carried any of the father's waywardness?" But the son's made decisions with faithfulness, kept all my laws and done them. He'll live. [20]The person who offends, he'll die. A son doesn't carry any of the father's waywardness and a father doesn't carry any of the son's waywardness. The faithfulness of the faithful person belongs to him and the faithlessness of the faithless person belongs to him. [21]But the faithless person when he turns back from all his offenses that he's done and keeps all my laws and makes decisions with faithfulness, he'll definitely live. [22]None of the rebellions that he's committed will be kept in mind for him; through the faithfulness with which he's acted, he'll live. [23]Do I really want the death of the faithless person (a declaration of the Lord Yahweh) and not his turning back from his ways so that he lives?

[24]But when the faithful person turns back from his faithfulness and does wrong in accordance with all the outrages that the faithless person did, and does them, is he to live? None of his faithful acts that he's done will be kept in mind because of the trespass that he's committed and the offenses that he's committed. Through them he'll die. [25]You say, "The Lord's way isn't right." Will you listen, Israel's household? Is it my way that isn't right? Isn't it your ways that aren't right? [26]When a faithful person turns back from his faithfulness and does wrong and dies for them, he dies for the wrong that he's done. [27]And when a faithless person turns back from his faithlessness that he's done and makes decisions with faithfulness, he keeps himself alive. [28]He's seen and turned back from all his rebellions that he's done. He'll definitely live. He won't die.

[29]Israel's household say, "The Lord's way isn't right." Are my ways not right, Israel's household? Isn't it your ways that are not right? [30]Therefore I shall decide about you, Israel's household, for each person in accordance with his ways (a

declaration of the Lord Yahweh). So turn, turn yourselves back from all your rebellions, and they won't become a wayward obstacle to you. [31]Send off from you all your rebellions that you've committed. Get yourselves a new mind and a new spirit. Why should you die, Israel's household? [32]Because I don't want the death of the person who dies (a declaration of the Lord Yahweh). So turn yourselves back and live!

Homeboy Industries in Los Angeles is a program that seeks to give a new start to gang members and people who've come out of prison. One of its recent trainees, Rasheena, describes how her parents were drug addicts and career criminals, in and out of prison for as long as she could remember. She started experimenting with drugs at age twelve. She was also sexually abused by one of her brothers and spent the next years in a cycle of manipulation and abuse. She ended up in prison, leaving her daughter alone as her mother had done to her. Realizing the error of her ways and having grown tired of running from her past, Rasheena vowed to be stronger, no longer falling victim to others around her.

Ezekiel works with a community that might assume that it's fatally constrained by its past. It might make its parents' lifestyle an excuse for making no effort to change. It might assume that God would want to have nothing to do with it because of the previous generation's lifestyle. The Ten Commandments reminded it that God "visits" the waywardness of parents on children to the third and fourth generation. This odd expression indicates that God makes that waywardness have an effect on the children and grandchildren. It couldn't be otherwise, as Rasheena's story shows (though she was fortunate in having a grandmother who looked after her and her siblings in her youngest years; maybe that's one reason why Rasheena kept some capacity for her vow). That's how family life works. Fortunately, God's grace extends to a thousand generations, several hundred times longer than the "visiting."

There's thus both encouragement and challenge that Ezekiel's audience needs to hear. The encouragement is that this "visiting" doesn't mean God punishes one generation for the previous generation's wrongdoing. God's relationship with people issues from what's happening now. What kind of a person would Yahweh be to want people to die rather than turn and live? I can make myself punish the faithless, Yahweh indicated in Lamentations 3, but it doesn't come naturally, so I seize the excuse to be merciful.

The challenge is that the people of Judah can't make the previous generation the excuse for their own lifestyle. They can make a vow like Rasheena's. Ezekiel's examples show he isn't talking about sinless perfection. His umbrella concept is the regular Old Testament principle of faithful decision-making. Is authority exercised in the community in a fair way? To spell out the point, he begins with faithfulness to Yahweh. Eating on the mountains refers to festival meals at the traditional shrines where people worshiped Baal or worshiped Yahweh as if he were so like Baal that it made little difference—so it's another way of looking to the lumps for help. There's the exercise of discipline in people's sexual lives, of which Ezekiel speaks in priestly terms. Adultery isn't only morally wrong but defiling. Other wrongdoing is also defiling, but there's something about adultery that's particularly antithetical to who Yahweh is; adultery means you can't go into God's presence. The reference to adultery follows on the references to false worship; the problem with adultery is its involving unfaithfulness, and mutual faithfulness is of the essence of relations between Israel and Yahweh. Sex during menstruation likewise perhaps clashes with who Yahweh is, because of the uncanny significance of menstruation as both a sign of life (because it signifies that a woman could become a mother) and a sign of death (because losing blood is a sign of death).

Ezekiel goes on to the need to have nothing to do with oppression, expressed when people take a tough stance toward poor people in their community and are more interested in using their assets in order to get better off than in using their assets to benefit the less well-off. None of his warnings concern anything very complicated. He's not talking about always feeling loving and nice, or never feeling envy or resentment, but about some basic outward expressions of living with God and living in community. Put those simple things right, and you'll be OK. Let them go wrong, and you're in trouble. "Get yourselves a new mind and a new spirit." Pull yourselves together. Take Rasheena as your example.

EZEKIEL 19:1–14

A Dirge for a Nation's Rulers

1   And you: take up a dirge for Israel's rulers.

2   What was your mother?—
       a lioness among lions.
    She bedded down among the great lions,
       reared her cubs.
3   She brought up one of her cubs,
       he became a great lion.
    He learned to hunt prey,
       he ate human beings.
4   Nations heard about him,
       he was caught in their pit.
    They brought him with hooks
       to the country of Egypt.

5   She saw that she'd hoped,
       her expectation had perished.
    She took another of her cubs,
       made him a great lion.
6   He went about among the lions;
       he became a great lion.
    He learned to hunt prey,
       he ate human beings.

7 He had sex with their widows,
　　wasted their cities.
　The country and its population were desolate
　　at the sound of his roaring.
8 But nations set against him
　　from provinces all around.
　They spread their net over him;
　　he was caught in their pit.
9 They put him in a cage with hooks,
　　brought him to the king of Babylon.
　They brought him under constraint,
　　so that his voice wouldn't make itself heard
　　anymore on Israel's mountains.

10 Your mother was a real vine (with your blood),
　　planted by water.
　It became fruitful and green
　　because of the abundant waters.
11 It had strong boughs
　　fit for the clubs of rulers.
　The stature of one grew high,
　　among the clouds.
　It was visible by its height,
　　by the abundance of its branches.
12 But [the vine] was uprooted in rage, thrown to the
　　earth,
　　and the east wind withered its fruit.
　[The branches] broke and withered, its strong
　　bough—
　　fire consumed it.
13 So now it's planted in the wilderness,
　　in a dry, thirsty country.
14 Fire came out from its bough,
　　consumed its branches with its fruit.
　It didn't have a strong bough,
　　a club for ruling.

That's a dirge. It's become a dirge.

It's a good day to raise a dirge about rulers. We've just been hearing about the fall of the director of the C.I.A., who was discovered to have had an affair with his biographer. In this context, the problem isn't that adultery is wrong but that affairs are a bad idea for people who work in the spy industry. And the director's successor as commander of U.S. forces in Afghanistan is under investigation on the discovery of inappropriate e-mails to a Florida socialite. Apparently Lyndon Johnson said there are two things that make leaders stupid: envy and sex; one could illustrate this aphorism from the stories of Israel's first two kings, Saul and David.

Ezekiel's dirge concerns three kings in his lifetime, though as usual Ezekiel doesn't call them "kings." The last kings of **Judah** were Josiah (640–609), Jehoahaz (609), Jehoiaqim (609–597), Jehoiakin (597), and Zedekiah (597–587). The first king in the dirge is Jehoahaz, who was deposed and taken into exile in Egypt. The last is the present king, Zedekiah, who will eventually suffer a similar fate. One would initially expect the second king to be Jehoiaqim, but the account of him ends with his being taken into exile, and the point of the dirge may be that this is the fate of all three that it mentions. Its bite then affects the current king, and declares that he'll indeed suffer the same fate as these predecessors.

A dirge is a composition expressing grief at someone's death. It can be addressed in part to the person who's died, like David's dirge over Jonathan in 2 Samuel 1; these poems, too, mix address to the person with talk about them. Like many other compositions expressing anguish, this poem differs from compositions expressing praise in the way the second half of a line is usually shorter than the first half. The poetic form mirrors how life has brought people up short. Much of Lamentations follows this form. While a dirge such as David's applies to a person who actually has died, the prophets utter more dirges about people who are still alive, bringing home the fate that lies ahead.

Initially, the Judahites listening to Ezekiel's dirge wouldn't know who he was talking about. The identity of the kings' mother would become clearer later in the poem, when she's identified as a vine, because that's a common image for **Israel**. It's Israel that births these three kings. Initially, the poem glories extravagantly over Jehoahaz, who reigned for only three months before being taken off to Egypt. Perhaps the imagery reflects the fact that he *is* the Davidic king, so by definition the glorious things said about him are true. Something similar applies to Jehoiakin, who also reigned for only three months before being taken off to **Babylon** in the company to which Ezekiel also belonged. The reference to having sex with women he made widows presupposes how armies kill a nation's men and rape its women.

The prophecy's real point comes in the last paragraph. Zedekiah is still reigning, but Ezekiel speaks of him as if he's already (a) in **exile**, (b) dead. It would presumably be worrying to Zedekiah if he ever heard the dirge, but we have to keep remembering that Ezekiel addresses his prophecies to Judahites in Babylon. They need to take seriously the fact that much further trouble is coming to Jerusalem. The reference to Zedekiah's blood perhaps indicates that he too was involved in the violence attributed to the previous kings. He is a branch from Israel's vine, but the branch is going to bring the death of the vine and the vine is thus not going to grow another branch. In other words, Zedekiah is going to be responsible for the nation's downfall and it isn't going to be able to give birth to another king.

The footnote says, "The prophecy came true. The pretend-dirge became an actual dirge."

EZEKIEL 20:1–44

When You Can't Inquire of God

[1]In the seventh year, in the fifth month, on the tenth of the month, some Israelite elders came to inquire of Yahweh,

and sat in front of me. ²Yahweh's message came to me: ³Young man, speak to Israel's elders. Say to them, The Lord Yahweh has said this: Is it to inquire of me that you're coming? As I live, if I shall let myself be inquired of by you (a declaration of the Lord Yahweh) . . .

⁴Will you sentence them, will you sentence them, young man! Get them to acknowledge their ancestors' outrages. ⁵Say to them, The Lord Yahweh has said this: On the day I chose Israel, I raised my hand [to swear] to the offspring of Jacob's household, and when I made myself known to them in the country of Egypt, I raised my hand to them, saying, I am Yahweh your God. ⁶On that day I raised my hand to them to get them out of the country of Egypt to a country that I'd sought out for them, flowing with milk and honey; it was the most attractive of all countries. ⁷I said to them, Each person, throw out the abominations before your eyes. Don't defile yourselves with Egypt's lumps. I am Yahweh your God. ⁸But they rebelled against me. They wouldn't listen to me. Each person, they didn't throw out the abominations before their eyes and abandon Egypt's lumps.

I said I'd pour out my rage on them, to spend my anger on them amid the country of Egypt. ⁹But I acted for the sake of my name, so that it might not be treated as ordinary in the eyes of the nations in whose midst they were, before whose eyes I'd caused myself to be acknowledged by them so as to get them out of the country of Egypt. ¹⁰I got them out of the country of Egypt and brought them into the wilderness. ¹¹I gave them my laws and made known to them my decisions, which a person might perform and live by. ¹²I also gave them my Sabbaths, to become a sign between me and them, so that they might acknowledge that I am Yahweh, who sanctifies them. ¹³But Israel's household rebelled against me in the wilderness. They didn't follow my laws. They rejected my decisions, which a person might perform and live by, and they quite treated my Sabbaths as ordinary.

I said I'd pour my rage on them in the wilderness, to make an end of them. ¹⁴But I acted for the sake of my name so that it might not be treated as ordinary in the eyes of the nations before whose eyes I got them out. [15]But I did also raise my hand to them in the wilderness not to bring them into the country that I'd given them, flowing with milk and honey, the most attractive of all countries, [16]because they'd rejected my decisions and not followed my laws, and treated my Sabbaths as ordinary, because their mind was following their lumps. [17]But my eye had pity on them so as not to destroy them. I didn't make an end of them in the wilderness. [18]I said to their children in the wilderness, Don't follow your parents' laws and don't keep their decisions, and don't defile yourselves with their lumps. [19]I am Yahweh your God. Follow my laws and keep my decisions and do them, [20]and sanctify my Sabbaths so that they're a sign between me and you, so that you acknowledge that I am Yahweh your God. [21]But the children rebelled against me. They didn't follow my laws and didn't keep my decisions by implementing them, which a person will implement and live by. They treated my Sabbaths as ordinary.

I said I'd pour my rage on them by spending my anger on them in the wilderness. [22]But I held back my hand and acted for the sake of my name so that it might not be treated as ordinary in the eyes of the nations before whose eyes I'd got them out. [23]I did also raise my hand to them in the wilderness to scatter them through the nations and disperse them through the countries, [24]because they didn't implement my decisions but rejected my laws, treated my Sabbaths as ordinary, and their parents' lumps were before their eyes. [25]I myself also gave them laws that weren't good and decisions they couldn't live by. [26]I defiled them by their gifts when they made every firstborn of the womb pass through [fire], so that I might desolate them, so that they might acknowledge that I am Yahweh. [27]Therefore speak to Israel's household, young man, and say to them, The Lord Yahweh has said this: Your ancestors further blasphemed me with this, by committing trespass against me. [28]I brought them into the country that I'd raised my hand to give them. But they looked at every high hill or leafy tree and slaughtered their sacrifices there, made the vexation of their offering there, produced their pleasing fragrance there, and poured their libations there. [29]I said to them, What is the shrine that you're coming to? (and they've called it Come-to-What? until this day).

³⁰Therefore say to Israel's household: The Lord Yahweh has said this: Are you defiling yourselves in the manner of your ancestors and whoring after their abominations, ³¹and in presenting your gifts by making your children pass through fire defiling yourselves in relation to all your lumps, until this day? And shall I let myself be inquired of by you, Israel's household? As I live (a declaration of the Lord Yahweh), if I let myself be inquired of by you . . . ³²What comes up into your spirit will simply not happen, that you're saying, "We'll be like the nations, like the countries' families, in ministering to wood and stone." ³³As I live (a declaration of the Lord Yahweh), if I don't reign over you with a strong hand and an arm stretched out and rage poured out . . . ³⁴I shall get you out from the peoples and gather you from the countries among whom you're scattered, with a strong hand and an arm stretched out and rage poured out. ³⁵I shall bring you into the wilderness of the peoples and enter into judgment with you there face to face. ³⁶As I entered into judgment with your ancestors in the wilderness of the country of Egypt, so I shall enter into judgment with you (a declaration of the Lord Yahweh). ³⁷I shall get you to pass under the club and bring you into the covenant bond. ³⁸I shall purge out from you the people who rebel and revolt against me; while I shall get them out from the country where they're staying, I shall not bring them into the land of Israel. And you will acknowledge that I am Yahweh.

³⁹You, Israel's household: the Lord Yahweh has said this: Each person, go, serve his lumps. But afterwards, if you don't listen to me, then you won't treat my sacred name as ordinary anymore with your gifts and your lumps. ⁴⁰Because on my sacred mountain, on Israel's high mountain (a declaration of the Lord Yahweh), there all Israel's household, all of it, will serve me in the country. There I shall favor them and there I shall ask after your donations and the finest of your offerings with all your sacred things. ⁴¹With your pleasing fragrance I shall favor you when I get you out from the peoples and gather you from the countries in which I've scattered you.

I shall sanctify myself through you in the eyes of the peoples.
[42]You will acknowledge that I am Yahweh when I bring you
into Israel's land, into the country that I raised my hand to
give your ancestors. [43]You'll be mindful there of your ways and
all your deeds by which you defiled yourselves. You'll be loathsome in your own sight for all your evils that you've done.
[44]You will acknowledge that I am Yahweh when I deal with you
for the sake of my name, not in accordance with your evil ways
and your ruinous deeds, Israel's household (a declaration of
the Lord Yahweh).

A friend asked me yesterday what I thought about a message
that had been delivered by one of his co-pastors. The preacher
had been reflecting on how the congregation should react to
Hurricane Sandy, which had devastated much of New York,
New Jersey, and other states. The preacher had commented
that his own instinct was to say, "That sucks," but had added
that he didn't really think he should react in that way. He
should accept all events because they issue from God's sovereignty. But he also noted that he wasn't a prophet and so
couldn't really comment on why the calamity had happened.
My friend wasn't sure about these observations.

Some of Judah's elders, the senior members of the community who have some responsibility for its guidance, have come
to consult Ezekiel in light of what's happened to them and out
of the feeling that they need to know what's going to happen.
He, after all, *is* a prophet. Can he tell them how long their **exile**
will last? Do they have to settle down for a long period (Jeremiah 29 says so)? Or can they hope for a quicker return?

Yahweh isn't going to give them that kind of information.
Yet Yahweh's refusal in this sense to be consulted by them doesn't
mean a refusal to say anything. Indeed, the question issues in
one of the longer prophecies in the book. One can imagine the
elders becoming gloomier and gloomier, and wishing they'd
never asked. That reaction would be intensified by the chapter's
comprising yet another repeating of an interpretation of their

people's story with which they're quite familiar from Ezekiel. It seems that they've still not owned that their story is one of rebellion and unfaithfulness. Yahweh extends his description of them as addicted to unfaithfulness ("outrages," **"lumps"**) even to their very beginnings as a people, in Egypt. He later adds a comment relating to the word for *shrine*, the word *bamah*. If you divide that word into two, *ba* means "coming" and *mah* means "what." So every time **Israelites** talk about going to a shrine, they're implicitly raising the question "What are you coming to?"

At the same time, Yahweh nuances the telling of the story. From that beginning, Yahweh acts for the sake of his **name**. That principle lies behind the series of occasions when Yahweh doesn't annihilate the people in rage in response to their serving other so-called gods. It would make him look stupid in the eyes of the world. It's a significant basis for the security of the people of God—God won't finally abandon us, because he'd look stupid. It's also a reason why Israel would be wise to give up its inclination to **faithlessness**, because that addiction also treats Yahweh's name as **ordinary** and makes Yahweh look stupid. Israel will surely not get away with it. Yahweh's concern for his reputation even undergirds and guarantees the promise of the community's restoration. Conversely, Yahweh simply won't tolerate their worshiping other deities. They'll submit themselves to him willingly or they'll do so under compulsion.

Yahweh emphasizes the gift of the Sabbath as a sign of the relationship between Israel and Yahweh. While other peoples had rest days, only Israel had the weekly Sabbath, so in a time and situation like that of Ezekiel it becomes a significant marker of Israel's distinctiveness. If Israel fails to keep the Sabbath, it's going back on its distinctive position. There's nothing wrong with Sunday to Friday being ordinary. But Israel mustn't treat the Sabbath as an ordinary day. It must treat it as belonging distinctively to Yahweh. It must sanctify it, let it be special and distinctive.

Yahweh's most extraordinary comment is that he gave Israel bad laws. The reference is to the law about offering the firstborn to Yahweh. They were to sacrifice the firstborn of their animals, but to make a substitutionary offering in respect of their human firstborn. But other peoples sometimes sacrificed their children, and Israel sometimes followed them in that practice, as Ezekiel's already noted. In effect Yahweh is accepting responsibility for their doing so. If Yahweh hadn't required them to make offerings at all, they might not have got involved in that repugnant practice. Indeed, Yahweh is claiming responsibility for doing so. It was an act of judgment.

The Old Testament often speaks of Yahweh as the people's shepherd, a more challenging image than it sometimes seems. A shepherd exercises **authority** over his sheep; they do what he says, in light of his waving his club. The Israelites will be like sheep submitting themselves to the Shepherd's club. In this way they will reenter their covenant relationship with Yahweh, unless they choose to exclude themselves. They'll loathe themselves, but the loathing will be strangely positive; it will be part of the process whereby they turn to Yahweh and start living faithfully instead of faithlessly. And then they'll be able to inquire of God.

EZEKIEL 20:45–21:32

The Sword Sharpened and Polished

[45]Yahweh's message came to me: [46]Young man, set your face toward Teman, preach against Dedan, prophesy against the open forest of the Southland. [47]You're to say to the Southland forest, Listen to Yahweh's message. The Lord Yahweh has said this: Here am I, I'm going to light a fire in you. It will consume every green tree and every dry tree in you. The burning flame won't go out. Every face from south to north will be scorched by it. [48]All humanity will see that I, Yahweh, lit it; it won't go out. [49]But I said, Oh, Lord Yahweh, they're saying of me, Isn't

he a teller of parables? [21:1]Yahweh's message came to me: [2]Young man, set your face against Jerusalem. Preach against the sanctuaries, prophesy against Israel's land. [3]You're to say to Israel's land, Yahweh has said this: Here am I, [acting] toward you. I shall get my sword out of its sheath and cut off from you the faithful and the faithless person. [4]Because I'm going to cut off from you the faithful and faithless person, therefore my sword will come out from its sheath against all humanity from south to north, [5]and all humanity will acknowledge that I, Yahweh, got my sword out of its sheath; it won't go back there.

[6]You, young man, sigh. With breaking of heart and with anguish you're to groan before their eyes. [7]When they say to you, Why are you groaning? you're to say, On account of the news, because it's coming. Every spirit will faint. All hands will go limp. Every heart will faint. All knees will turn to water. There, it's coming, it will happen (a declaration of the Lord Yahweh).

[8]Yahweh's message came to me: [9]Young man, prophesy and say, The Lord Yahweh has said this: Say, A sword. A sword is sharpened, yes, and polished. [10]It's sharpened so that it can bring slaughter, it's polished so that it can be a lightning flash. Otherwise, could we rejoice, club of my son, which rejects every tree? [11]Someone gave it for polishing and for grasping in the hand. The sword is sharpened and polished, for putting into the hand of a slayer. [12]Cry and howl, young man, because it will happen among my people, among all Israel's rulers. They're going to be thrown to the sword, with my people. Therefore strike your thigh. [13]Because there's going to be a testing, and what if it scorns the club? Will it not happen? (a declaration of the Lord Yahweh).

[14]So you, young man, prophesy, clap hand against hand. The sword will come twice, a third time it will be the sword of the slain, a sword of great slaughter, which surrounds them, [15]so that the spirit will melt and the fallings will be many. At all their gateways I've set the sword's slaughter. Aaaagh! It's made to be a flash of lightning, grasped for slaughter. [16]Slash to the right, set yourself to the left, wherever your edges are appointed. [17]I too will clap my hands and lay to rest my rage. I Yahweh have spoken.

[18]Yahweh's message came to me: [19]You, young man, set for yourself two roads for the king of Babylon's sword to come. They'll go out from one country. Choose a place; choose it at the beginning of the road to the city. [20]You're to set a road for the sword to come to Rabbah of the Ammonites, and one to Judah against fortified Jerusalem. [21]Because the king of Babylon is standing at the split on the road, at the beginning of the two roads, to perform divination. He's shaking the arrows, he's asking the effigies, he's looking at a liver. [22]In his right hand the divination for Jerusalem's come up, for setting battering rams, for giving the word for slaughter, for lifting up his voice in the battle shout, for setting battering rams against the gateways, for constructing a ramp, for building a tower. [23]To them it will be like empty divination, in the eyes of the people who've been sworn with oaths. But he's one who keeps waywardness in mind, so that they'll be taken. [24]Therefore the Lord Yahweh has said this: Because you've caused your waywardness to be kept in mind, as your rebellions reveal themselves, as your offenses become visible, in all your doings— because you've caused it to be kept in mind, you'll be taken in hand. [25]And you, Israel's ordinary, faithless ruler, whose day's come at the time of final waywardness . . . [26]The Lord Yahweh has said this: Remove the miter, lift off the crown. This won't [continue to be like] this. Exalt the lowly, lower the exalted. [27]Ruin, ruin, ruin, I shall make it (indeed, this hasn't happened [thus before]) until the one comes to whom authority belongs, and I shall give it to him.

[28]And you, young man, prophesy, and say: The Lord Yahweh has said this about the Ammonites and their reviling. You're to say, Sword, sword, unsheathed for slaughter, polished to consume, so as to be a flash of lightning, [29]because of their seeing empty prophecy for you, because of their divining falsehood for you, they are to give you to the necks of the ordinary, faithless people whose day has come at the time of final waywardness.

[30]Return it to its sheath. In the place where you were created, in the country of your origin, I shall decide about you. [31]I shall pour out my wrath upon you. With my furious fire I

shall blow on you. I shall give you into the hand of brutal people, craftsmen in destruction. [32]You will be for fire to consume. Your blood will be in the midst of the country. You won't be remembered. Because I, Yahweh, have spoken.

The Coptic Church in Egypt elected its new pope this month. Its complex process of nomination by bishops and laypeople eventually issues in the identification of three possible appointees. Their names are written on pieces of paper and placed in a box on the altar in the cathedral in Cairo during a Sunday Eucharist. At this service a five-year-old child from the congregation draws the next patriarch's name from the box. In my seminary we were recently seeking to appoint a new president. Would we dare utilize such a procedure?

Ezekiel's latest acted parable involves as bold a step of faith. His presentation portrays the **Babylonian** king, Nebuchadnezzar, deciding on his next military action. His army stands at a fork in the road. Should he take the road to Jerusalem, or to Ammon across the river Jordan, the modern kingdom of Jordan? He seeks guidance in the manner used in traditional societies. Shaking the arrows involves marking arrows "Jerusalem" or "Ammon," shaking them in a sheath, then drawing one out. The effigies were perhaps images representing dead family members whom one might consult for advice, as people having more insight and information available to them than people who are alive (Genesis 31 refers to Rachel's stealing such effigies). Divination might involve examining an animal's body parts, especially the liver, and looking for distinctive features. Diviners had records of how such features had previously correlated with events, which they could use as a basis for predicting future events. Asking the question issues in clear advice: Nebuchadnezzar should attack Jerusalem. The Jerusalemites are skeptical about such a way to get direction. Ironically, their attitude is appropriate to a people who know that **Yahweh** alone is the real God and the only reliable source of such direction (hence **Israelites** aren't allowed to engage in divination; it was forbidden even if it did work). Yet Yahweh can say that the divination has led Nebuchadnezzar to a decision that fits Yahweh's purpose.

Because Nebuchadnezzar is the means of implementing Yahweh's terrible will for Jerusalem, Ezekiel starts with a warning to the land lying to the south, **Judah** itself (the three names, Teman, Dedan, and Southland, are all ways of saying "south"). It's not directly south of Babylon, but Babylonians reach Judah by arriving from the north—hence the image of the northern enemy in the Prophets. The Babylonians will come like a fire consuming the country. But Ezekiel expresses the warning only in parabolic form, and it's easy for people to dismiss. The following prophecy is more explicit. Maybe its three terms (Jerusalem, the sanctuaries, the land) exactly correspond to those earlier three names, and directly interpret them. The prophecy is still expressed in an image; it pictures Yahweh as a warrior unsheathing his sword that's sharp and flashing. But there's no missing the meaning of this "parable."

Before picking up the sword image again, Ezekiel is commissioned to groan. It's maybe both a groan expressing his grief at what's going to happen, and one anticipating the groan to overwhelm Judah itself. The sword prophecy is enigmatic in detail, but its general point is clear. In the midst of it, Ezekiel is commissioned to cry out and howl, because Judah is destined to do so.

Its point about rulers is picked up later in the section when Ezekiel confronts "Israel's **ordinary**, faithless ruler," Zedekiah, who will be deposed as his predecessor had been. Yahweh puts down the majestic and exalts the insignificant. It's the principle embodied in the exaltation of little David to be king, but you can't have one half of the principle without the other half. The threefold repetition of "ruin" scarily parallels the threefold "holy, holy, holy" in Isaiah 6. It suggests not just ruin to the power of one or of two but ruin to the power of three.

But such ruin won't be the end. Zedekiah will be deposed, but there'll come one to whom Davidic **authority** will properly belong (compare the cryptic promise to Judah in Genesis 49).

Finally, Ezekiel comes back to Ammon, in another prophecy that's obscure in detail but clear in general. Ammon's escape through Nebuchadnezzar's divination will not help in the long run. The day will come when the sword is returned to its sheath, and the one who wielded it (Nebuchadnezzar) will pay for doing so.

EZEKIEL 22:1–31

Unfaithfulness to People and Unfaithfulness to God

[1]Yahweh's message came to me: [2]You, young man, will you exercise authority, will you exercise authority, over the city of bloodshed, and cause it to acknowledge all its outrages. [3]You're to say, The Lord Yahweh has said this: City that sheds blood in its midst, so that its time is coming, and makes lumps for itself, so that it becomes defiled! [4]Through your blood that you've shed, you're guilty, and through the lumps that you've made, you're defiled. You've brought your days near; you've come to your years. Therefore I shall make you an object of reviling for the nations, an object of scorn for all the countries. [5]The ones near and the ones far away from you will scorn you, defiled of name, abounding in tumult. [6]There: Israel's rulers were in you, each one with his power, in order to shed blood. [7]People have belittled father and mother in you. Toward the alien they've practiced fraud in your midst. Orphan and widow they've wronged in you. [8]You've despised my sanctuaries and treated my Sabbaths as ordinary. [9]People who spread lies were in you in order to shed blood. In you they've eaten on the mountains. They've implemented scheming in your midst. [10]In you a man's exposed his father's nakedness. They've raped a woman defiled by taboo. [11]One man's performed an outrage with his neighbor's wife and another man's defiled his daughter-in-law by scheming. In you a man's raped his sister, his father's

daughter. ¹²In you they've taken a bribe so as to shed blood. You've taken interest and profit. You've looted your neighbors by fraud and disregarded me (a declaration of the Lord Yahweh). ¹³So there: I'm going to clap my hands regarding your loot that you've made and over your bloodshed that's been in your midst. ¹⁴Will your mind stand firm or your hands be strong for the days when I'm dealing with you? I Yahweh have spoken and I shall act. ¹⁵I shall scatter you among the nations and disperse you among the countries. I shall consume your defilement out of you. ¹⁶You'll be treated as ordinary in yourself in the eyes of the nations, and you will acknowledge that I am Yahweh.

¹⁷Yahweh's message came to me: ¹⁸Young man, Israel's household's become slag to me. All of them are the copper, tin, iron, and lead inside a furnace. Silver's become slag. ¹⁹Therefore the Lord Yahweh has said this: Because all of you've become slag, therefore here am I, I'm going to gather you into the midst of Jerusalem. ²⁰[Like] the gathering of silver, copper, iron, lead, and tin inside the furnace, for blowing fire on it to smelt it, so I shall gather in my anger and wrath, and lay you down, and smelt you. ²¹I shall collect you and blow on you with my furious fire and smelt you inside it. ²²Like the smelting of silver inside a furnace, so you'll be smelted inside it, and you will acknowledge that I, Yahweh, have poured out my wrath upon you.

²³Yahweh's message came to me: ²⁴Young man, say to it: You're a country that's not been cleansed, not rained on, in the day of wrath. ²⁵Its conspiracy of prophets in its midst is like a roaring lion tearing prey. They've consumed human beings, taken riches and wealth, made many widows in its midst. ²⁶Its priests have violated my teaching and treated my sanctuaries as ordinary. They haven't distinguished sacred and ordinary. They haven't enabled people to know the difference between clean and defiled. They've closed their eyes to my Sabbaths. I'm treated as ordinary in their midst. ²⁷Its officials within it are like wolves tearing prey, shedding blood to destroy lives for the sake of gaining loot. ²⁸Its prophets have coated them with paint, seeing emptiness and divining lies for them, saying,

"The Lord Yahweh has said this" when Yahweh hasn't spoken. [29]The country's people have practiced fraud and committed robbery. They've wronged the lowly and needy, and defrauded the alien without right judgment. [30]I sought from them someone building up the wall or standing in the break in front of me on behalf of the country, so I might not destroy it, but I didn't find anyone. [31]So I'm pouring out my wrath on them. In furious fire I'm putting an end to them. I'm bringing their way on their head (a declaration of the Lord Yahweh).

At Thanksgiving Dinner this week, I was talking to my stepson's brother, a prison chaplain. He manages to be both distressed and positive about situations he faces every day. The United States sends far more people to prison as a proportion of the population than anyone, but its citizens aren't distinctively wicked. The majority of people in federal prison are there for crimes with no direct victim, such as offenses related to drugs, drunkenness, or immigration. Distressingly, however, imprisonment leads to people becoming habitual criminals. We also discussed how few people see themselves as wicked. We all have ways of justifying our actions. Stealing from my workplace (for instance) is justified because my boss is dishonest anyway.

The long list of wrongs compiled by Ezekiel covers crimes with victims and offenses against God. It stresses crimes involving bloodshed, and no doubt there were acts of murder in the city. But when he elaborates his references to bloodshed, he speaks of fraud, lying, and taking bribes rather than of people wielding a club. The prophets often refer to powerful and wealthy people cheating ordinary people out of their land, or just taking advantage of the vulnerability of the aged, the orphan, and the widow. Losing your land is quite likely to mean losing your life. These offenders wouldn't see themselves as murderers ("those people should have been more efficient in running their farms, or they should have worked harder;

their fate is their own fault"). Ezekiel sees them as murderers. Belittling father and mother would involve not merely insults but depriving them of the possibility of living off their land. Turning lending into a way of making a profit likewise takes advantage of the vulnerable and pushes them further into a pit.

The city is also unfaithful to **Yahweh.** Ezekiel first sets the making of **lumps** alongside the shedding of blood. The two offenses are related. Serving other gods, or serving Yahweh in the way people served other gods, could involve sacrificing a child. Here, too, people didn't see themselves as murderers. They were making an ultimately costly offering to God. But murderers they are. Faithfulness to God and faithfulness to people (or the opposite) are related. The way you think about God and about what God wants of you makes a difference to your life. If these are in separate compartments, it's odd. They'll interrelate either to positive ends, or to negative ones.

The two realms shouldn't simply be identified. Making images is wrong not only because it easily links with bloodshed but because in its own right it conveys defilement. If no one was left in the world to be the victim of one's actions, making images would still be wrong. It would still dishonor God and bring defilement on oneself. Sexual sin likewise offends in more than one connection. The illicit relationships Ezekiel condemns make family relationships and community relationships collapse; further, sexual relationships and marriage can be another means of annexing property.

Some people listening to the final paragraph of this section would recognize that it's taking up earlier prophets' messages. It adapts a series of phrases from Zephaniah 3—these messages come from fifty years previously; from a bit later, Jeremiah 5 uses the image of looking for one faithful individual but finding none. This prophecy in Ezekiel implies that nothing has changed. Although there have been prophets such as Zephaniah and Jeremiah who've brought Yahweh's message and with whom Ezekiel could identify, and priests who were also faithful, most prophets and priests identified with the leadership that used its position to shed blood and dishonor Yahweh. Indeed, they encouraged it by giving it a stamp of (alleged) divine approval, like people painting a wall to hide its cracks.

EZEKIEL 23:1–27

You Can Serve Only One Master

[1]Yahweh's message came to me: [2]Young man, there were two women, the daughters of one mother. [3]They lived immorally in Egypt. They lived immorally in their youth. Their breasts were pressed there. There men squeezed their girls' nipples. [4]Their names: the bigger one was Oholah, and her sister Oholibah. They became mine, and they had sons and daughters. Their names: Oholah was Samaria, and Oholibah was Jerusalem. [5]Oholah was immoral though she was under me. She doted after her lovers, doted on Assyria, guardsmen [6]clothed in blue, governors and overseers, all of them desirable young men, cavalry riding horses. [7]She gave her immoralities to them, all of them the pick of the Assyrians, and with each one on whom she doted, with all their lumps, she defiled herself. [8]She didn't abandon her immoralities from Egypt, because men had slept with her in her youth, when they'd squeezed her girl's nipples and poured out their immorality upon her. [9]Therefore I gave her into the hand of her lovers, into the hand of the Assyrians on whom she'd doted. [10]When they exposed her nakedness, took her sons and daughters, and slew her with the sword, she became well-known to women, when they implemented decisions against her.

[11]Her sister Oholibah saw, but her doting was more ruinous than [Oholah's], and her immoralities than her sister's. [12]She doted on the Assyrians, governors and overseers, guardsmen clothed in perfection, cavalry riding horses, all of them desirable young men. [13]I saw that she defiled herself. The two of them had one way, [14]but she increased her immoralities. She saw

men engraved on the wall, images of Kaldeans engraved in vermilion, [15]girded with a belt on their waists, flowing turbans on their heads, all of them with the appearance of officers, the form of Babylonians, Kaldea the country of their birth. [16]She doted on them at their appearing to her eyes. She sent aides for them to Kaldea. [17]So the Babylonians came to her, to her love bed. They defiled her with their immorality. She defiled herself with them, then tore herself away from them. [18]So she exposed her immoralities and revealed her nakedness, and I tore myself away from her, as I'd torn myself away from her sister. [19]She multiplied her immoralities in being mindful of her young days when she was immoral in the country of Egypt. [20]She doted on their concubinage, whose flesh was the flesh of donkeys, and their emission the emission of horses. [21]You revisited your youthful scheming, when men from Egypt squeezed your nipples for the sake of your young breasts.

[22]Therefore, Oholibah, the Lord Yahweh has said this: Here am I, I'm going to arouse your lovers against you, the ones from whom you tore yourself away. I shall bring them against you from all around: [23]the Babylonians, all the Kaldeans, Peqod, Shoa, and Koa, all the Assyrians with them, desirable young men, governors and overseers all of them, officers and men of renown, riding horses all of them. [24]They'll come against you, armory, chariot, and wheel, and with an assembly of peoples. They'll set buckler, shield, and helmet against you all around. I shall give over the decision to their eyes and they'll decide about you with their decisions. [25]I shall give over my passion toward you, and they'll deal with you in fury. They'll remove your nose and ears and the last of you will fall by the sword. Those people will take your sons and your daughters, and the last of you will be consumed by fire. [26]They'll strip you of your clothes and take your majestic things. [27]I shall put a stop to your scheming from you, and your immorality from the country of Egypt. You won't lift up your eyes to them. You won't be mindful of Egypt anymore.

It's the festival of Christ the King today, which follows Thanksgiving and is the Last Sunday before Advent. Thinking about my sermon for the day, I wondered why the Last Sunday before Advent should be a celebration of Christ the King, and found that the festival was established by a pope less than a century ago, at a time when he thought the nations were more and more inclined to live their lives and conduct their policies autonomously, taking less and less notice of the fact that Christ is King and needs to be acknowledged as such.

Ezekiel has talked much about the people's unfaithfulness and has used sexual unfaithfulness as a metaphor for this failing, but he's usually been referring to their inclination to enter into relationships with other gods. Here the focus lies on entering into relationships with other nations, as in chapter 16. Faithfulness to **Yahweh** means treating Yahweh as key to the people's political destiny. The Old Testament's talk of covenant relationships helps make the point. The Hebrew word for "covenant" also means "treaty" or "alliance." Israel's covenant relationship with Yahweh excludes entering into treaties or alliances with other peoples. Ezekiel starts from **Israel**'s time in Egypt, because Egypt is **Judah**'s current "lover." For more than a century Judah has made alliances with the great regional power to the south. One shouldn't press the details of the allegory: Exodus doesn't speak of Israel's unfaithfulness in Egypt, and Samaria and Jerusalem weren't sisters, or even brothers (Judah was **Ephraim**'s uncle). The focus lies on Israel's relationship with **Assyria** and **Babylon**, the two big political powers over the 150 years before Ezekiel's day. Admittedly, one shouldn't draw the boundary between politics and religion too sharply. A treaty with another nation involves some acknowledgment of its gods. Doting on Assyria means acknowledging its **lumps**.

The first part of the name of the two sisters comes from the Hebrew word for a tent. The two names mean "her/its tent" and "my tent is in her/it," with reference to a family tent or a worship tent or a bridal tent. It would be ambiguous whether it would be a good tent or a tent that suggested unfaithfulness. But the main point is that the names belong to the sister cities

Samaria and Jerusalem, the capitals of Ephraim and Judah. Ephraim fell under Assyria's spell first; it was nearer Assyria and it was geographically more exposed. It was unfaithful to Yahweh in allying with Assyria and then unfaithful to Assyria in allying with Egypt, and it had paid the penalty for its unfaithfulness from both parties when the Assyrians took Samaria and transported its population in 722. The odd thing (as the Prophets saw it) was that Judah failed to learn the lesson, and followed its big sister's example. Indeed, it did worse, following its affair with Assyria by having an affair with Babylon. Judah, too, tried to make treaty commitments and then not keep them. It's about to pay the same penalty, which will stop it being so attracted to Egypt as an ally.

The **Kaldeans** were the dominant group in Babylonia and thus the term usually refers to Babylonians in general. Here the general term is followed by the names of three other Mesopotamian tribes within the Babylonian Empire. The people from whom Judah asserted independence won't let Judah behave as if it can determine its own destiny. The forces that looked so impressive as potential allies will now be frightening avengers. Yahweh is going to give over to Babylon his strong feelings about Judah and his power to decide on what should be done about Judah. It's a frightening warning. In 2 Samuel 24 David recognizes that when you're in trouble for your wrongdoing, it's better to fall into God's hands than into human hands, which may not be held back by mercy.

EZEKIEL 23:28–49

Ezekiel Writing for *The Onion*

[28]Because the Lord Yahweh has said this: Here am I, I'm going to give you into the hand of the people you repudiate, into the hand of the people from whom you tore yourself away. [29]They'll act toward you with repudiation and take all you've toiled for and abandon you naked and bare. Your immoral

nakedness will be visible, your scheming, and your immorality. ³⁰They'll do these things to you because of your whoring after the nations, on account of the way you defiled yourself with your lumps. ³¹You've walked in the way of your sister, so I shall put her chalice into your hand.

³² The Lord Yahweh has said this:

> You're to drink your sister's chalice,
> deep and wide.
> It will bring laughter and scorn,
> in containing much.
> ³³ You'll be full of drunkenness and sorrow,
> the chalice of desolation and devastation,
> your sister Samaria's chalice,
> ³⁴ but you'll drink it and drain it.
> And you'll break it into shards
> and tear your breasts.
> Because I have spoken
> (a declaration of the Lord Yahweh).

³⁵Therefore the Lord Yahweh has said this: Because you've disregarded me and thrown me behind your back, you yourself—carry your scheming and your immorality.

³⁶Yahweh said to me, Young man, will you pass judgment on Oholah and Oholibah. Tell them their outrages. ³⁷Because they've committed adultery and there's blood on their hands. They've committed adultery with their lumps. Furthermore, they've made their children, whom they bore for me, pass through [the fire] as food for them. ³⁸They've also done this to me: defiled my sanctuary and treated my Sabbaths as ordinary. ³⁹When they'd slaughtered their children for their lumps, they came into my sanctuary that day, to treat it as ordinary. There. That's what they did within my house. ⁴⁰Furthermore they'd send for men coming from afar to whom an aide was sent. There, they came, men for whom you bathed, painted your eyes, and donned jewelry. ⁴¹You sat on an elegant couch with a table spread in front of it, and you put my incense and my oil on it. ⁴²The sound of a carefree horde was in it, with men

from the human horde brought in, drunkards from the wilderness. They put bracelets on the women's hands and a majestic crown on their heads. [43]I said of one worn out by adultery, Even now they act immorally, she and her immorality, [44]and they've had sex with her. As men have sex with an immoral woman, so they've had sex with Oholah and Oholibah, scheming women. [45]But faithful men—they'll pass judgment on them, the judgment on women who commit adultery and the judgment on women who've shed blood, because they're women who commit adultery and there's blood on their hands.

[46]Because the Lord Yahweh has said this: Bring up an assembly against them, give them over to terror and plunder. [47]The assembly is to pelt them with stones and cut them down with their swords. They're to slay their sons and their daughters and burn their houses in fire. [48]I shall put a stop to scheming from the country, and all the women will accept discipline and won't act in accordance with your scheming. [49]They'll bring your scheming upon you. You'll carry the offenses involved in your lumps. And you will acknowledge that I am the Lord Yahweh.

Most days I check on *The Onion*, a collection of fanciful and whimsical fictional news items, slightly more curious than the factual ones in the real news. On Black Friday *The Onion* reported that 20,000 people were sacrificed in the annual blood offering to Corporate America, continuing the age-old annual rite to ensure bounteous profits in the coming fiscal year. A day or two previously, it reported that as civilian casualties continue to mount amid the conflict along the Gaza Strip, an eight-year-old Palestinian boy expressed both joy and astonishment that he'd yet to be killed in an Israeli military attack. A few days previously, it reported that the suicide rate in the United States was up amid the economic crisis ("nothing boosts morale or whisks your blues away quite like a full-time job"). Such reports are in bad taste, but make important points and sometimes get the point home.

Ezekiel would have no trouble getting a job with *The Onion*. It's possible to be offended by his bad taste and the demeaning way he speaks of the women in his allegory, but he's concerned about another question. Somehow he has to get through to the Judahite community in Babylon, and specifically to the men. He takes up again the tactic he tried in chapter 16. Maybe they've paid for sex, though it's misleading to think of Oholah and Oholibah as prostitutes. The word used to describe them simply denotes a woman who doesn't live by the sexual standards that society (officially) recognizes; it could refer to anyone who's sexually active outside marriage. It needn't imply being paid for sex, but it carries some of the connotations of the word *whore*. If the men didn't know anyone involved in the sex trade, they might know someone with a reputation for being an easy lay. Officially they'd strongly disapprove of such women, but their fantasies and their actions might be different from their public stance.

"You know that woman you call a whore?" Ezekiel asks. "It's you." You know you're so superior in relation to Ephraim, your sister nation to the north that the Assyrians had put out of existence? You're as bad or worse, and your fate will be the same. Judah will be treated the way the men can pruriently imagine treating a woman who's been caught in immorality (compare the story in John 8). The immoral action involves entering into political relationships with people such as Assyria, Babylon, and Egypt. They've tried to get out of their commitments but they'll find they can't do so with impunity. With some irony, nations such as Assyria and Babylon will turn out to be the "faithful men" who'll implement Yahweh's judgment on the two sisters. (Assyria had acted thus against Oholah long ago, but Ezekiel stands outside the chronological framework of Israel's history and speaks as if looking at the two peoples' history as a whole.)

Ezekiel again assumes that political unfaithfulness and religious unfaithfulness go together. Serious commitment to

Yahweh means not worshiping other gods and not seeking to safeguard the future by alliances with other nations. If people aren't seriously committed to Yahweh, they'll be living by an alternative spirituality and an alternative politics. They haven't formally given up on Yahweh. They believed they could have it both ways: engage in the forms of worship associated with other gods, including the sacrifice of children, and then show up in the temple. They could offer sacrifice in the temple, and then conduct their political life as if Yahweh didn't exist.

EZEKIEL 24:1–27

The Cooking Pot and the Bereavement

[1]Yahweh's message came to me in the ninth year, on the tenth month, on the tenth of the month: [2]Young man, write for yourself the date today, this very day. The king of Babylon's set himself against Jerusalem on this very day. [3]And tell a parable to the rebellious household. You shall say to them: The Lord Yahweh has said this:

> Put the pot on, put it on,
>   and pour water into it also.
> [4] Collect its pieces into it,
>   every good piece.
> Leg and shoulder,
>   the choicest of the bones, fill it.
> [5] Take the choicest of the flock,
>   pile the bones under it, too.
> Get it to boil;
>   its bones are to cook inside it, too.
> [6] Therefore the Lord Yahweh has said this:
> Oh, city of blood,
>   pot in which there's rust,
>   whose rust hasn't come out from it!
> Get [the contents] out piece by piece;
>   no lot has fallen on it.

7 Because its blood was inside it;
    she put it on a crag's surface.
  She didn't pour it on the earth
    to cover over it with dirt.
8 To arouse rage,
    to take redress,
  she put her blood on a crag's surface
    so that it wouldn't be covered.
9 Therefore the Lord Yahweh has said this:
  Oh, city of blood,
    I shall make the pile great, too.
10 Get much wood, light the fire,
    cook the meat through.
  Mix the spices;
    the bones must burn.
11 Stand it on the coals empty,
    so that it may get hot and its copper burn
  and its defilement may smelt inside it,
    its rust be consumed.
12 It's wearied vigor;
    the abundance of its rust doesn't come out from it,
    the rust in the fire.

¹³Your scheming is your defilement, because I'd have cleansed you, but you wouldn't be clean from your defilement. You won't be clean again until I've spent my rage on you. ¹⁴I Yahweh have spoken. It will come about. I shall do it. I won't hold back. I won't spare. I won't relent. In accordance with your ways and in accordance with your deeds they are deciding about you (a declaration of the Lord Yahweh).

¹⁵Yahweh's message came to me: ¹⁶Young man, here am I, I'm going to take from you the delight of your eyes through an epidemic. But you're not to mourn, you're not to weep, your tears aren't to come. ¹⁷Groan quietly. Don't make mourning for the dead. Put on your hat. Put your sandals on your feet. Don't cover your lips. Don't eat people's food.

¹⁸I spoke to the people in the morning, and my wife died in the evening. I did in the morning as I'd been commanded,

[19]and the people said to me, "Won't you tell us what these things mean for us, that you're acting so?" [20]I said to them, Yahweh's message came to me: [21]Say to Israel's household: The Lord Yahweh has said this: Here am I, I'm going to treat my sanctuary as ordinary, the strong object of your pride, the delight of your eyes, the object of your heart's pity. Your sons and your daughters whom you abandoned will fall by the sword. [22]You'll do as I've done. You won't cover your lips. You won't eat people's food. [23]Your hat on your head, your sandals on your feet, you won't mourn and you won't weep. You'll waste away because of your wayward acts and you'll groan one to another. [24]So Ezekiel is to be a sign for you. In accordance with all that he's done, you'll do, when it comes about. And you will acknowledge that I am the Lord Yahweh.

[25]You, young man, is it not the case that on the day I take from them their stronghold, their splendid object of celebration, the delight of their eyes, the longing of their heart, their sons and their daughters—[26]on that day a survivor will come to let you hear it with your ears. [27]On that day your mouth will open to the survivor. You'll speak and no longer be dumb. You'll be a sign to them, and they will acknowledge that I am Yahweh.

I know what it means for one's marriage and the death of one's wife to be a sign. I didn't know when my first wife was about to die and it didn't happen suddenly, though the end was sudden in its way. She'd been disabled for years and had pneumonia several times. Each time people said, "This is it," but it wasn't. So I wasn't thinking that this infection would lead to her death. In a way it was our having to live with her illness for all those years that was the sign—the sign that it was possible to do so, that there need be nothing to be afraid of, that life could still be worth living, that God could accompany you along a hard road.

I don't infer from our story that God caused Ann to get ill in order to generate that sign. Likewise one needn't infer from

Ezekiel's story that God made his wife die in order to generate a sign (though I don't think Ezekiel with his strong affirmation of God's sovereignty would object to that idea as we Westerners would). In a traditional society like that of **Babylon** and **Judah**, people get infections and die. The story need imply only that Ezekiel's wife got ill and God told him she wouldn't recover. The sign lies not in the death but in the way Ezekiel is to react. He isn't to grieve in the natural way. Normally a man would lament loudly, wouldn't dress in his usual formal way, and would cover his face. People would bring him food and he'd eat it. Ezekiel won't follow these natural instinctive and cultural practices.

People will want to know why. They know him well enough to assume that his strange actions likely carry a message. Now sometimes an event can be so devastating that you're simply stunned and paralyzed, which is how Ezekiel is behaving. He's a sign because the terrible event that's about to happen in Jerusalem will be so devastating that people will be stunned and paralyzed.

Although the two halves of the chapter are different in that one half comprises three related prophecies about Jerusalem, while the second half involves Ezekiel and his personal experience, both parts relate to the moment referred to at the chapter's beginning. Back in Jerusalem, Nebuchadnezzar has begun his final siege. His records provide the date, 15 January 588 in our terms. It would take days or weeks for news of the event to reach Babylon, but God reveals that fact to Ezekiel. He writes it down, as prophets sometimes do. When the news reaches Babylon in the regular way, it will provide one piece of evidence that he's a real prophet. He doesn't make up this stuff.

The succeeding prophecies take up the image of Jerusalem as a cooking pot, which came previously in chapter 11. It's a troublesome image. The "meat" in the pot is the family and friends that the people in **exile** left behind. The second prophecy takes the image in a different direction. Now the pot is rusty, so the meat is thrown out of it. The rust suggests the blood that stains the city. Blood has to be treated with some reverence because it symbolizes life (when blood flows out, life flows out). People in Jerusalem haven't cared about such principles. They've shed blood casually and flagrantly. Such improperly shed blood cries out from the ground. It's doing so in Jerusalem. So once the cooking is done, the rusty (that is, blood-stained) pot is going to be heated really hot, to decontaminate it. That's the kind of action that's needed, given the way all effort to cleanse it has gotten nowhere.

Jerusalem's fall will be a turning point for Ezekiel himself, as his wife's death would be a turning point in his personal life. For five years he's been dumb. He did utter his prophecies, and maybe he spoke normally at home. But he didn't take part in regular community life; he stayed quiet except when he had a message from **Yahweh**. But when the city's fall happens, in a few months' time, Yahweh says it will be permissible for Ezekiel to speak normally. The event will vindicate the message he's been giving with wearisome consistency for five years. And he will have something new to say.

EZEKIEL 25:1–17

Vengeance Is Mine

[1]Yahweh's message came to me: [2]Young man, set your face against the Ammonites and prophesy against them. [3]Say to the Ammonites, Listen to the message of the Lord Yahweh. The Lord Yahweh has said this: Because you said "Aaah" about my sanctuary when it was treated as ordinary, and about Israel's land when it became desolate, and about Judah's household when it went into exile, [4]therefore, here am I, I'm going to give you to the Qedemites as a possession. They'll set up their encampments in you and put their dwellings in you. Those people will eat your fruit. Those people will drink

your milk. [5]I shall make Rabbah a pasture for camels and the Ammonites a fold for sheep, and they will acknowledge that I am Yahweh. [6]Because the Lord Yahweh has said this: Because you clapped your hands and stamped your feet and celebrated with all your contempt in your heart about Israel's land, [7]therefore here am I, I'm going to stretch out my hand against you, and I shall give you as plunder to the nations. I shall cut you off from the peoples, wipe you out from the countries, destroy you, and you will acknowledge that I am Yahweh.

[8]The Lord Yahweh has said this: Because Moab and Seir said, There—Israel's household is like all the nations, [9]therefore here am I, I'm going to open up Moab's flank from the cities, from its cities on its extremity, the country's glory—Bet-jeshimot, Baal-meon, and Qiriataim—[10]to the Qedemites, along with the Ammonites. I shall give it as a possession, so that the Ammonites may not be remembered among the nations [11]and I may implement decisions against Moab, and they will acknowledge that I am Yahweh.

[12]The Lord Yahweh said this: Because of Edom's action in exacting redress on Israel's household and incurring guilt when they took redress against them, [13]therefore the Lord Yahweh has said this: I shall stretch out my hand against Edom and cut off from it human being and animal. I shall make it a ruin from Teman to Dedan. They'll fall by the sword. [14]I shall inflict my redress on Edom by the hand of my people Israel. They'll act against Edom in accordance with my anger and my fury, and they will acknowledge my redress (a declaration of the Lord Yahweh).

[15]The Lord Yahweh has said this: Because of the Philistines' action in taking redress and because they've exacted redress with contempt in heart in destroying with ancient enmity, [16]therefore the Lord Yahweh has said this: Here am I, I'm going to stretch out my hand against the Philistines and cut off the Kerethites, and wipe out what remains of the seacoast. [17]I shall implement great acts of redress against them with acts of furious reproof, and they will acknowledge that I am Yahweh when I inflict my redress on them.

A few weeks ago, the president of the Palestinian National Authority, Mahmoud Abbas, spoke of his attachment to the city of Safed in Galilee, where he was born; his family fled to Syria during the 1948 war, when the city ended up as part of Israel. He knows he can never live there again, but to him it's still home. Last week hostilities broke out between the state of Israel and the people of the Gaza Strip, which generated panic on the part of Israelis who now know that Gazan rockets can more or less reach Tel Aviv, brought some Israeli deaths, and brought many more deaths and much destruction in Gaza. For people outside the situation it's hard not to take sides, but it's important to understand the tragedy of this situation in which two peoples both have an attachment to the same land, and a history of that land being home.

It's then ironic to read these prophecies that include **Philistia**, of which the Gaza Strip is part (with further irony, the other four chief Philistine cities, Ashdod, Ashqelon, Eqron, and Gath, are all within modern Israel). Ammon, Moab, and Edom, too, are mostly outside the bounds of modern Israel, mostly in the kingdom of Jordan, east of the river Jordan, though relations between Israel and Jordan are much better than relations between Israel and Gaza, even though many citizens of Jordan once lived in the area of what are now Israel and Palestine or are the immediate descendants of people who lived there.

At one level, the hostility between Israel and Gaza mirrors that between Old Testament **Israel** and Ammon, Moab, Edom, and Philistia. Christians can therefore slide from identifying with Old Testament Israel into identifying with modern Israel ("Do you believe Jerusalem is the rightful capital of Israel? The Bible does. Support Israel. Sign the Petition," I read the other day). Alternatively we can slide from identifying with the Palestinians into identifying with Ammon, Moab, Edom, and Philistia. So we need to try to think in Ezekiel's framework.

Several Prophets include messages about the destiny of other peoples, but each has a different reason for doing so. Ezekiel is distinctive in the placing of them. In terms of the numbers of chapters, we're exactly halfway through the book. The first half has focused resolutely on the bad news for the **Judahite** community, but chapter 24 has heralded a moment of transition. Jerusalem's fall means Ezekiel moves from being a prophet of bad news to being a prophet of good news. (But the way this chapter follows chapter 24 encourages reflection on how Ezekiel's wife never knows about this transition and on the contrast between the transition to good news in Ezekiel's message that's unmatched by any such transition in his personal life.)

The prophecies about **Yahweh**'s judgment on other peoples constitute the first stage in that transition. While Judah is to be on the receiving end of Yahweh's judgment, other peoples are to have the same experience, particularly peoples who've been Judah's troublemakers.

Morally or theologically speaking, there are two reasons. Ezekiel deals with Ammon, Moab, Edom, and Philistia in clockwise order from Jerusalem's perspective, from northeast to east to southeast to west. Beginning with Ammon also corresponds to its place in the acted parable about the two roads (chapter 21). There its narrow escape simply made it congratulate itself and laugh at Judah's misfortune. Ezekiel may be referring back to the fall of Jerusalem that led to his own **exile** in 597, or the prophecy may come from after the city's final fall in 587. The basis for Yahweh's action isn't merely Ammon's attitude to Judah but its attitude to Judah's God. In 597 and in 587 Yahweh's sanctuary was treated as **ordinary**, and Yahweh doesn't stand by when that happens. (This consideration suggests another reflection on the contemporary Middle East. The Palestinian people has included a substantial Christian community, but one aspect of the Middle Eastern tragedy is the extra level of loss that the Christian communities have experienced as they've been neglected or marginalized. It's easy to think about the Middle Eastern questions in a way that ignores our family relationship with the church there.)

Ezekiel accuses Moab of a similar cynical reaction to Jerusalem's fall, and its comment about Judah experiencing a fate like that of any other nation hints at another form of irreverence: they're referring to Yahweh's people! Ezekiel warns Moab of a similar fate to Ammon's. Nebuchadnezzar did invade and devastate Ammon and Moab five years after the fall of Jerusalem.

The basis for judging Edom and Philistia is suggested by the eight occurrences of the word *redress* (nine in the Hebrew). Twice each, Ezekiel speaks of the two peoples exacting redress on Judah; twice each, he speaks of Yahweh exacting redress in return for these peoples' actions. We don't have any information from the Old Testament histories or from outside the Old Testament to tell us what Edom and Philistia did, though there were long-standing bad relations or an "ancient enmity" between Edom and Philistia on one hand and Israel on the other. This fact would make it entirely plausible for the two peoples to see Nebuchadnezzar's action as giving them a chance to add to Judah's troubles in a way they might think entirely justified. The moral or theological principle assumed by Ezekiel is the regular one that redress is God's business, though here, unusually, Israel is to be the means of God's redress; prophets hardly ever refer to Israel's having a role in this connection. But we never hear of Israel actually taking action against Edom after Ezekiel's day.

Kerethites is another word for Philistines, maybe linking with their origin in Crete. Using that term makes for a neat link with the Hebrew for *cut off*. It's almost as if their destiny is advertised in their name.

EZEKIEL 26:1–21

(The Love of) Money Is the Root of All Evil?

¹In the eleventh year on the first of the month, Yahweh's message came to me: ²Young man, because Tyre has said about Jerusalem, "Aaah, the people's gateway has broken, it's turned

to me, I shall be full, it's been laid waste," ³therefore the Lord Yahweh has said this: Here am I against you, Tyre; I shall bring up many nations against you, like the sea bringing up its waves. ⁴They'll destroy Tyre's walls and demolish its towers. I shall scrape off its soil and make it into the surface of a crag. ⁵It will become a place for spreading nets in the midst of the sea. Because I have spoken (a declaration of the Lord Yahweh). It will become plunder for the nations. ⁶Its daughter-towns that are in the countryside will be slain by the sword. And they will acknowledge that I am Yahweh.

⁷Because the Lord Yahweh has said this: Here am I, I'm going to bring against Tyre from the north Nebuchadnezzar, king of Babylon, the king of kings, with horse, chariotry, cavalry, an assembly, and a great company. ⁸Your daughter-towns in the countryside he'll slay with the sword. He'll build a tower against you, construct a ramp against you, and set a buckler against you. ⁹He'll set the force of his battering ram against your walls and demolish your towers with his axes. ¹⁰From the profusion of his horses their dust will cover you. From the sound of the cavalry, wheel, and chariot, your walls will shake, when he comes through your gateways like people coming into a breached city. ¹¹With the hooves of his horses he'll trample all your streets. He'll slay your people with the sword. Your strong columns will fall to earth. ¹²They'll plunder your wealth and loot your merchandise. They'll tear down your walls and demolish your desirable houses. Your stones, your wood, and your soil they'll lay in the midst of the waters. ¹³I shall put a stop to the clamor of your songs, and the sound of your guitars will make itself heard no more. ¹⁴I shall make you into the surface of a crag. You'll become a place for spreading nets. You won't be built up anymore. Because I, Yahweh, have spoken (a declaration of the Lord Yahweh).

¹⁵The Lord Yahweh has said to Tyre: At the sound of your downfall, at the groan of the slain, at the making of slaughter within you, will foreign shores not shake? ¹⁶All the sea's rulers will come down from their thrones. They'll remove their robes, strip off their embroidered clothes, and put on great trembling. They'll sit on the ground and tremble at every

moment and be desolate because of you. [17]They'll take up a dirge over you and say to you:

> Oh! You've perished, you who were peopled from
> the seas,
>   renowned city,
> one that was mighty on the sea,
>   it and its inhabitants,
> people who put their terror
>   on all [the sea's] inhabitants.
> [18] Now the foreign shores tremble
>   on the day of your downfall.
> The foreign shores that are by the sea
>   panic at your passing.

[19]Because the Lord Yahweh has said this: When I make you a ruined city, like cities that are uninhabited, when I bring up the deep over you and the mighty waters cover you, [20]I shall make you go down with the people who go down to the Pit, to the people of old, and I shall make you live in the world deep below, like the ruins from of old, with the people who go down to the Pit, so you won't be inhabited. I shall make "Splendor in the land of the living"—[21]I shall make you a horror. There'll be nothing of you. You'll be sought out, but you won't be found again, ever (a declaration of the Lord Yahweh).

Today's *The Onion*, which I mentioned in connection with chapter 23, has a message from its advertising supremo (I'm not sure it's genuine, but it makes no difference) begging people to read the advertisements alongside the "news" items. After all, he explains, that's why the entire journalism industry exists: to sell ads. The only reason a site or newspaper wants people to pay attention is so that their eyes might wander over to a nearby ad. What readers are taking part in is "a scam in which people are tricked into looking at ads so that some large, omnipotent corporation will give us a big stack of cash." It's the aim of every newspaper, magazine, and television program.

"You're merely part of a grand commercial enterprise that has existed, in one form or another, since long before you were born and that will continue to exist long after you're dead."

Tyre would understand. It existed to be a great commercial enterprise. The city lies fifty miles south of Beirut and even today is one of the biggest cities and ports in Lebanon. In ancient times, Tyre itself was strictly the small island that lies just off the shore. Its "suburbs" lay on the mainland, and were key to the provision of its supplies. It had one of the best harbors on the eastern Mediterranean, and a strategic location between Mesopotamia to the east, North Africa to the south and southwest, and Greece, Italy, and Spain across the Mediterranean to the west, where it had colonies. It was heavily fortified to safeguard its role as a great trading center.

Its position was the foundation for its role as a mercantile center, like a great hub such as London Heathrow or Singapore; hence Ezekiel's declaration that people "will plunder your wealth and loot your merchandise." The only question for Tyre to ask about any world event would be, "What are the implications for our trading position?" It would ask that question about the fall of Jerusalem. While the date of Ezekiel's prophecy oddly lacks a month, the city's fall hasn't happened yet, so one should perhaps think of Ezekiel imagining the Tyrians asking about the implications of this event that seemed pretty certain. It will mean Jerusalem ceasing to have any significance in the economy and trade of Syria-Palestine, so Tyre can increase its commercial domination of the area. That's all that matters. In later times Tyre was in ongoing tension with Galilee over food. Galilee provided much of Tyre's food, which meant shortages for Galilee itself. It wouldn't be surprising if there were similar dynamics in Old Testament times.

There are thus several reasons why **Yahweh** might determine that Tyre must be put down. The city that seems to embody "Splendor in the land of the living" will be turned into a horror. One principle that prophets commonly assume is that any nation that gets big must be put down, not least because it's virtually impossible for a powerful nation to avoid thinking that it's God. Another consideration is the attitude Tyre shares with Ammon, Moab, Edom, and **Philistia**: its contempt for Jerusalem, Yahweh's own city. Tyre has something else in common with Ammon, Edom, and Philistia. Jeremiah 27 relates how these four peoples sent envoys to Zedekiah, apparently to propose rebellion against **Babylon**. It was an idea to which Zedekiah was only too sympathetic. Jeremiah is against it, and so is Ezekiel. His prophecy about Tyre is for **Judahites** to hear. They should have nothing to do with Tyre.

The consideration distinctive to Tyre is that when a nation sees commerce as the only thing that matters, it's lost its way. Karl Marx described money as "the universal agent of separation." It divides people from one another, alienates us from our true humanity and from our fellow human beings. Tyre had become alienated in this way. Money isn't the root of all evil, but the love of money is the root of all evil (1 Timothy 6), and maybe there's little difference. God means us to enjoy life's good things such as food and clothes, which in a Western context money buys. But it's easy for trade to become something simply designed to benefit the traders.

Nebuchadnezzar arrived at Tyre and besieged it a couple of years after Ezekiel uttered this prophecy, and laid siege to it for thirteen years. Finally both sides were perhaps tired; the Tyrians submitted to Nebuchadnezzar and he didn't destroy the city. Yet Ezekiel and his fellow Judahites preserved his prophecy in his book; they didn't infer that Nebuchadnezzar's failure to destroy Tyre had invalidated the prophecy. Maybe they assumed one shouldn't be literalistic in interpreting prophecy. The threats Yahweh utters use the same language and imagery as the threats he utters against Jerusalem, which hints that we shouldn't assume he's being literal in either context. The devastating siege and eventual surrender of Tyre would be enough to count as Yahweh doing what he promised.

EZEKIEL 27:1–36

The Wreck of the *Titanic*

[1]Yahweh's message came to me: [2]You, young man, take up a dirge over Tyre. [3]You're to say to Tyre, which lives at the entrance to the sea, which trades with the peoples at many foreign shores: The Lord Yahweh has said this:

> Tyre, you said,
>> "I'm perfect in beauty."
> [4] Your borders were in the heart of the seas;
>> your builders perfected your beauty.
> [5] With juniper from Senir
>> they built all your planks.
> They took a cedar from Lebanon
>> to make a mast for you.
> [6] With oaks from Bashan
>> they made your oars.
> Your boarding they made of ivory inlaid in cypress
>> from the shores of Cyprus.
> [7] Linen with embroidery from Egypt became your spread,
>> to be an ensign for you.
> Blue and purple from the shores of Elishah
>> became your covering.
> [8] The inhabitants of Sidon and Arvad
>> were your rowers.
> Your experts, Tyre, were within you;
>> they were your sailors.
> [9] The elders of Gebel and its experts were within you,
>> fixing your cracks.
> All the ships of the sea and their mariners were in you
>> to deal in your merchandise.
> [10] Persia, Lydia, and Libya were in your forces,
>> your fighting men.
> They hung shield and helmet in you;
>> those men gave you your splendor.
> [11] People from Arvad and Helek
>> were on your walls all around.

Gammadites were in your towers,
  they hung their quivers on your walls all around;
  these men completed your beauty.

[12]Tarshish was your dealer because of the abundance of all your wealth; they gave your wares in exchange for silver, iron, tin, and lead. [13]Javan, Tubal, and Meshek were your traders; they gave your merchandise in exchange for human life and copper things. [14]From Beth-togarmah they gave horses, horsemen, and mules in exchange for your wares. [15]The Dedanites were your traders. Many foreign shores were dealers under your control. They brought back to you ivory tusks and ebony as your payment. [16]Aram was your dealer because of the abundance of your products; they gave your wares in exchange for turquoise, purple, embroidery, fine linen, coral, and ruby. [17]Judah and the country of Israel were your merchants; they gave your merchandise in exchange for wheat from Minnith and Pannag, honey, oil, and balm. [18]Damascus was your dealer because of the abundance of your products, because of the abundance of all your wealth, in wine of Helbon and white wool. [19]Vedan and Javan gave yarn in exchange for your wares; there was wrought iron, cassia, and cane among your merchandise. [20]Dedan was your trader in saddlecloths for riding. [21]Arabia and all Qedar's rulers were dealers under your control in lambs, rams, and goats, as your dealers in these. [22]The traders of Sheba and Ra'amah were your traders; they gave your wares in exchange for the finest of all spice and for all precious stone and gold. [23]Haran, Kanneh, and Eden, the traders of Sheba, Assyria, and Kilmad, were your traders. [24]Those were your traders in fine things, in blue embroidered cloths, and in colored rugs bound with cords and preserved with cedar, in your market. [25]Tarshish ships were your ministers for your merchandise.

You were full and very heavy
  in the heart of the seas.
[26] Into the mighty waters
  the rowers brought you.

The east wind broke you
    in the heart of the seas.
27 Your wealth and your wares, your merchandise,
    your mariners and your sailors,
the men who fixed your cracks
    and the people who handled your merchandise,
all your fighting men who were in you,
    and in all your assembly that was in your
        midst,
will fall in the heart of the seas
    on the day of your downfall.
28 At the sound of your sailors' cry,
    the shorelands will shake.
29 All the oarsmen
    will come down from their ships.
The mariners, all the sailors of the sea,
    will stand on the earth.
30 They will let their voice be heard concerning you,
    and cry in distress.
They will put dirt on their head
    and cover themselves in ash.
31 For you, they will shave their head
    and wind on sackcloth.
They will weep for you with distress of spirit,
    with distressed lament.
32 For you they will take up a dirge as they groan,
    and lament for you:
"Who was like Tyre,
    like the one silenced in the midst of the sea?
33 When your wares came forth from the seas,
    you filled many peoples.
With the abundance of your wealth and your
        merchandise
    you enriched earth's kings.
34 When you broke because of the seas,
    in the depths of the waters,
your merchandise and all your assembly
    fell in the midst of it.

³⁵ All the inhabitants of foreign shores
    are desolate over you.
Their kings bristled with horror,
    their faces went dark.
³⁶ The dealers among the peoples whistled at you;
    you became a horror, and you're no more forever."

Among the Roman cities in Turkey to which John wrote the letters that appear in the book of Revelation, the one that makes for the most spectacular visit is Ephesus, a monumental site, with a population of several hundred thousand in Christ's day. It still contains the reconstructed huge façade of the library that forms a monument to the Roman governor Tiberius Julius Celsus Polemaeanus. The nearby temple of Artemis was her most important shrine. The theater, where the assembly gathered to argue for the arrest or execution of Paul and his associates, is larger than the Hollywood Bowl. But it was destroyed (and all the library's books burned) by the Goths in the third century. It was partly rebuilt, but eventually abandoned. In Paul's day, it would have been hard to imagine such a fate. But it shares that fate with all seven of those cities. They're either abandoned, or survive only as hard-to-find enclaves within a modern city.

Tyre's destruction would be as unimaginable, but Ezekiel imagines it. He here gives more detail on Tyre's powerful place in the Mediterranean and Middle Eastern world. The first poem pictures the great maritime power as if it were itself a ship. The best materials from all over the world came together to build this magnificent "vessel." Literal reality pokes through as Ezekiel describes Tyre's military forces as well as its "sailors." The middle paragraph catalogs the merchandise Tyre traded in and the city's trading partners. They cover a world that extends to the far west (Tarshish, in Spain), the far east (**Assyria**), the north (Beth-togarmah, in Armenia), and the south (Sheba, in Arabia). They cover a bewildering variety of goods.

Finally Ezekiel reverts to picturing Tyre as a ship, exploiting the devastating potential of the image. Traveling from Greece to Ephesus, we crossed the Aegean Sea; even in Paul's day it was a busy sea route (as busy as the air route from New York to Chicago or the train line from London to Birmingham, it's been said, with a little exaggeration). It was quicker and safer than the land route, as it is today. Yet Paul also found that travel by sea could be hazardous, and the people of Tyre were used to there being occasions when one of its ships failed to make it home and the sailors' families mourned their loss. That destiny lies ahead of the ship of Tyre itself, **Yahweh** declares. The opening of this last paragraph perhaps hints that business generates temptation and the ship is over-full. The east wind takes cargo and crew to the ocean bottom. Only metaphorically do people on the shore hear the sailors' cry, but in literal reality they howl in grief when it becomes clear that neither ship nor crew are coming home. More discreetly, the business people who were wise enough to stay home set about calculating how much they've lost.

It's an image for the coming destruction of the good ship Tyre itself. The east wind is the cause of the wreck. There are no doubt meteorological reasons lying behind the shipwreck, but it's no coincidence that the east wind destroying Tarshish ships provides an image for Yahweh's destroying Jerusalem's attackers in Psalm 48. The wind is Yahweh's agent. That psalm begins with a comment on Jerusalem's beauty, and Ezekiel starts from Tyre's self-assessment as "complete in beauty." Similar phrases come twice more in the poem. They come twice earlier in the Old Testament, in Lamentations 2 and Ezekiel 16, both times applied to Jerusalem—though both times with some irony. Such standing belonged to Jerusalem, not because it was architecturally so magnificent (it wasn't) but because of the significance Yahweh had given it as his city, with a key place in the world as his dwelling place. So when Jerusalem failed to live up to the implications of this significance, it paid for it.

But when another city such as Tyre claimed such significance, it was taking a risk. **Israel** didn't have to do anything about it, such as attack Tyre in Yahweh's **name**. But it could be sure that Yahweh would do something about it (so it would be foolish to start believing Tyre's publicity).

EZEKIEL 28:1–26

The Fall of a King

[1]Yahweh's message came to me: [2]Young man, say to Tyre's ruler: The Lord Yahweh has said: Because your mind has been lofty and you've said, "I am God, enthroned as a deity—I've taken my seat in the heart of the seas," when you're a human being and not God, but you made your mind like a deity's mind:

[3] There, you're shrewder than Danel;
    nothing hidden baffles you.
[4] Through your shrewdness and your insight
    you've made wealth for yourself.
  You've made gold and silver in your treasuries
[5]   through the abundance of your shrewdness
      and through your trading.
  You've made your wealth great;
    but you've made your mind lofty because of your
      wealth.
[6] Therefore the Lord Yahweh has said this:
  Because of your making your mind
    like the mind of a deity,
[7] therefore here am I, I'm going to bring against you
    strangers, the most violent of nations.
  They'll draw their swords against your shrewd beauty
    and pierce you in your splendor.
[8] Down to the Pit they'll bring you;
    you'll die the death of the slain
    in the heart of the seas.
[9] Will you actually say "I am a deity"
    before your slayers,

given that you're a human being and not God—
    at the hand of the people who pierce you?
¹⁰ You'll die the death of the uncircumcised
    at the hand of strangers,
because I have spoken
    (a declaration of the Lord Yahweh).

¹¹Yahweh's message came to me: ¹²Young man, take up a dirge over the king of Tyre. You're to say to him: The Lord Yahweh has said this:

You were an exact seal,
    full of shrewdness, perfect in beauty.
¹³ You were in Eden, God's garden,
    with every precious stone your covering:
carnelian, topaz, and diamond,
    beryl, onyx, and jasper,
sapphire, turquoise, and emerald,
    and gold, the work of your tambourines,
and your sockets that were in you,
    prepared on the day of your creation.
¹⁴ You were a cherub,
    anointed as the protector, and I placed you—
    you were on God's sacred mountain.
When you walked about amid the fiery stones,
¹⁵   you were a person of integrity in all your
        ways,
from the day of your creation,
    until wrong appeared in you.
¹⁶ Through the abundance of your trading,
    people filled the midst of you with violence.
You committed offenses, and I am profaning you
    from God's mountain and destroying you,
cherub the protector,
    from the midst of the fiery stones.
¹⁷ Your mind became lofty because of your beauty;
    you ruined your shrewdness on account of
        your splendor.

I'm throwing you out to the earth;
    before kings I'm making you something to stare at.
¹⁸ Because of the abundance of your wayward acts,
    through the wrongdoing of your trading,
    you've treated your great sanctuary as ordinary.
I'm making fire go out from your midst
    and it's devouring you.
I'm making you into ash on the earth
    before the eyes of all who look at you.
¹⁹ All who acknowledge you among the peoples
    are desolate at you.
You're becoming a horror,
    and you'll be no more, forever.

²⁰Yahweh's message came to me: ²¹Young man, set your face toward Sidon and prophesy against it. ²²Say, The Lord Yahweh has said this:

Here am I against you, Sidon;
    I shall get honor in your midst.
They will acknowledge that I am Yahweh,
    when I implement decisions against you.
I shall show myself holy in you
²³   and let loose epidemic in it and blood in its
        streets.
The slain will fall in its midst
    through the sword that's against it from all around,
    and they will acknowledge that I am Yahweh.

²⁴No more will there be for Israel's household prickling brier and piercing thorn from all the people around them who treat them with contempt, and they will acknowledge that I am the Lord Yahweh.

²⁵The Lord Yahweh has said this: When I've gathered Israel's household from the peoples among whom they're dispersed and I've shown myself holy among them before the eyes of the nations, they'll live on their land that I gave my servant Jacob, ²⁶and live on it with assurance. They'll build houses and plant

vineyards and live with assurance, when I've implemented decisions on all the people who treat them with contempt, who are around them. And they will acknowledge that I Yahweh am their God.

In our church Bible study on Wednesday, some people were noticing things in Genesis that they hadn't previously seen, such as the difference in the creation account in Genesis 1 and in Genesis 2, and one person asked, "Where was the Garden of Eden?" I gulped, because people can be disturbed by the issues that such questions raise, but I went on to explain how I see the question. Genesis 1–2 is talking about real events: God did create the world, God did provide for humanity, humanity had the chance to live in a relationship with God but chose to go its own way. But Genesis tells this story in a form that's more like a parable or painting than a photograph. Its geographical points illustrate both these aspects. Genesis tells you about four rivers, which suggests a place with real geography, but we can't match its geography with literal geography.

Outside Genesis, Ezekiel is the book with most references to Eden (there's also an ordinary place named Eden in chapter 27, but the name is spelled slightly differently). This prophecy to the king of Tyre is also talking about a real event, though it's an event to come, not an event way back at the beginning. In this connection it recycles the imagery of the Eden garden in a new direction, with a new profile. The passage has been understood to describe the fall of Satan, but in the context it's a warning about the coming fall of the Tyrian king. The king in Ezekiel's day was Ithobaal, but the king isn't named; the prophecy's concern isn't with one particular or particularly wicked king but with the kingly line at Tyre. Promising the fall of Tyre's king is another way of promising Tyre's own fall.

In this warning, the garden becomes a picture of Tyre's magnificent position in the world in Ezekiel's day—not on land but at sea. Adam becomes the king of Tyre. The **cherub** protecting the garden from further encroachment also becomes a figure for the king in his position as protector of his city and people. Insight becomes something he already possesses rather than something he desires that becomes his downfall. He's as discerning as Danel, the mythical hero mentioned in Ezekiel 14, who appears appropriately here in light of the fact that his story was told by people not far from Tyre, in a city called Ugarit—it is from findings there that we know the story. The garden is a place with gold and precious stones, but these become the king's own. It's not merely God's garden but God's **sacred** mountain, and the list of precious stones parallels the list of the stones in the high priest's breastplate. The king is in a quasi-priestly position as well as a kingly one (in the Middle East, the king of a city was often also a priest). Whereas we don't know that Adam ever had time to become a person of integrity (his yielding to temptation may have happened soon after his creation), the king did have a period as a person of integrity, but then let himself be led astray. Whereas the desire that led Adam astray was a desire to make his own **decisions**, the desire that led the king astray related to stuff. Whereas violence emerged in Adam's family, violence comes to characterize the king's city. Whereas Adam aspired to being like God, being like God is something the king claims as a present achievement on the basis of his insight and his achievements. Whereas Adam was threatened with the loss of his life but this threat was not immediately implemented, the threat made to Adam will be a reality for this king. Instead of being able to live on God's sacred mountain, he'll be removed from the realm of the sacred because he's desecrated it.

When describing the fate that threatens the king, Ezekiel becomes more literal and repeats his earlier threat of enemy attack, but gives it more precision in working out its implications for the king. Unlike a series of **Judahite** kings in the last years of Judah's independent existence, he won't merely be deposed by a foreign power—he'll lose his life. The king would likely be circumcised, as circumcision is a common Middle Eastern practice; to be uncircumcised is uncivilized. Describing him as uncircumcised is to say that he'll die a disgraceful death; to die in battle at the hand of strangers is likely to mean being deprived of a decent burial.

Sidon is another strong seaport, twenty-five miles north of Tyre and thus halfway to Beirut. The brief warning about its fall provides background to a promise of relief for **Israel**, and that promise in turn leads into a more positive promise for Israel that looks way beyond the **exile** to the people's restoration and their freedom to resume a quiet life.

EZEKIEL 29:1–21

"My Children Have Defeated Me!"

¹In the tenth year, in the tenth month, on the twelfth of the month, Yahweh's message came to me: ²Young man, set your face against Pharaoh, king of Egypt, and prophesy against him and against Egypt, all of it. ³Speak as follows: The Lord Yahweh has said this:

> Here am I against you,
>   Pharaoh, king of Egypt,
> big monster stretching out
>   in the middle of its channels,
> that said, "My Nile is mine;
>   I'm the one who made it."
> ⁴ I shall put hooks in your jaws
>   and make the fish in your channels stick to your
>   scales.
> I shall get you up from the middle of your channels,
>   with all the fish in your channels that stick to
>   your scales.
> ⁵ I shall abandon you to the wilderness,
>   you and all the fish in your channels.

You'll fall on the face of the countryside;
  you won't be collected and you won't be gathered.
I'm giving you as food to the creatures of the earth
  and the birds of the heavens.
6 And all the inhabitants of Egypt
  will acknowledge that I am Yahweh.
Because they were a support made of reed
  for Israel's household.
7 When they grasped you in their hand, you'd fracture,
  and tear their entire shoulder.
When they leaned on you, you'd break,
  and make their entire side collapse.

8Therefore the Lord Yahweh has said this: Here am I, I'm going to bring a sword against you. I shall cut off from you human being and animal. 9The country of Egypt will become desolation and ruin. And they will acknowledge that I am Yahweh. Because [Pharaoh] said, "The Nile is mine; I'm the one who made it," 10therefore here am I toward you and toward your channels. I shall make the country of Egypt an utter ruin and desolation, from Migdol to Syene, as far as the border with Sudan. 11Human foot won't pass through it and animal foot won't pass through it. It won't be inhabited for forty years. 12I shall make the country of Egypt a desolation in the middle of desolate countries, and its cities amid ruined cities will be a desolation for forty years. I shall scatter the Egyptians among the nations and disperse them among the countries.

13Because the Lord Yahweh has said this: At the end of forty years I shall gather the Egyptians from the peoples where they've scattered. 14I shall restore the fortunes of the Egyptians and bring them back to the country of Pathros, upon the country of their origin. They'll be a lowly kingdom there. 15They'll be the lowliest of the kingdoms; they won't arise again over the nations. I shall make them small so they don't have dominion over the nations. 16They won't again be an object of trust for Israel's household, making it mindful of its waywardness in turning after them. And they will acknowledge that I am the Lord Yahweh.

[17]In the twenty-seventh year, on the first of the first month, Yahweh's message came to me: [18]Young man, Nebuchadnezzar king of Babylon has made his forces serve with great servitude against Tyre. Every head is rubbed bare. Every shoulder is scraped. But he and his forces have no wages from Tyre for the servitude they've expended on it. [19]Therefore the Lord Yahweh has said this: Here am I, I'm going to give Nebuchadnezzar, king of Babylon, the country of Egypt. He'll carry off its wealth, take spoil from it, and seize booty from it, and it will be the wages for his forces. [20]As his compensation for which he served, I'm giving him the country of Egypt, because they acted for me (a declaration of the Lord Yahweh). [21]On that day I shall make a horn grow for Israel's household, and to you I shall give an opening of your mouth among them, and they will acknowledge that I am Yahweh.

There are two great but solemn stories involving Rabbi Eliezer, a Jewish teacher before and after the fall of Jerusalem in AD 70. He lived at a time when the Jewish people needed to discern what Jewish faith would mean when it could no longer focus on the temple. He took a conservative stance about possible changes. Other theologians disagreed with him: Moses said the **Torah** "isn't in heaven" (Deuteronomy 30); they inferred that it had been given to the scholars to interpret, its implications being determined by their decision. They can overrule not only Rabbi Eliezer but even God himself! Elijah the prophet is said to have reported that God laughed and said, "My children have defeated me!" Later, when he was near death, Rabbi Eliezer is said to have placed his arms on his heart and in anguish to have declared, "Woe to you, my two arms, which are like two Torah scrolls that have been tied up. . . . Much Torah have I taught, but my students took from me less than can fit into an eye dropper."

I can imagine Ezekiel nodding at both these stories. He's referred nearly fifty times so far in the book to people coming to acknowledge who **Yahweh** is, but he's seen no evidence of their doing so, and as far as we know he never did. To judge from the dates he gives, his message about Nebuchadnezzar in this chapter is his very last (it comes here, before messages that were actually given earlier, because it concerns Egypt, the subject of this chapter). The date is 571, two or three years after Nebuchadnezzar raised the siege of Tyre, and three or four years before Nebuchadnezzar indeed invaded Egypt and fought a battle that he, at least, claims to have won. Maybe Ezekiel saw that event, and had things to say after it happened, but if so, these words weren't preserved. The point he makes here concerns a question that might be raised by his words about a kind of obligation Yahweh feels toward Nebuchadnezzar, who has been his agent in bringing judgment. Here in his closing comment Ezekiel reaffirms that judgment isn't Yahweh's last word. Yahweh will make a horn grow for **Israel**. Israel is like a bull for whom its horn is a symbol of its strength; Yahweh might seem to have cut off its horn, but its horn will grow again. In due course Yahweh indeed makes it happen, though not (as far as we know) in Ezekiel's lifetime. Like Jeremiah, he ends his ministry and dies with **Judah** still in **exile**, living in hope and speaking words of hope, but not seeing hope become reality.

The story of Nebuchadnezzar and Tyre also provides an example of God's willingness to let his children defeat him. One might have thought that there was a tight link between God's declarations of intent and events that take place in the world, but one glance at how things are in the world shows that it's not so. God's sovereignty and human decision-making interweave in the way things happen. No doubt God could ensure that the only things that happen are what he really wants, but he doesn't operate that way. He'll fulfill his purpose, but he's always willing to take the long view. He even let his Son be crucified and turned that event into something that could contribute to the fulfillment of his purpose rather than frustrate it.

In speaking of Egypt in this chapter, Ezekiel moves from the regional power to the north (Tyre) to the regional power to the south, which will occupy him for the next four chapters. Even though he's in **Babylon**, he doesn't give the attention to Babylon that Isaiah or Jeremiah do. It's hardly because he's scared to do so. The point of turning to Egypt is that Egypt is the power that people in Judah see as their salvation, and thus that Judahites in Babylon also have hope in. Egypt is like a cane that breaks when you lean on it, and takes you down with it.

Ezekiel speaks of Egypt's empty pretensions in order to discourage the Judahites from believing Egypt's publicity out of their own wishful thinking. As if Egypt could really claim to have made the Nile! There's hardly a more impressive example of a people so blessed by having in their midst such a wondrous resource that they didn't create or earn. The Egyptians implicitly acknowledged the point in other contexts when they contrasted Egypt favorably with Canaan, where people had to rely on the uncertainty of rain, a kind of second-best substitute for the Nile, if they were to hope that their crops would grow.

After Yahweh's envisaging a bleak future for Egypt, his promises in the third paragraph are a surprise. Again we need to see his words in the context of points he's seeking to get home to Judah. Judah mustn't treat Egypt as its salvation. But on the other hand, Yahweh cares about the Egyptians as he cares about the Judahites. He uses the same terms about them as he uses about Judah—he talks about gathering the scattered people and about restoring their future (Pathros is a name for Upper Egypt). Yahweh won't let Egypt be a regional power again, because it illustrates the principle that power corrupts and absolute power corrupts absolutely. It needs to be protected from itself, and Judah needs to be protected from ever trusting Egypt as its salvation in the future.

EZEKIEL 30:1–26

The Day of the Lord for Egypt

¹Yahweh's message came to me: ²Young man, prophesy, and say, Yahweh has said this:

> Howl, "Aaaagh for the day,"
> ³   because Yahweh's day is near.
> A day of cloud,
>   a time of nations, it will be.
> ⁴ A sword will come upon Egypt,
>   anguish will fall upon Sudan,
> when the slain fall in Egypt, and people take its wealth,
>   and its foundations collapse.

⁵Sudan, Libya, Lydia, the entire foreign group, Cyrenaica, and members of the covenanted country will fall by the sword with them.

> ⁶ Yahweh said this:
> The people who support Egypt will fall;
>   its strong majesty will sink down.
> From Migdol to Syene
>   they'll fall there by the sword
>   (a declaration of the Lord Yahweh).

⁷They'll be desolate amid desolate countries, and its cities will be amid ruined cities. ⁸And they will acknowledge that I am Yahweh when I put fire in Egypt, and all its helpers break. ⁹On that day aides will go out from before me in ships to terrify confident Sudan. Anguish will be upon them on Egypt's day, because there—it's coming.

¹⁰The Lord Yahweh has said this: And I shall put a stop to Egypt's horde by the hand of Nebuchadnezzar, king of Babylon. ¹¹He and his company with him, the most violent of nations, are going to be brought to ruin the country. They'll draw their swords against Egypt and fill the country with the slain. ¹² I shall make the channels dry ground and sell the

150

country into the hand of evil people. I shall desolate the country and everything in it by the hand of strangers. I, Yahweh, have spoken. ¹³The Lord Yahweh has said this: I shall wipe out the lumps and stop the nonentities from Memphis. There'll no longer be a ruler from the country of Egypt. I shall put fear in the country of Egypt. ¹⁴I shall desolate Pathros. I shall put fire in Zoan. I shall implement decisions in Thebes. ¹⁵I shall pour out my fury on Pelusium, Egypt's stronghold. I shall cut off the horde of Thebes. ¹⁶I shall put fire in Egypt. Pelusium will writhe and writhe. Thebes will be torn apart. Memphis: adversaries daily. ¹⁷The young men of Heliopolis and Pi-beseth will fall by the sword. Those—they'll go into exile. ¹⁸In Tehaphnehes the day will be dark when I break Egypt's yokes there, and its strong majesty comes to a stop in it. Cloud will cover it and its daughter towns will go into captivity. ¹⁹I shall implement decisions in Egypt, and they will acknowledge that I am Yahweh.

²⁰In the eleventh year, in the first month, on the seventh of the month, Yahweh's message came to me: ²¹Young man, I'm breaking the arm of Pharaoh, king of Egypt. There, it's not bound up so as to give healing, by putting a bandage to bind it up to strengthen it for grasping a sword. ²²Therefore the Lord Yahweh has said this: Here am I toward Pharaoh, king of Egypt. I shall break his arms, the strong one and the breaking one. I shall make the sword fall from his hand. ²³I shall scatter the Egyptians among the nations and disperse them among the countries. ²⁴I shall strengthen the arms of the king of Babylon and put my sword in his hand. I shall break the arms of Pharaoh. He'll groan before him with the groans of the slain. ²⁵I shall strengthen the arms of the king of Babylon, but Pharaoh's arms— they'll fall. And they will acknowledge that I am Yahweh, when I put my sword into the hand of the king of Babylon and he stretches it out against the country of Egypt. ²⁶I shall scatter the Egyptians among the nations and disperse them among the countries, and they will acknowledge that I am Yahweh.

It was Advent Sunday yesterday, so in church we started thinking about "the day of the Lord." In the Gospel passage from

Luke 21, Jesus encouraged us not to be anxious about distress among the nations and warned us not to be weighed down with dissipation and drunkenness, lest "that day," the day when the Son of Man appears, should catch us unexpectedly, like a trap. The Advent prayer thus speaks of the link and the contrast between the time of our mortal life in which Jesus came to visit us in lowliness, and the last day when he will come again in glorious majesty to judge the living and the dead. I was reminded of the movie we watched a few nights ago, *Seeking a Friend for the End of the World*, whose premise was that an asteroid was about to hit earth. It portrayed different ways of coping with that realization. Jesus' point is that we won't get three weeks' notice. Indeed, Jesus' twenty-first-century disciples are not inclined to be in awe of his coming. He might want to encourage us to be more anxious.

In effect, Ezekiel gives Egypt and its allies three weeks' notice; except that as far as we know, it never hears about his prophecy, and anyway it would have taken no notice. The **Judahites** in **exile** are Ezekiel's audience. Earlier in his ministry, Ezekiel has reversed the implications of "**Yahweh**'s day," like Amos. Amos's audience thought of it as a day of blessing when their enemies would be put in their place; Amos warned them that it would be a day of darkness and trouble, when their enemies would be God's means of causing them trouble. Ezekiel agreed.

Is Ezekiel is here reversing that reversal? Not really. Yahweh's day is indeed being turned back into bad news for the nations (specifically, for Egypt), but Egypt is Judah's ally and resource for help against the **Babylonians**, so bad news for Egypt is bad news for Judah. The Prophets have the recurrent task of reframing Israel's thinking about the nations of its world, and one of the significances of these prophecies about the nations is to enable Jews and Christians to reframe our thinking about the nations in our world.

One way Ezekiel does so lies in the radical nature of his belief in Yahweh's sovereignty. He actually believes that Yahweh makes things happen in the world. It's possible to think and talk about God's sovereignty in a way that doesn't seem to imply that this sovereignty has much purchase in the world. It has purchase for Ezekiel. There are about twenty-eight verbs in this chapter of which Yahweh is the subject: "I shall desolate, I shall wipe out, I shall put fire," and so on.

Yet Ezekiel isn't thinking in terms of a divine intervention in the world that involves no human agents. There are no miracles in Ezekiel's scenario. It's the king of Babylon who will physically wield the sword and light the fire in Egypt. Like other prophets, Ezekiel understands events at two levels. In our world we've become used to questions such as "Did my neurons make me do it?" (it's the title of a book by one of my colleagues and friends). To say "My neurons made me do it" isn't incompatible with saying "I did it." Indeed, my wife suggests, you can reverse the statement—"I make my neurons," I shape them. Likewise, to say "Nebuchadnezzar did it" (of his own free will) isn't incompatible with saying "Yahweh did it."

One can't move from Ezekiel's statement about Pharaoh and Nebuchadnezzar to the idea that God has a hand in all events in the same way. There's special significance about these events because of their interweaving with Israel's history, in which God is involved in order to achieve special ends. It does open up the possibility of asking the question about God's involvement in events in our own time. Yet some events are just things that happen. When Jesus talks about distress among the nations, about wars and rumors of wars, he's talking about events that have no ultimate meaning.

There's another sense in which Ezekiel invites us to reframe our understanding of events in history. In speaking of Yahweh's day coming for Egypt, Ezekiel isn't talking about the end of history but about an event within history. On the way to Yahweh's day as one that brings history to its radical transformation, Yahweh's day comes a number of times as Yahweh acts in a particularly significant fashion to bring trouble or blessing.

EZEKIEL 31:1–18

On Which the Sun Never Sets

[1]In the eleventh year, in the third month, on the first of the month, Yahweh's message came to me: [2]Young man, say to Pharaoh, king of Egypt and to his horde:

> To whom are you like in your greatness?—
> [3]   there: Assyria was a cedar in Lebanon,
> beautiful in boughs,
>   and a shady thicket,
> lofty in height,
>   and its top was among the clouds.
> [4] Waters made it big, the deep made it high,
>   going with its rivers around its plantation.
> It sent its channels
>   to all the trees of the countryside.
> [5] As a result its height was loftier
>   than all the trees of the countryside.
> Its branches abounded, its boughs extended,
>   because of the abundant water in its channel.
> [6] All the birds of the heavens
>   nested in its branches.
> All the animals of the countryside
>   gave birth under its boughs.
> All the great nations
>   were living in its shade.
> [7] It was beautiful in its great size, in the length of its
>   branches,
>   because its root was by abundant waters.
> [8] Cedars in God's garden didn't overshadow it,
>   junipers didn't equal its branches,
>   plane trees didn't compare with its branches.
> No tree in God's garden
>   equaled it in its beauty.
> [9] I made it beautiful
>   in the abundance of its branches.
> All the trees of Eden were jealous of it,
>   the ones in God's garden.

154

¹⁰Therefore the Lord Yahweh has said this: Because its height was lofty and it put its top into the midst of the clouds, and its attitude became lofty in its height, ¹¹I gave it into the hand of the leader of the nations so that he'd deal effectively with it. In accordance with its faithlessness I dispossessed it. ¹²Strangers, the most violent of nations, cut it down and left it. Its branches fell on the mountains and in all the valleys. Its boughs broke into all the ravines in the earth. All the peoples of the earth went down from its shade and left it. ¹³Upon it, fallen, all the birds of the heavens dwell, and to its boughs have come all the animals of the countryside—¹⁴so that no trees by water should become lofty in their height or put their top among the clouds, nor should any mighty ones, drinkers of water, stand up in their loftiness, because all of them were given over to death, to the country below, amid all human beings, with the people who go down to the Pit.

¹⁵The Lord Yahweh has said this: On the day it went down to Sheol, I caused mourning, I closed the deep over it. I held back its rivers; the abundant waters held back. I made Lebanon grieve over it. All the trees of the countryside languished over it. ¹⁶At the sound of its fall I made the nations shake, when I made it go down to Sheol with the people who go down to the Pit. In the country below, all the trees of Eden, the choicest and best of Lebanon, all the drinkers of water, found consolation. ¹⁷Those also went down with it to Sheol, to the people slain by the sword, and its support, the people who'd lived in its shadow amid the nations.

¹⁸To whom are you like in this way, in honor and greatness among the trees of Eden? You'll be brought down with the trees of Eden to the country below. Among the uncircumcised you'll lie, with the people slain by the sword. That's Pharaoh and his entire horde (a declaration of the Lord Yahweh).

I recently read a history of everyday life in Britain after the Second World War, which took me back to my childhood with memories of rationing and of playing in a bomb crater. Those years followed on a great victory, yet they were years of shortages and scarcity. Then, as Britain started to emerge from its austerity, they were years of rebellion in different parts of the empire. The British prime minister recognized that a "wind of change" was blowing in Africa, and it was blowing elsewhere, too. A United States secretary of state declared that Britain "has lost an empire, and has yet to find a role." The good news was that, roleless, it seemed to become as happy as anywhere else.

Ezekiel's comment is that the great power in **Judah**'s world needs to be prepared to learn the lessons that emerge from the story of an earlier great power. "Remember **Assyria**?" he asks. It didn't describe itself as the empire on which the sun would never set, the term applied to the position in the world occupied by Spain, then by Britain, then by the United States. It could easily have done so. But within the lifetime of many of Ezekiel's readers, it had collapsed. Ezekiel continues to address Pharaoh, but his actual audience continues to be the Judahites in **Babylon**. It's just a few weeks later than the last paragraph of the previous chapter, still during the siege of Jerusalem. The Jerusalemites in Babylon are still hoping against hope for the city's deliverance, in keeping with promises prophets have made in the past and are making in the present. They're not looking for a miracle. They just need Egypt to fulfill its treaty obligations. It's not going to happen, says Ezekiel.

The tree image is a recurrent one to describe a king or an empire. It suggests beneficence—the king is good for you, the empire is good for you. It protects you. It's big and impressive; it gives you something to be proud of. The Assyrian "tree" grew by a plentiful water supply, like the tree in Psalm 1. No other "tree" could rival it. Even the trees in God's own garden envied it. According to later writers, it was in Ezekiel's day that Nebuchadnezzar built the Hanging Gardens of Babylon with their many trees, imitations of the gardens his Median wife knew in **Persia**. If Nebuchadnezzar did construct these gardens, Ezekiel's audience would make a link with that work.

The nation's leader to whom **Yahweh** then gives power over Assyria is none other than Nebuchadnezzar (his father Nabopolassar was king when Assyria collapsed into Babylon's arms, but it was his son Nebuchadnezzar who won the final victory at Carchemish in 605 and was reigning in the time of Ezekiel and his community). The reason for its downfall is the one that recurs in the Prophets. While they critique the empires' self-indulgence and violence, the dominant note is the very fact that they're empires. They're concentrations of human power that rival God. They come to think of themselves as God. So for their sake, and for other people's sake, and for God's sake, and for truth's sake, they must be put in their place.

It's strange that the nations within the empire grieve its passing. But there's security in being under a big power's authority (as well as material advantage in the markets it provides and the trade routes it safeguards). It does offer protection and order in return for the price you pay in literal terms in taxation and tribute, and in the power you surrender. In contrast to their mourning, the representatives of other nations who are already present in Sheol gain satisfaction from the empire's fall. The talk about the felling of a tree and about descending to Sheol combines two motifs that are both applicable to a great king in the Old Testament. Daniel 4 describes Nebuchadnezzar as a tree that almost gets felled. Isaiah 14 describes the fall of the Babylonian king and his descent to Sheol, and his "greeting" by the kings already there. The *Pit* is simply another word for Sheol. The literal grave pit in which people's bodies might be buried (ironically, these would especially be poor people, not kings) provides an image for the location of the king's burial.

The last little paragraph returns to the point made at the chapter's beginning. The point about the long recollection of Assyria's fate is that Egypt needs to learn the lesson from it. And the point about urging Egypt to learn the lesson is to get Judah to learn the lesson. God's people are really stupid if they think there's a worldly empire that will last and can be their protection.

EZEKIEL 32:1–32

The Great Leveler

[1]In the twelfth year in the twelfth month on the first of the month, Yahweh's message came to me: [2]Young man, take up a dirge over Pharaoh, king of Egypt. You're to say to him:

> You think of yourself as the lion of the nations,
>   but you're like the dragon in the waters.
> You've thrust forth with your rivers,
>   you've stirred up the water with your feet,
>   you've muddied their rivers.
> [3]   The Lord Yahweh has said this:
> And I shall spread my mesh over you
>   in an assembly of many peoples;
>   I shall lift you up in my net.
> [4]   I shall leave you on the earth;
>   I shall throw you on the face of the countryside.
> I shall get all the birds of the heavens to settle on you;
>   I shall get the animals of the entire earth
>   to be full from you.
> [5]   I shall put your flesh on the mountains
>   and fill the valleys with your height.
> [6]   I shall drench the earth
>   with the flow
>   of your blood upon the mountains,
>   and the ravines will fill from you.
> [7]   I shall cover the heavens when I put you out,
>   and make their stars dark.
> I shall cover the sun with cloud,
>   and the moon won't give its light.
> [8]   All the bright lights in the heavens
>   I shall darken above you.
> I shall bring darkness on your country
>   (a declaration of the Lord Yahweh),

⁹ and I shall vex the mind of many peoples,
    when I bring you broken among the nations,
    to countries that you haven't known.

¹⁰ I shall make many peoples desolate because of you;
    their kings will bristle with horror because of you.
  When I whirl my sword in their faces,
    they'll tremble at every moment,
  each for his own life,
    on the day of your downfall.

¹¹ Because the Lord Yahweh has said this:
    The king of Babylon's sword will come to you.

¹² By warriors' swords I shall make your horde fall,
    the most violent among the nations, all of them.
  They'll destroy Egypt's majesty;
    the entire horde of it will be obliterated.

¹³ I shall wipe out all its cattle
    from beside abundant waters.
  Human feet will no more muddy them,
    and animal hooves won't muddy them.

¹⁴ Then I shall settle their waters,
    make their rivers run like oil
    (a declaration of the Lord Yahweh).

¹⁵ When I make the country of Egypt a desolation
    and the country is desolate of what filled it,
  when I strike down all the inhabitants in it,
    then they will acknowledge that I am Yahweh.

¹⁶ That's a dirge, and people will lament with it;
    the nations' daughters will lament with it.
  Over Egypt and over its entire horde
    they'll lament with it
    (a declaration of the Lord Yahweh).

¹⁷In the twelfth year, on the fifteenth day of the month, Yahweh's message came to me: ¹⁸Young man, wail for Egypt's horde. You're to send them down, it and the daughter-towns of mighty nations, to the country deep below, with the people who go down to the Pit. ¹⁹"Than whom are you more beautiful? Go down and be laid down with the uncircumcised." ²⁰They'll

fall among people slain by the sword. The sword's been given over. They're dragging it off with all its hordes. [21]The mightiest of warriors speak to him from the midst of Sheol, with his supporters. The uncircumcised, people slain by the sword, have gone down and lain down. [22]Assyria is there, and all its assembly, around him his graves, all of them slain, people fallen by the sword, [23]whose graves were put in the Pit's far parts and its assembly was around its grave, all of them slain, fallen by the sword, people who'd spread terror in the country of the living. [24]Elam is there, and all its horde, around its tomb, all of them slain, fallen by the sword, people who went down uncircumcised to the country deep below, people who'd spread their terror in the country of the living but come to carry their shame with the people who go down to the Pit. [25]Among the slain they've given it a bed, with all its graves around him, all of them uncircumcised, slain by the sword. Because their terror was spread in the country of the living, they've come to carry their shame with the people who go down to the Pit; among the slain he is put.

[26]Meshek and Tubal and their entire horde are there. Their graves are around him. All of them are uncircumcised, pierced through by the sword, because they spread their terror in the country of the living. [27]They don't lie with warriors of the uncircumcised who fell, who went down to Sheol with their battle equipment and put their swords under their heads. Their wayward acts were upon their frames, because the warriors' terror had been in the country of the living. [28]And you yourselves will break among the uncircumcised and will lie down with people slain by the sword. [29]Edom is there, its kings and all its rulers, who despite their might are put with the people slain by the sword. Those people lie with the uncircumcised and with the people who go down to the Pit. [30]The leaders of the north, all of them, are there, and all the Sidonians, who went down with the slain despite the terror that issued from their might, disgraced, and lie uncircumcised with the people slain by the sword, and carry their shame with the people who go down to the Pit. [31]These Pharaoh will see, and he'll be consoled for his entire horde, Pharaoh's men who

were slain by the sword, and all his forces (a declaration of the Lord Yahweh). ³²Because I'm spreading my terror in the country of the living. He'll be laid down among the uncircumcised with the people slain by the sword, Pharaoh and his entire horde (a declaration of the Lord Yahweh).

Each New Year the "Rose Parade" passes our house in Pasadena, with the "Rose Queen" prominently enthroned. My wife's cousin, Nancy, was Rose Queen in 1952. She keeps an eye on which of the rose queens is still alive; she doesn't look forward to the time when she's the oldest living rose queen. Her year was also the year Queen Elizabeth came to a different throne. In both age and duration of her reign, she has passed Queen Victoria. I don't know if she thinks about such questions. Thinking about my own pension prospects, I recently discovered that statistically a man of my age could expect to live until he's eighty-five. I'm less worried about whether I shall live to complete The Old Testament for Everyone, now that I need only another four months.

No normal human being wants to think too much about such questions. Ezekiel wants Pharaoh to face dying, though he talks about it for the sake of his compatriots in **Babylon**. The date has again moved on a year, in a way that's more significant than we might at first realize. Not only has Jerusalem fallen; the next chapter will tell us that the news of its fall actually reached the **Judahites** in Babylon a few weeks previously. There's no question now of hoping that Jerusalem might be saved and that the Egyptians might be its saviors. It wouldn't be inappropriate to read Lamentations before reading this chapter. Jerusalem is dead. In light of people's hopes in Egypt, they might read this chapter as a consolation; at least it really is true that Egypt is going to die, too. But the book of Ezekiel is about to make a transition from talking about the death of **Yahweh**'s people to talking about their resurrection, and one effect of this chapter is to underscore the stark reality of death.

Death takes you down into the earth. It's the whole person that goes down into the earth. The earth is full of dead people. You can picture them gathered there, beneath the earth. It's the Pit, "the country deep below." No one escapes this experience. Being more beautiful doesn't exempt you. Being a mighty warrior doesn't exempt you. Ezekiel underlines the grimness of the experience by pointing to the company you find yourself in there. It's uncircumcised people—in other words, barbarians. It's people slain by the sword, who likely didn't receive a decent burial. It's violent, trouble-making people, like the **Assyrians**. It's people who ought therefore to be ashamed of the lives they lived, like the Elamites; Elam was a big power away to the east, in Iran, but it had come under Babylon's domination, so its great days were also over. Meshek and Tubal, to the north, we know from chapter 27; in chapters 38–39 they will be great powers that take part in a last great battle with Yahweh, his people, and his purpose. They're not allowed to die with warriors who died an honorable death. Egypt will join all these and others, and will find an odd form of comfort from being no worse off than these other war-makers.

Death is the great leveler. Egypt had thought of itself as a lion among nations, but it's just a crocodile or a hippopotamus making a mess. It's a nice way of dismissing Egypt, because the sea monster provided Middle Eastern peoples with a frightening image for dynamic power asserted against God. Psalm 104 demythologizes it into a kind of Loch Ness Monster playing in the water. Isaiah 30 makes fun of it as an allegedly dynamic entity that actually just sits there and does nothing (which fits Ezekiel's warnings about the folly of trusting in Egypt). Ezekiel downgrades it another way. It's just a tiresome water creature that Yahweh will have no trouble catching in his net, hurling onto the ground, and leaving for other creatures to eat. Whereas that second paragraph has Pharaoh finding consolation in sharing the same fate as other great peoples, this first paragraph has other, less significant, peoples troubled by mighty Egypt's so easily being picked up and thrown down.

EZEKIEL 33:1–20
London Bridge Is Falling Down (So Do Something)

[1]Yahweh's message came to me: [2]Young man, speak to the members of your people and say to them, Regarding a country: when I bring the sword against it, and the country's people take someone from their number and make him into their lookout, [3]and he sees the sword coming against the country, and blows the horn and warns the people, [4]and someone who hears the sound of the horn hears but doesn't take warning, and the sword comes and takes him—his blood will be on his head. [5]He heard the sound of the horn but didn't take warning; his blood will be on him. Had that person taken warning, he'd have saved his life. [6]But should the lookout, when he sees the sword coming, not blow the horn, and the people don't take warning, and the sword comes and takes one of them, that person gets taken because of his own waywardness, but I shall seek his blood from the lookout. [7]So now, young man, I've made you a lookout for Israel's household. You'll hear a message from my mouth, and you're to warn them from me. [8]When I say to the faithless person, "Faithless one, you shall definitely die," and you haven't spoken to warn the faithless person from his way, that faithless person will die because of his waywardness, but I shall seek his blood from your hand. [9]But you—when you've warned the faithless person from his way, to turn from it, and he hasn't turned from his way, he'll die because of his waywardness, but you'll rescue your life.

[10]So you, young man, say to Israel's household: You've said this: "Our rebellions and our offenses rest upon us. Because of them we're wasting away, and how can we live?" [11]Say to them, As I live (a declaration of the Lord Yahweh), if I want the death of the faithless person . . .—rather that the faithless person should turn from his way and live. Turn, turn, from your evil ways. Why should you die, Israel's household?

163

¹²So you, young man, say to the members of your people: The faithfulness of the faithful person won't rescue him on the day of his rebellion, and the faithlessness of the faithless person—he won't fall because of it on the day he turns from his faithlessness, and the faithful person won't be able to live because of it on the day he commits offenses. ¹³When I say of the faithful person, "He'll indeed live," but he trusts in his faithfulness and does wrong, none of his faithfulness will be kept in mind. Because of the wrong that he's done—he'll die because of it. ¹⁴And when I say to the faithless person, "You shall definitely die," and he turns from his offenses and makes faithful decisions ¹⁵(the faithless man returns a pledge, restores what was stolen, walks by the laws of life, so as not to do wrong), he'll definitely live, he won't die. ¹⁶None of his offenses that he's committed will be kept in mind for him. He's made faithful decisions. He'll definitely live.

¹⁷The members of your people say, "The Lord's way isn't right." But they—their way isn't right. ¹⁸When a faithful person turns from his faithfulness and does wrong, he'll die because of them. ¹⁹When a faithless person turns from his faithlessness and makes faithful decisions, on account of them that person will live. ²⁰And you say, "The Lord's way isn't right." I shall decide about each person in accordance with his ways, Israel's household.

My wife was just getting me to look at some projections she's made for work that needs to be done in the condominium building in which we live. When I watch residential buildings being constructed in our city, I'm always worried that they seem to be built of chipboard and chicken wire, but I've often been assured that this method is a wise one in earthquake country. Brick such as we use in Britain wouldn't be a good idea. But now I learn, not to my surprise, that the walls and foundations of our forty-year-old building are in danger of rotting. It's OK; we can do something about it. But will we do so? My wife has to persuade the rest of the homeowners that we must. If we don't, in due course the building will fall down.

Jerusalem has fallen (down). Prophecies about Judah's neighbors and allies have occupied eight chapters, but these form a segue into the last third of the book of Ezekiel. They do so chronologically; they mostly come from the last months of the city's siege. They also do so in subject; they include declarations of judgment on peoples who were inclined to rejoice in the city's fall, and thus they indicate a move toward Ezekiel's saying something more hopeful.

He begins with a restatement of Yahweh's commission; the first paragraph restates part of chapter 3. He reminds people of the commission he's been fulfilling for seven years. The implication is, "You can be deeply distraught about what's happened to Jerusalem, but don't think that the Jerusalemites have had a rough deal. They've ignored the warnings Yahweh gave them." We again recall that the people to whom Yahweh sent Ezekiel as lookout weren't the people living in a city that was under attack. They were people already in exile, who nevertheless still needed to examine their own lives, the worship they engaged in or would engage in if they could, and the forms of community life they engaged in or would if they had the chance. Ezekiel has blown his horn—they can't deny it. If he hadn't done so, they'd still be guilty, and if they forfeited their lives, they couldn't complain. But if he hadn't done so, he'd have become guilty of a capital offense. It's not explicit what would then happen—how Yahweh would seek the guilty person's blood from the lookout's hand. But he risks Yahweh behaving toward him as a member of a murder victim's family might behave toward the person's killer.

The exiles feel hopeless about their situation, Ezekiel goes on to note. They're marking time. They can't see any future as a people. Yet there's a new note in what they say, one contrasting with what we've heard from them so far. They know that they're in this situation because their rebellions and their offenses rest upon them. They're not talking merely about feeling overwhelmed. They're talking about the objective fact that they're stuck in exile with no future because of their rebellions and offenses. Jeremiah 24 had described them as the good figs who contrasted with the bad figs left in Jerusalem, but Jeremiah had meant they were lucky figs, not wholesome figs. If they were ever pretending they were wholesome figs, they've given up the pretense. The trouble is, they're in danger of ricocheting from "We're OK" to "We're hopeless."

One effect of Ezekiel's reminder of his commission is to underscore the moral nature of Yahweh's relationship with them. It's not so complicated. Yahweh doesn't send trouble without sending a warning. Simply pay attention. Ignore the lookout—you lose your life. Listen to the lookout—you save your life.

In his follow-up comments about the faithful and the faithless person, the latter is the focus. There aren't really many faithful people to think about. His point lies in the promise that it's never too late to turn. The prophet again makes clear that Yahweh's declarations of judgment are always meant to be self-frustrating, to cause themselves not to come true. The harsher Yahweh's words and the more unequivocal his declarations, the more certain it is that he's longing for people to respond and make it unnecessary to fulfill them. So instead of moaning, the exiles need to start taking responsibility for themselves. There are just a few basic attitudes to other people that they need to put right, like stop making other people's need a chance for me to make a buck.

EZEKIEL 33:21–33

On How Not to Listen to a Singer-songwriter

[21]In the twelfth year of our exile, in the tenth month, on the fifth of the month, a survivor came to me from Jerusalem, saying, "The city's been struck down." [22]Yahweh's hand had come upon me in the evening before the survivor came, and he'd opened my mouth, before he came to me

in the morning. So my mouth had opened. I was no longer dumb.

²³Yahweh's message came to me: ²⁴Young man, the people living in these ruins on Israel's land are saying, "Abraham was one man, but he came to possess the country, whereas we're many. The country is given to us as a possession." ²⁵Therefore say to them, The Lord Yahweh has said this: You eat with the blood, you raise your eyes to your lumps, and you shed blood—and you'll enter into possession of the country? ²⁶You've stood by your sword, you've committed outrage, and you've each defiled his neighbor's wife—and you'll enter into possession of the country? ²⁷You're to say this to them: The Lord Yahweh has said this: As I live, if the people in the ruins don't fall by the sword and I don't give the people in the countryside to the animals for them to eat, and the people in the strongholds and in the caves don't die in an epidemic . . . ²⁸I shall make the country desolation and devastation. Its strong majesty will cease, Israel's mountains will be desolate, with no one passing through, ²⁹and they will acknowledge that I am Yahweh, when I make the country desolation and devastation because of all their outrages that they've committed.

³⁰But you, young man: the members of your people are speaking about you by the walls and in the doorways of the houses. One speaks to another, a man to his brother: "Come on, listen to what message is coming out from Yahweh." ³¹They'll come to you like a people coming, and sit in front of you, my people, and listen to your words. But they won't do them, because while they're making amorous sounds with their mouths, their mind is going after their loot. ³²And there are you, like a singer of amorous sounds to them, beautiful in voice and doing well in playing. They listen to your words but none of them are doing them. ³³But when it comes about (there, it's coming), they will acknowledge that a prophet's been among them.

I've noted that it's Advent as I write, and a few days ago I was planning the Christmas services and sorting out when we shall sing different carols. We have our biggest Christmas service on Christmas Eve, not near midnight like many churches, but at 6.30—I think it's so that people don't have to be out too late and so that children can be there. We shall begin with informal carol singing by candlelight from 6.00. But it's easy for "Carols by Candlelight" sung in front of a nice manger set, preferably with some children singing "Away in a Manger," to be simply a piece of touching, emotive entertainment.

People can be making heartfelt sounds with their mouths, but is that all it is? They can be appreciating the choir, the organist, and maybe even the pastor, but is that all it is? Ezekiel's question is, does it make a difference to their lives tomorrow?

News has arrived that Jerusalem's finally fallen (the date is earlier than a couple of those in preceding chapters, because sometimes the book is arranged more by subject than by chronology). Whereas we talk about Jerusalem's "fall," it didn't "fall"; it was pushed. Ezekiel speaks more vividly and more painfully of its being struck down. Something had happened to him the previous evening that made the arrival of the news not a surprise. He doesn't quite say that he knew the report would arrive the next day, but he knew Yahweh had removed the restraint that he'd placed on Ezekiel's speech, and we know from chapter 24 that this experience would link with the arrival of the news. Maybe he implies that he'd already made clear to people that the restraint had gone and that he expected the news to come any day, which would also have the effect of adding to the evidence that Yahweh really had been speaking through him.

The first message he reports after the news arrives continues to concern the people back in Jerusalem, about whom he's so often spoken to their relatives and friends in Babylon. The arrangement of the prophecies need not imply that it was the first message he received after the news arrived. It might seem more likely that a little while has elapsed before people in Jerusalem have picked themselves up enough to make the encouraging and encouraged noises that Ezekiel here reports. But in due course, at least, they can see the possibility of getting their lives back together. The Babylonian army's gone, and people can't imagine the exiles coming back, which neatly leaves the land to people who never left, or people who'd taken refuge across the Jordan or elsewhere and were now free to come back to the city.

Ezekiel continues to look at the situation religiously and morally, not merely politically. Politically the situation has changed. Religiously and morally, it hasn't. There's no political basis for saying that more trouble is going to come on **Judah**. But there's a religious and moral basis for saying so. There can be no future if there's no change. As far as we know, there were no more military disasters in Judah over the next fifty years, but neither was there positive development.

The Judahites in Babylon might enjoy listening to Ezekiel speaking thus, but if so (in the manner of other prophets such as Amos) he's thereby softened them up before he puts the boot in. If they affirm his message, they're condemning themselves. It's quite pleasant listening to a preacher denounce other people, especially if his message has positive implications for you. His closing words are teasingly ambiguous. In the broad context, one would have thought that the "it" must be the content of the "songs" that the people have enjoyed that describe Yahweh's positive purpose for the community, which contrasts with the talk of yet more trouble for people back in Judah. But following on the critique of people who like listening to their singer-songwriter but don't take any notice of what he says, the talk in terms of something coming about and of people then acknowledging Yahweh might more likely have its usual implication: it's more trouble that's coming for them, as for the people in Jerusalem. How they respond will determine whether what comes about will be good news or bad news.

EZEKIEL 34:1–31

The Good Shepherd

¹Yahweh's message came to me: ²Young man, prophesy against Israel's shepherds. Prophesy and say to them, About the shepherds, the Lord Yahweh has said this: Hey, Israel's shepherds, who've been shepherding themselves! Isn't it the flock that shepherds shepherd? ³You eat the fat and clothe yourselves in the wool, you sacrifice the fatlings, you don't shepherd the flock. ⁴You haven't strengthened the weak, nor healed the sick, nor bandaged the broken, nor brought back the scattered, nor sought the missing, but ruled them with harshness and cruelty. ⁵They've scattered for lack of a shepherd, and become food for any animal of the countryside when they scattered. ⁶My flock wanders through all the mountains and on every high hill. My flock's scattered over the face of the country. There's no one seeking and no one looking.

⁷Therefore, shepherds, listen to Yahweh's message. ⁸As I live (a declaration of the Lord Yahweh), because my flock's become plunder and my flock's become food for any animal of the countryside through the lack of anyone shepherding, and my shepherds haven't sought my flock, but the shepherds have shepherded themselves and not shepherded my flock, if I don't . . . ⁹Therefore listen, you shepherds, to Yahweh's message. ¹⁰The Lord Yahweh has said this: Here am I toward the shepherds. I shall seek my flock from their hand. I shall make them stop from shepherding the flock, and the shepherds won't shepherd themselves anymore. I shall rescue my flock from their mouth. They won't be food for them.

¹¹Because the Lord Yahweh has said this: Here am I, I myself, and I shall seek my flock and inquire after them. ¹²Like a shepherd inquiring after his herd when he's among his dispersed flock, so I shall inquire after my flock and rescue them from all the places where they've scattered on the day of cloud and gloom. ¹³I shall get them out from the peoples, gather them from the countries, and bring them to their land. I shall shepherd them on Israel's mountains by the watercourses and by all the country's settlements. ¹⁴I shall shepherd them on

good grazing; their pasture will be on Israel's high mountains. There they'll lie down in good pasture, and they'll graze on rich grazing on Israel's mountains. [15]I myself shall shepherd my flock and I myself shall get them to lie down (a declaration of the Lord Yahweh). [16]I shall seek the missing, bring back the scattered, bandage the broken, and strengthen the weak. But the fat and strong I shall destroy. I shall shepherd with judgment.

[17]So you, my flock (the Lord Yahweh has said this): Here am I, I'm going to decide between one animal and another. About rams and he-goats: [18]is it too little for you that you graze on good grazing, but you trample with your feet what's left of your grazing, and that you drink the clearest of the water, but muddy what's left with your feet, [19]so that my flock grazes on what your feet have trampled and your feet have muddied? [20]Therefore the Lord Yahweh has said this to them: Here am I, and I shall decide between fat animal and thin animal. [21]Because you were pushing with flank and shoulder, and butting with your horns against all the sick, until you scattered them abroad, [22]but I shall deliver my flock, and it will no longer be plunder. I shall decide between one animal and another.

[23]And I shall set up over them one shepherd and he'll shepherd them, my servant David. He's the one who will shepherd them. He'll be their shepherd. [24]I, Yahweh, will be their God, with my servant David ruler among them. I Yahweh have spoken. [25]I shall seal a covenant of well-being for them. I shall stop evil creatures from the country. They'll live in the wilderness with assurance and sleep in the forests. [26]I shall make them and the environs of my hill a blessing. I shall make the rain come down in its season; they'll be showers that bring blessing. [27]The trees of the countryside will give their fruit; the earth will give its produce. They'll be with assurance on their land, and they will acknowledge that I am Yahweh, when I break the bars of their yoke and rescue them from the people who make them serve them. [28]They'll no longer be plunder for the nations. The country's creatures won't eat them, but they'll live with assurance with no one disturbing them. [29]I shall set

up for them a plantation of renown, and they'll no longer be carried off by famine in the country. They'll no longer bear the nations' shame. ³⁰And they will acknowledge that I Yahweh their God am with them and they, Israel's household, are my people (a declaration of the Lord Yahweh). ³¹You, my flock, the flock I shepherd, you're human, and I am your God (a declaration of the Lord Yahweh).

We were watching an Armenian movie that had been accurately described as maudlin and quirky. In the middle, for no apparent reason as far as I remember, a flock of sheep occupied the bulk of the screen, and my wife commented, "There'll be wolves around." "Why do you say that?" I asked. "When there are sheep, there are always wolves."

I don't know if it was an overly gloomy remark, but the way Ezekiel looks at Israel, it's true in his day. The image of the people as a flock and of the leader as shepherd is common in the Old Testament. Mesopotamian peoples described the king as their shepherd, though the Old Testament speaks more of shepherds (plural), referring to priests and prophets as much as rulers. The image has a background in **ordinary** life, where people were familiar with flocks and shepherds. The way Ezekiel has spoken of prophets and priests means he'd have no objection if his readers applied his message to priests and prophets, but the chapter ending suggests he's thinking especially of kings. The sequence of kings that has led up to this moment in **Judah**'s story would justify some cynicism about them; the longer sequence going back over four or five centuries would provide more evidence. When **Israel** first expressed the desire for kings, Samuel had warned them that it would cost them, and Ezekiel is essentially pointing out that Samuel was right. Yet not calling them kings draws attention to the way kingship isn't the only form of leadership that's wolf-like. King, queen, president, prime minister, premier, governor, chief: all are susceptible to the temptation Ezekiel describes. Our use of the word *shepherd* or *pastor* to describe a congregation's leader draws attention to how the temptation applies within the church as well as within the state.

The fundamental temptation is that leadership becomes a way of getting your own needs met rather than seeing to the needs of the people you're supposed to be caring for. The shepherds' priority is making sure they themselves are doing well. To that end they're prepared to ill-treat the animals that are already doing badly. Not having shepherds doesn't solve the problem. It just means the members of the flock wander about unsupervised and become the victims of those wolves. The encouragement in the present context is that **Yahweh** intends to act as the good shepherd. He'll bring them back to lush, grassy land with a good water supply.

Ezekiel likes elaborating an image until it becomes an allegory; he does so with the shepherd–flock image. The shepherds and the wolves aren't the only ones taking advantage of the flock. It's divided within itself. The reference to rams and he-goats presupposes that flocks include both sheep and goats ("sheep and goats" doesn't here imply animals that really belong and animals that don't, as in Jesus' story about sheep and goats). The strong rams and he-goats can ensure that they get the best grass and water, and they don't worry about spoiling things for others. Ezekiel thus avoids implying that Judah can blame its kings for everything. The members of the flock must look at themselves, too. Leadership abhors a vacuum. If there's no king, other forms of leadership will arise, and the powerful in the community may be as much a drain on the community as a king was. The question the members of the flock have to ask is, "Does someone else look less well-fed than me? If so, is it because I'm monopolizing the sustenance and/or getting in the way of other people reaching it?"

It might seem surprising that Yahweh then speaks of setting a human good shepherd over his flock. There'll be a new David on David's throne. Why doesn't Yahweh carry on shepherding it in person? Perhaps it's significant that the sending of a new David follows on Yahweh's personally having put things right for the flock; the job that now needs doing is more the maintaining of the situation. And it's noteworthy that Ezekiel doesn't call this new David a king but a ruler—the Hebrew word is often translated "prince." In the event, the Davidic ruler after the **exile**, Zerubbabel, will be a governor, not a king. Eventually, Jesus will be born as a new David, and he'll also not be a king in the literal sense.

Further, by no means will Yahweh have absented himself from the scene. He'll see to the maintaining of the work he's done to restore a good life for his flock. They'll be his people and he'll be their God, and they'll know it.

EZEKIEL 35:1–36:15

Two Peoples, One Land

[1]Yahweh's message came to me: [2]Young man, set your face against Mount Seir and prophesy against it. [3]You're to say to it: The Lord Yahweh has said this: Here am I toward you, Mount Seir. I shall stretch out my hand against you and make you a desolation and devastation. [4]Your cities I shall make into a ruin and you'll be a desolation, and you will acknowledge that I am Yahweh. [5]Because you had an ancient enmity and you hurled the Israelites into the sword's power at the time of their calamity, at the time of their final waywardness, [6]therefore, as I live (a declaration of the Lord Yahweh), I shall make you into blood; blood will pursue you. Given that you didn't repudiate blood, blood will pursue you. [7]I shall make Mount Seir desolation and devastation, and I shall cut off from it passerby and returner. [8]I shall fill its mountains with its slain. Your hills, your valleys, and all your watercourses—people slain by the sword will fall in them. [9]I shall make you a lasting desolation, your cities won't be inhabited, and you will acknowledge that I am Yahweh. [10]Because you said, "The two nations and the two countries will be mine, and we shall possess them" (but

Yahweh was there), [11]therefore as I live (a declaration of the Lord Yahweh), I shall act in accordance with your anger and with your passion with which you acted out of your repudiation of them. I shall cause myself to be acknowledged among them as I judge you. [12]You will acknowledge that I Yahweh have heard all your insults, which you've uttered about Israel's mountains, "They're desolate, they've been given to us as food." [13]You acted big against me with your mouth and you made your words proliferate against me. I myself heard. [14]The Lord Yahweh has said this: In accordance with the celebrating over the entire country, I shall make you a desolation. [15]In accordance with your celebrating over the possession that belonged to Israel's household, because it became desolate, so I shall act toward you. You'll become a desolation, Mount Seir and all Edom, all of it. And they will acknowledge that I am Yahweh.

[36:1]And you, young man, prophesy to Israel's mountains. Say, Mountains of Israel, listen to Yahweh's message. [2]The Lord Yahweh has said this: Because the enemy said over you, "Aaah, the ancient high places have become ours as a possession," [3]therefore prophesy and say, The Lord Yahweh has said this: Because, yes because of the great desolation and trampling upon you from all around, so that you became the possession of the remaining nations, and you were taken up onto the lip of the tongue and the slur of the people, [4]therefore, Israel's mountains, listen to the Lord Yahweh's word. The Lord Yahweh has said this to the mountains and hills, to the watercourses and desolate ruins and abandoned cities that have become plunder and derision to the remaining nations, which are from all around—[5]therefore the Lord Yahweh has said: If I haven't spoken in my passionate anger against the remaining nations and against Edom, all of it, which made my country a possession for itself with wholehearted celebration and contempt of spirit, as plunder for the sake of open space . . . [6]Therefore prophesy about Israel's land. You're to say to the mountains and hills, to the watercourses and valleys, The Lord Yahweh has said this: Here am I, I'm going to speak in passion and fury, because you've carried the nations' shame. [7]Therefore the Lord Yahweh has said this: I myself have raised my hand [to swear]: If the nations that are from all around you don't carry their shame . . .

⁸But you, Israel's mountains, will produce your boughs and bear your fruit for my people Israel, because they're near returning. ⁹Because here am I toward you, and I shall turn to you, and you'll be served and sown. ¹⁰I shall make the people on you abundant, Israel's entire household, all of it. The cities will be inhabited, the ruins built up. ¹¹I shall make many upon you the human beings and the animals; they'll be many and they'll be fruitful. I shall populate you as you were before and make things good for you, better than you were before, and you will acknowledge that I am Yahweh. ¹²I shall get people, my people Israel, to walk upon you. They'll come to possess you and you'll be their own. You won't bereave them ever again.

¹³The Lord Yahweh has said this: Because they're saying to you, "You've been one who devours human beings, who bereaves your nations," ¹⁴therefore you'll no more devour human beings, you'll no more bereave your nations again (a declaration of the Lord Yahweh). ¹⁵I shall not let the nations' shaming be heard anymore. You'll no more carry the peoples' reviling. You'll no more make your nations collapse (a declaration of the Lord Yahweh).

My heart sank when I saw that one of the resolutions presented to our church convention last Saturday concerned Israel and Palestine. I've noted earlier how it's so easy for Christians (and others) to be committed to Israel and then demonize the Palestinians, or to be committed to the Palestinians and then demonize Israel. But then I discovered that the resolution recognized the tragedy in two peoples' attachment to the same land and expressed concern both at Islamic movements that want to eliminate Jews from the area and at exclusivist Israeli policies.

It's both encouraging and discouraging to see how tensions and rivalry over this land go back three thousand years, though the dynamics of that tension change in different centuries. Ezekiel's prophecy about it reflects one dynamic. *Mount Seir* is a term for Edom, the area south and southeast of **Judah**. Chapter 25 already mentioned Edom and referred to Edom's "ancient enmity." Within the Old Testament, it goes back to the relationship between Jacob and Esau, the ancestors of **Israel** and Edom, then to the story in Numbers 20. After Ezekiel's time, the Edomites took over much of the southern part of Judah's land. The references in the Prophets to Edom's hostile action imply that in Ezekiel's day the Edomites were taking advantage of Judah's defeat and weakness, and that in this connection they collaborated with the **Babylonians** in return for some reward in terms of land. But the Old Testament doesn't give us hard information on what happened. Ezekiel certainly sees the Edomites as partly responsible for Judah's troubles. It was the time of Judah's "final waywardness"—the waywardness that finally made God act in judgment. But that fact didn't mean the Edomites should get away with action that was purely an expression of enmity and ambition. They'd been willing to shed blood, and God had declared near the beginning of the entire human story that people who shed blood get their blood shed (Genesis 9). There and here, it's a law of human behavior and also a law that God is prepared to affirm and use.

The two nations to which Ezekiel refers, which the last paragraph describes simply as "the nations," are **Ephraim** and Judah. There's some hyperbole in his declaration that the Edomites aspired to taking over the whole of the two nations' territory, and some hyperbole in his description of the retribution **Yahweh** will bring—Yahweh didn't bring calamity on Edom in the way he pictures it. One indication that we shouldn't take his language too literally is his repeating similar phrases in different chapters to describe different peoples' wrongdoing and punishment; it's conventional and figurative language.

The "remaining nations" are then the peoples who weren't as seriously devastated as Judah by the Babylonians—the

177

peoples mentioned in chapter 25. As Ezekiel speaks to Edom and other nations but Judahites in **exile** are his "real" audience, so he speaks to Israel's mountainous country but Judahites in exile are his "real" audience. Yahweh's message to the land is good news for the people who'll be the means of Yahweh's fulfilling his promises to the land. To his actual audience, "They're near returning" means "You're near returning." Paradoxically, the arrival of the bad news that Judah has been punished for its "final waywardness" is encouraging; it opens up the way to restoration. Its land has been one that devours and bereaves its people, because it belongs to Yahweh and it acts as Yahweh's agent when they're in the wrong. But that dynamic is to be abolished.

We have no way of checking whether Judah in general or Ezekiel in particular are justified in their accusations of Edom, which form the basis for Ezekiel's declarations about its fate. What we can say is that they show how these declarations presuppose a moral basis for Yahweh's actions. When Judah does wrong, it loses its land. Yahweh doesn't take Judah's side against Edom just because he has favorites. In our own context, God doesn't favor Israelis or Palestinians just because he has favorites. They have to ask themselves about their ancient enmity and their recent enmity, about their involvement in bloodshed, about their waywardness, about the nature of their desire for land and their attitude to other peoples' attachment to the same land, about how they see God's involvement in their conflict. They can do so in hope, knowing God's positive purpose for this land, though also with some fear, knowing his anger about what goes on there.

EZEKIEL 36:16–38

There's No Cure

[16]Yahweh's message came to me: [17]Young man, Israel's household were living on their land, but they defiled it with their

way and with their deeds. In my eyes their way was like the defilement of a woman who's taboo. [18]So I poured out my fury on them because of the blood they poured out on the earth, and they defiled it with their lumps. [19]I scattered them among the nations and they were dispersed among the countries. In accordance with their way and their deeds I judged them. [20]They came to the nations, wherever they came, and treated my sacred name as ordinary, when people said of them, "These are Yahweh's people, but they left his country." [21]But I've taken pity on my sacred name, which Israel's household caused to be treated as ordinary among the nations where they came. [22]Therefore say to Israel's household: The Lord Yahweh has said this: It's not for your sake that I'm going to act, Israel's household, but for my sacred name, which you've caused to be treated as ordinary among the nations where you came. [23]I shall make my great name sacred, which has been treated as ordinary among the nations in whose midst you've caused it to be treated as ordinary, and the nations will acknowledge that I am Yahweh (a declaration of the Lord Yahweh) when I show myself holy through you before their eyes.

[24]I shall take you from the nations, gather you from all the countries, and bring you to your land. [25]I shall toss clean water over you and you'll be clean. From all your defilements and all your lumps I shall cleanse you. [26]I shall give you a new mind and put a new spirit inside you. I shall remove the stony mind from your flesh and give you a fleshy mind, [27]and I shall put my spirit inside you. I shall make it so that you walk by my laws and keep my decisions and do them. [28]You'll live in the country that I gave your ancestors, and you'll be my people and I shall be your God. [29]I shall deliver you from all your defilements. I shall call to the grain and make it abundant, and not bring famine upon you. [30]I shall make the fruit of your trees and the produce of the fields abundant, so that you no more receive reviling among the nations because of famine. [31]You'll be mindful of your evil ways and your deeds that weren't good, and you'll be loathsome in your own sight because of your wayward acts and because of your outrages. [32]It's not for your sake that I'm going to act (a declaration of

the Lord Yahweh), be it known to you. Be disgraced and ashamed because of your ways, Israel's household.

³³The Lord Yahweh has said this: On the day I cleanse you from all your wayward acts, I shall people your cities, the ruins will be built up, ³⁴and the desolate country will be served instead of being a desolation in the sight of every passerby. ³⁵People will say, "That country that was desolate has become like Eden Garden, and the cities that were ruined and desolate and devastated, people live in, fortified." ³⁶And the nations that remain around you will acknowledge that I Yahweh have built up the devastations; I've planted the desolations. I Yahweh have spoken and I shall act.

³⁷The Lord Yahweh has said this: Further, in this I shall let myself be sought out by Israel's household, to act for them. I shall make people as abundant as sheep. ³⁸Like the sacred flocks, like the Jerusalem flocks at its set occasions, so the ruined cities will be full of human flocks, and they will acknowledge that I am Yahweh.

Another highlight of our church convention, which I mentioned in connection with Ezekiel 35, was a celebration of the fiftieth anniversary of a center for the treatment of addicts, located just a few blocks from where I live. In a film, a recovering alcoholic spoke more than once of the "miracle" (his word) of the fact that he's still alive, that somehow he came to stop living in denial, own his problem, be able to seek help, and open up the possibility of getting his life back together and saving his family as well as himself. Yet he still described himself as a "recovering alcoholic" and spoke of there being no cure for addiction. He can't have one drink, as I can. If he walked into a bar and ordered a beer tomorrow, he'd be back where he started. He doesn't even take a mouthful of wine at communion. He's been transformed; yet he's not been transformed.

Ezekiel speaks of **Israel** being transformed, and it was transformed; and yet it wasn't. It needed to change, to become willing to worship **Yahweh** alone, give up using images, cease taking Yahweh's **name** in vain, keep the Sabbath, stop sacrificing children, and so on. Israel heeded those challenges in the centuries that followed. God gave them a new attitude and a new spirit. In Ezekiel's day, it was as if they had a mind made of stone—hard and inflexible. God promised to give them a mind made of flesh—alive, soft, and malleable (in the Old Testament, the idea of "flesh" doesn't carry the negative connotations that it often has in Paul's letters). God did so. Yet Israel remained like a recovering alcoholic. It could still fall. It could still make big mistakes. But it could look back on how things once were and be astonished that it was still alive. Thus Ezekiel continues to speak in hyperbole. God will give people a new attitude and spirit; yet it will transpire that the old attitude and spirit are still there.

Through Jesus, that transformation was extended to the Gentile world, but the Church also exists as a body that's transformed, and yet it isn't. One can look at the church in another country or another time and be horrified at its blindness and failure; churches in other countries look at my church that way, and churches in other times would do the same. The Church is a body with a new attitude and new spirit; and it's not. The imagery again involves hyperbole. So we read Ezekiel's promise in a way that arouses a longing for the miracle to happen to us that the recovering addict in that film describes, the miracle whereby we own that we have a problem and that we can't solve it ourselves.

Ezekiel is someone who speaks tough. "You know why God will bring about a transformation of your life? Don't think it's for your sake. It's for God's own sake. God's own name is discredited by the mess you're in as a result of your sin. So God is going to sort the mess out for his own sake." It puts us in our place and declares that we humans and our needs aren't the center of the universe, but it does so in an encouraging way. It gives us a powerful basis for confidence and prayer. Ezekiel's talk about defilement and cleansing and about self-loathing, shame, and disgrace has similar implications. One effect of our wrongdoing is to make it impossible for us to come into God's presence. We'd spoil it. But God wants us in his presence. So he doesn't just urge Israel to clean itself up before approaching him. He'll take action to clean them up. He'll pour water over them (he won't just sprinkle them—he'll douse them). An excess of self-loathing, shame, and disgrace is debilitating and paralyzing, but a little can be motivating and galvanizing.

EZEKIEL 37:1–14

Dem Bones, Dem Bones, Dem Dry Bones

[1]Yahweh's hand came on me and took me out by Yahweh's wind, and set me down in the middle of a vale. It was full of bones. [2]He got me to pass through them, all the way around. There—they were very many on the surface of the valley. And there—they were very dry. [3]He said to me, "Young man, can these bones come to life?" I said, "Lord Yahweh, you know." [4]He said to me, "Prophesy to these bones. Say to them, You dry bones, listen to Yahweh's message. [5]The Lord Yahweh has said this to these bones: Now: I'm going to bring breath to you, and you'll come to life. [6]I shall put muscles on you, bring up flesh on you, spread skin on you, and put breath into you, and you'll come to life, and you will acknowledge that I am Yahweh." [7]I prophesied as I was commanded, and a sound came as I prophesied, and there—a shaking, and the bones drew near bone to its bone. [8]I looked, and there, muscles were on them, and flesh came up, and skin spread on them above. But there was no breath in them. [9]He said to me, "Prophesy to the breath, prophesy, young man. You're to say to the breath, The Lord Yahweh has said this: Come from the four winds, breath, and breathe into these slain people, so that they come to life." [10]So I prophesied as I was commanded, and the breath came into them. They came to life and stood on their feet, a very, very great force.

[11]He said to me, "Young man, these bones are Israel's entire household. There, they're saying, 'Our bones are dry, our hope

has perished. We're totally finished.' [12]Therefore prophesy and say to them, The Lord Yahweh has said this: Now. I'm going to open your graves and get you out of your graves, my people, and bring you to Israel's land. [13]You will acknowledge that I am Yahweh when I open your graves and get you out of your graves, my people. [14]I shall put my spirit in you and you'll come to life and I shall set you down on your land, and you will acknowledge that I Yahweh have spoken and acted (Yahweh's declaration)."

We watched the old movie version of Rodgers and Hammerstein's *Carousel* the other night, and were wondering about the significance of one of its great songs, "You'll Never Walk Alone." Hold your head up high when you walk through a storm, because at the end of the storm is a golden sky, it promises. You can walk on with hope in your heart and you'll never walk alone. Really? In the 1960s the fans of Liverpool Football Club adopted the song as their anthem, in the context of recession and depression in Liverpool. Is it whistling in the wind? Is it a promise like the one in Hammerstein's later song, "Whistle a Happy Tune": if you whistle like that, no one will know you're afraid? Or like Charlie Chaplin's promise in his song "Smile," that if you smile, you'll find that life is worthwhile?

Ezekiel wants the **Judahites** in **Babylon** and in Jerusalem to hold their head up high and not be afraid of the dark, but knows they need to avoid being in the denial that those songs imply, or living on the basis of the assumption that holding your head up high or whistling a happy tune can solve your problems. To be fair to them, he speaks as if they're not in denial. The background to his vision of the dry bones is their sober assessment of their situation. Their bones are dry: in other words, they're utterly and irredeemably dead. When **Israelites** roll away the stone from the family tomb because someone in the family has died, all that remains of people who died earlier is their dry bones. That fact provides a metaphor for the community's understanding of itself. It's finished. In other words, its hope has perished. While Ezekiel may include an allusion to their subjective hope (the hope they feel), he's at least as concerned about their objective hope. They're finished as a people. They have no future.

There's thus little prospect of their being able to encourage themselves by whistling a happy tune or assuring themselves that they'll never walk alone, unless they can be given some reason for doing so. Fortunately, Ezekiel can provide them with some reason. It's regularly a prophet's job to disturb the comfortable and comfort the disturbed. Prophets exist to disagree with their people. When his people thought they had a future, Ezekiel's job was to tell them they had none. Now that they think they have no future, his job is to tell them that they have one. They feel like a people who are dead and buried. OK, says God, I shall open your graves and bring you back to life. Ezekiel is thus not talking about the resurrection of individuals but the resurrection of the nation. When the people of God seems to be finished, it's not finished.

His parabolic vision or visionary parable makes this point. The Hebrew word *ruah* means both wind, breath, and spirit. By "spirit," it denotes the dynamic life power inherent in a person that finds expression in dynamic action. "You need to be born of the spirit," Jesus will comment in John 3, utilizing the same broad meaning of the word. God is the ultimate in dynamic life power. In Ezekiel's day and in Isaiah's earlier day, the Judahites had been tempted to trust in Egypt's military resources, but Isaiah 31 had noted that the Egyptians were human beings, not God, and their horses flesh, not spirit. Because spirit suggests extraordinary, forceful liveliness, the same word means wind, a mysterious embodiment of extraordinary, forceful power; it's invisible, yet it can fell a tree. And because spirit suggests dynamic life power, the same word means breath, the mysterious movement of air that's much less dramatic yet also vital and life-giving; if there's no breath, there's no life.

184

It's impossible to bring out in English Ezekiel's utilizing the same Hebrew word that refers to wind, breath, and spirit. In his vision he's plucked up and carried by **Yahweh's** *ruah*. He sees the remains of a defeated army scattered over a plain, their bones glistening white in the sun. There's no prospect of this army ever fighting again. But he's told to preach to the bones, which is as silly as Jesus' later address to Lazarus when he's four days dead in the tomb. He's to tell them that Yahweh is going to reconstitute them as bodies and then put *ruah* into them so that they're living bodies, not just reformed skeletons and not even just reconstituted corpses, neither of which is much improvement on being scattered bones. He prophesies to the fourfold *ruah* and summons *ruah* to come into the reconstituted corpses, which happens. They stand up, an army ready to fight again.

Judah is dead. But Yahweh intends to bring it back to life and reestablish it on its land, full of new life. It can therefore whistle and walk head high. The people of God isn't dependent on denial. It's dependent on God's promise.

Preachers today can feel that they stand before people who can only think within a framework determined by our culture, and that it's like preaching to dry bones. They may then be tempted to accept the terms of that framework for their preaching, but thereby risk losing the content of the gospel, which presupposes a different framework. Ezekiel's parable encourages them to resist the temptation and allow for the possibility that their words might play a part in bringing the bones back to life.

EZEKIEL 37:15-28

On Being Post-denominational

[15]Yahweh's message came to me: [16]And you, young man, get yourself a piece of wood and write on it, "Belonging to Judah and to the Israelites who are its associates," and get a piece of

wood and write on it, "Belonging to Joseph (Ephraim's piece of wood) and all Israel's household that are its associates." [17]Bring them close one to the other so they become one piece of wood. They're to become one in your hand. [18]And when members of your people say to you, "Won't you tell us what these things of yours are?", [19]tell them, The Lord Yahweh has said this: Here am I, I'm going to take Joseph's piece of wood that's in Ephraim's hand, and the Israelite clans that are his associates, and I shall put them on it, Judah's piece of wood, and make them one piece of wood. They'll be one in my hand.

[20]The pieces of wood on which you've written are to be in your hand before their eyes, [21]and you're to tell them, The Lord Yahweh has said this: Here am I, I'm going to get the Israelites from among the nations where they've gone, gather them from all around, and bring them to their land. [22]I shall make them into one nation in the country, on Israel's mountains. One king will be king for all of them. There won't be two nations again. They won't divide into two kingdoms ever again. [23]They won't defile themselves again with their lumps and their abominations and all their rebellions. I shall deliver them from all their settlements in which they committed offense, and cleanse them, and they'll be my people and I shall be their God. [24]My servant David will be king over them and they'll all have one shepherd. They'll walk by my decisions, and keep my laws and do them. [25]They'll live in the country that I gave to my servant, to Jacob, in which your ancestors lived. They'll live in it, they and their children and grandchildren, forever, with David my servant as their ruler forever. [26]I shall seal a covenant of well-being for them. It will be a lasting covenant with them. I shall give it to them and cause them to increase, and I shall put my sanctuary amid them forever. [27]My dwelling will be with them. I shall be their God and they'll be my people. [28]And the nations will acknowledge that I am Yahweh, the one who sanctifies Israel, when my sanctuary is in their midst forever.

My final comment arising from our church convention, I promise, concerns a distinctively Episcopal resolution. It was a proposal to require that members of a church council (what we call the vestry) should have to be people who've been confirmed, which rules out most people who don't have an Episcopal background. I was pleased when the rector of the biggest church in the diocese (with whom I often disagree) stood up to declare that it was a step backward, as we live in a "post-denominational" age. Nowadays people are more likely to go to a church near where they live and where they feel at home than to join a church on the basis that it's Episcopal or Presbyterian or Baptist. The resolution was defeated.

You could say that Ezekiel is promising the arrival of a post-denominational time, though that assessment is anachronistic. For a century many denominations have been seeking to move to more structural unity, though the "post-denominational" image suggests sidestepping a concern for formal unity and ignoring the different labels churches wear. Ezekiel's action with the two pieces of wood that are turned into one, as if by magic, is another symbolic action, but his symbolic action now models a promise, not a threat. His image implies something structural, though something more like post-denominationalism was what Israel came to experience. The background to his promise is that **Judah** and **Ephraim** had split into two nations with two monarchies more than three centuries before his day. Indeed, after two centuries Ephraim had ceased to exist as a nation. Ezekiel's promise is thereby doubly bold.

Its background is a theological fact that also underlies concern about church unity. **Israel** is one people; the Church is one body. How, then, can Israel be two nations with two governments, sometimes at war with one another? How can the Church be hundreds of denominations with hundreds of governments, sometimes excommunicating each other or martyring each other's members? I'm inclined to think that Jesus' prayer in John 17 that "they all may be one" is the least-answered prayer in history.

Naming the two peoples is complicated. Judah was the name of one of the nations, but it had absorbed Simeon, and for practical purposes it more or less included Benjamin; further, there were people from Ephraim who had come and settled in Judah but knew they weren't actually Judahites. While Ephraim was one of the names for the other nation, it could also be referred to as Joseph (Joseph was father of Ephraim and Manasseh, the ancestors of the clans that dominated the Northern Kingdom), and more often as Israel, but that was also a name that applied to the entire people. The unity **Yahweh** promises is implicit in the clans tracing their common descent back to Jacob. It will be safeguarded by their return to the situation in which they have one king, a descendant of David, as was so in David's own day. The promise speaks in terms of the clans' situation back in the homeland, but Ezekiel is still speaking to people in **Babylon**, and therefore speaks in terms of Yahweh bringing all the exiles back to form this one new people. The promise about a sanctuary will be developed in the last nine chapters of Ezekiel.

EZEKIEL 38:1–23

The Last Great Battle (1)

[1]Yahweh's message came to me: [2]Young man, set your face toward Gog, in the country of Magog, the highest ruler in Meshek and Tubal. You're to prophesy against him [3]and say, The Lord Yahweh has said this: Here am I toward you, Gog, highest ruler in Meshek and Tubal. [4]I shall turn you around and put hooks in your jaws and bring out you and your entire force, horses and cavalry, clothed in perfection all of them, a great assembly, with buckler and shield, grasping swords, all of them. [5]Persia, Sudan, and Put are with them, all of them with shield and helmet; [6]Gomer and all its legions, Beth-togarmah in the far parts of the north and all its legions—many peoples with you. [7]Be ready, get yourselves ready, you and your entire

assembly who are assembling around you. You're to be a watch for them. [8]After many days you'll be assigned; at the end of the years you'll come to a country restored from the sword, gathered from many peoples, against Israel's mountains, which have been a ruin continually—but it will have been taken out from the peoples, and they'll be living with assurance. [9]When you go up, you'll come like a storm; you'll be like a cloud to cover the country, you and all your legions and the many peoples with you.

[10]The Lord Yahweh has said: On that day, words will come up into your mind. You'll formulate an evil plan. [11]You'll say, "I shall go up against a country of open villages. I shall come to quiet people living with assurance, all of them, living without walls and without bars or gateways, [12]to take plunder and seize spoil," to turn your hand against ruins that have become populated, and upon a people gathered from the nations, making cattle and possessions, living at the center of the earth. [13]Sheba and Dedan, the traders of Tarshish and all its magnates will say to you, "Is it to take plunder that you're coming? Is it to seize spoil that you've put together your assembly, to carry off silver and gold, to take cattle and possessions, to take a great plunder?"

[14]Therefore prophesy, young man, and say to Gog: The Lord Yahweh has said this: On that day, when my people Israel are living with assurance, is it not the case that you'll acknowledge it, [15]and come from your place, from the far parts of the north, you and many peoples with you, riding horses all of them, a great assembly, a huge force. [16]You'll go up against my people Israel like a cloud to cover the country. At the end of the days it will come about. I shall bring you to my country so that the nations may acknowledge me when I show myself holy through you before their eyes, Gog.

[17]The Lord Yahweh said this: Are you the one of whom I spoke in earlier days by the hand of my servants Israel's prophets, who prophesied in those days for years that I'd bring you against them? [18]On that day, on the day Gog comes onto Israel's land (a declaration of the Lord Yahweh), my angry blazing will go up. [19]In my passion, in my furious fire,

I've spoken. If on that day a great earthquake doesn't happen in Israel's land ... [20]Before me the fish in the sea, the birds in the heavens, the animals of the countryside, everything that moves on the ground, and all the human beings that are on the surface of the ground will quake. Mountains will collapse, cliffs will topple, every wall will fall to the earth. [21]I shall summon the sword against him through all my mountains (a declaration of the Lord Yahweh). Each person's sword will be against his brother. [22]I shall judge him with epidemic and with bloodshed, and pour torrential rain, hailstones, fire, and sulfur on him and on his legions and on the many peoples that are with him. [23]I shall show I'm great and show I'm holy and cause myself to be acknowledged before the eyes of many nations, and they will acknowledge that I am Yahweh.

Yesterday a twenty-year-old-man in Connecticut shot his mother, drove to the school where she worked and shot twenty-six more adults and children, then finally shot himself. Last night my wife commented on how "disappointing" such an event was for what it said about our humanity and our human "civilization." We went on to wonder whether the future of humanity seems gloomier than it did (say) fifty years ago, and whether we were glad that we aren't beginning our lives at this moment in history. They're strange questions to be asking a few days before Christmas.

In previous chapters, Ezekiel has spoken of wonderful days coming when **Yahweh** will bring his people back to life, put his spirit into them, and reunite them as a people. You could have got the impression that the day when Yahweh finally fulfills his promises to Abraham has arrived. In light of these restated promises, it's surprising to find Yahweh now speaking of more invasion and war after **Israel**'s country has been restored from the sword. One might also describe it as disheartening, though perhaps in a sense it's a relief, because it corresponds to how life is. The reestablishing of **Judah** as a semi-independent entity in a few decades' time won't herald the arrival of a totally new age of blessing, **well-being**, and peace. There'll be more invasion and more war. Humanly speaking, one reason is the fact that Israel sits geographically at the center of the earth, at the meeting point of Europe, Asia, and Africa. Maybe that fact underlies God's choice of this land. It also makes it a natural point of conflict, a land over which there's fighting between major powers and trading peoples.

Ezekiel speaks of these conflicts by recycling the way he and other prophets have described the coming of an enemy from the north—because that's the obvious way for an enemy to arrive. Typically, Ezekiel paints the picture in an exotic fashion. The enemy won't be an entity such as **Assyria** or **Babylon**, with whom Judah is quite familiar. It will be strange people from the far north (from Judah's perspective). Meshek and Tubal were tribes in northeastern Turkey, already mentioned in Ezekiel 27 and 32. It's been suggested that the names are connected with Moscow and Tobolsk, but Moscow is named after the river on which it sits, and Tobolsk is the capital of Siberia, which also seems a stretch. The idea of this link was most attention-grabbing when it suited people in the West to be able to say that God planned judgment on Russia. Earlier, Gomer was similarly identified with Germany, while Luther took Gog as the leader of the Turks, which worked neatly in his context. "Gog" actually looks like a variant on the name of a Turkish king called Gyges or Gugu; it's harder to know who or where Magog was.

The Judahites who received this prophecy would have known even less than us about such questions; the point is that these are strange, far-off, frightening places and people. Yahweh speaks of an alliance of these northern peoples and of eastern and southern peoples that will attack little Judah. Yahweh will inspire this attack, as Yahweh inspired earlier invaders. Those earlier commissions were responses to Israel's waywardness; the invaders were Yahweh's agents in bringing Yahweh's punishment. Here there's no such suggestion. Yahweh inspires this confederation of powers to attack Judah so they can be defeated there. The attack will lead to Yahweh's displaying his holiness and greatness in demonstrating the power to put down great human powers.

A phrase such as "the end of the years" doesn't imply Ezekiel is speaking about "the End," the last days, here. The phrase doesn't denote a time more final than he's previously been describing. It's not a technical term for "the last days" but simply an expression denoting the end of some time period. Yet there's another sense in which he's been speaking about "the End," the ultimate fulfillment of Yahweh's purpose, all through his prophecies, and here he does imply that Gog is the ultimate embodiment of that destructive military power arriving from the north of which prophets such as Jeremiah spoke. When God asks whether Gog does embody that power, it's perhaps a rhetorical question, or perhaps Ezekiel provides another hint that the fulfillment of God's purpose involves some interaction between God's own initiative and the will of human powers such as Nebuchadnezzar, the people of Tyre, and now Gog. Yet there's indeed something final about the defeat Yahweh will impose on Gog. When more trouble arises after Israel has been restored on its land, Israel isn't to assume that something odd has happened. The event need only herald a magnificent deliverance that Yahweh will bring.

EZEKIEL 39:1–29

The Last Great Battle (2)

[1]And you, young man, prophesy against Gog. You're to say, The Lord Yahweh has said this: Here am I toward you, Gog, the highest ruler of Meshek and Tubal. [2]I shall turn you around, lead you along and take you up from the far parts of the north and bring you to Israel's mountains. [3]But I shall strike your bow from your left hand and make your arrows fall

from your right hand. ⁴You'll fall on Israel's mountains, you and all your legions and the peoples that are with you. I shall give you as food to birds of prey of every kind and to the animals of the countryside ⁵when you fall on the surface of the countryside, because I've spoken (a declaration of the Lord Yahweh). ⁶I shall send off fire against Magog and against the people who live with assurance on far shores, and they will acknowledge that I am Yahweh. ⁷I shall cause my sacred name to be acknowledged among my people Israel and not let my sacred name be treated as ordinary anymore, and the nations will acknowledge that I Yahweh am holy in Israel. ⁸There, it's coming, it's happening (a declaration of the Lord Yahweh). ⁹The inhabitants of Israel's cities will go out and make a fire and burn the weaponry, shield and buckler, bow and arrows, hand pike and spear. They'll make a fire with them for seven years. ¹⁰They won't carry wood from the countryside and they won't cut it from the forests, because they'll make a fire with the weaponry. They'll plunder their plunderers and despoil their despoilers (a declaration of the Lord Yahweh).

¹¹On that day I shall give Gog a place where there'll be a grave in Israel, Travelers Canyon, east of the sea. It will obstruct travelers; they'll bury Gog and his entire multitude there. They'll call it Gog's Multitude Canyon. ¹²Israel's household will bury them to cleanse the country, for seven months; ¹³the entire people of the country will bury them. It will mean renown for them, the day I show my splendor (a declaration of the Lord Yahweh). ¹⁴They'll set apart permanent people as travelers in the country, burying (the travelers) ones that remain on the surface of the country, to cleanse it. At the end of seven months they'll search. ¹⁵As travelers travel in the country and see human bones, they're to construct a marker by it, until the buriers have buried it in Gog's Multitude Canyon ¹⁶(and the name of the city will also be Multitude) and cleansed the country.

¹⁷And you, young man (the Lord Yahweh has said this), say to birds of every kind and to every animal of the countryside, Assemble and come, gather from all around to my sacrifice that I'm going to make for you, a great sacrifice on Israel's

mountains. You'll eat flesh and drink blood. [18]You'll eat warriors' flesh and drink the blood of earth's rulers: rams, lambs, goats, bulls, fatlings of Bashan, all of them. [19]You'll eat fat until you're full and drink blood until you're drunk from my sacrifice that I shall have made for you. [20]At my table you'll become full of horses, chariotry, warriors, every fighting man (a declaration of the Lord Yahweh). [21]I shall put my splendor among the nations, and all the nations will see my decision that I've put into effect and my hand that I've set against them. [22]Israel's household will acknowledge that I Yahweh am their God from that day onward. [23]And the nations will acknowledge that Israel's household went into exile for their waywardness, because they trespassed against me. I hid my face from them and gave them into the hand of their adversaries, and all of them fell by the sword. [24]It was in accordance with their defilement and with their rebellions that I dealt with them and hid my face from them.

[25]Therefore the Lord Yahweh has said this: Now I shall restore Jacob's fortunes and have compassion on Israel's entire household and be passionate about my sacred name. [26]They'll carry their shame and all their trespass that they committed against me when they live on their land with assurance, with no one disturbing them, [27]when I bring them back from the peoples and gather them from their enemies' countries and show myself holy among them before the eyes of many nations. [28]They will acknowledge that I Yahweh am their God, when I've exiled them to the nations but gathered them on their land. I shall leave none of them there anymore. [29]I shall not hide my face from them anymore when I've poured out my spirit on Israel's household (a declaration of the Lord Yahweh).

Two Armenian Christian women from Iraq, mother and daughter, found refuge here in California from the turmoil in Iraq, settling in the next town to us. A couple of hours in the other direction, in San Diego, there lives a former U.S. marine, who in April 2003 was part of a company that found itself under fire in the streets of Baghdad and poured gunfire into three cars in which an Iraqi family, including these two women, was simply hurrying to get to the safety of home. The mother's husband and her two sons died. The two women have found a kind of peace, but the marine hadn't. Like thousands of soldiers, he lives with the horror of what he had to do that day, though he's made some progress through being able to meet the two women and to know of their forgiveness.

I have the impression that in biblical times people in general weren't overwhelmed by war's horror to the extent that we now are. It may be partly because our weaponry is so much more devastating, partly because urban warfare (in particular) makes it harder to distinguish combatants from non-combatants. I guess it's partly war's horror that makes seeking peace important to us, even while we seem ever further from attaining it. In Ezekiel, the end of the previous chapter promised a covenant of **well-being**, and well-being isn't confined to peace, but it surely includes it; the Hebrew word *shalom* has this implication. The point was more explicit in the previous occurrence of this promise in chapter 34. There **Yahweh** glossed the promise by speaking in terms of stopping **evil** creatures from entering the country and making it possible for people even to live in the wilderness with assurance and sleep in the forests (that chapter's image of the people as sheep lies in the background).

Maybe another, more paradoxical, reason for the difference in attitudes is that my home country and my adopted country aren't little nations but big nations with big war machines. We're more like Meshek and Tubal than **Judah**. We have bad consciences about being among the world's great war-makers. **Israel** was never in that position (except perhaps in David's day); it was usually the victim of the great powers. It's reduced (!) to trusting God to bring peace, by putting down the great war-makers. In this vision God again promises to do so. Their weapons aren't going to be turned into farming implements, as Isaiah 2 envisages, but into fuel for fires that will make it unnecessary to collect any other fuel for seven years. The recurrent sevens in the prophecy suggest completeness; they remind us again not to be literalistic in interpreting the prophecy. All earth's war-makers are going to be eliminated.

The writer who told the story about the marine and the Armenian women noted that Numbers 31 has a purifying ritual for soldiers returning from war, and that Iraqi tribal tradition also has procedures for dealing with the consequences of a killing in a way that stops it escalating into inter-familial and inter-tribal conflict. Western society lacks such procedures. Ezekiel speaks at great length about the need to **purify** the land after the massacre it speaks of. Last night we watched a movie that began with a teacher committing suicide in her classroom; the principal had the classroom redecorated before it was used again, but the children remained aware of the place where the teacher had hanged herself. A parent whose child survived this week's Connecticut massacre commented, "There's going to be a black cloud over this area forever. It will never go away." To put his point in biblical terms, the victims' blood will always cry out from the ground. Maybe there's a need of cleansing that would require tearing down the school and building a new one.

Like the **Torah,** Ezekiel recognizes that even a massacre undertaken by God defiles the land with the blood of the slain. Israel was accepting of death at the end of a full life, but recognized that there's something horrible and defiling about violent death. The burying of the slain is to be done east of the Dead Sea and thus not in the holy land proper. Even there it requires the purifying of the land where it happens, and the taking of great care to ensure that all remains are buried. (The paragraph about the birds and animals coming to a grisly feast refers to a stage before the collection and burial of the remains.)

Yahweh doesn't encourage in Israel the delusion that they're somehow morally better than the war-making nations, just because they're not great war-makers. Ezekiel reminds them of their waywardness and trespass and their shame and defilement; conversely, the ultimate object of Yahweh's action is that foreign nations as much as Israel will come to acknowledge Yahweh. Neither do these two chapters about Gog close on a negative note, the destruction of violent forces, but with a restatement in the closing paragraph of Yahweh's positive promises.

EZEKIEL 40:1–37

Who Can Ascend the Hill of the Lord?

[1]In the twenty-fifth year of our exile, at the beginning of the year, on the tenth of the month, in the fourteenth year after the city was struck down, on this very day Yahweh's hand came upon me, and he brought me there. [2]In a great appearance of God he brought me to Israel's country and set me down on a very high mountain. On it was the very structure of a city to the south. [3]He brought me to it, and there—a man, his appearance the very appearance of bronze, a linen cord in his hand, and a measuring rod. He was standing in the gateway. [4]The man spoke to me: "Young man, look with your eyes, listen with your ears, and give your mind to everything that I'm going to show you, because you've been brought here to show you. Tell Israel's household everything you see."

[5]There—a wall outside the house, all the way around. In the man's hand was a six-cubit [ten and a half feet or just over three metres] measuring rod, by the cubit-plus-a-handbreadth. He measured the structure's width, one rod, and its height, one rod. [6]He came to the gateway whose face was toward the east, and went up its steps. He measured the gateway's threshold, one rod in depth (the one threshold, one rod in depth). [7]Each alcove was one rod in length and one rod in width. Between the alcoves it was five cubits.

The gateway's [other] threshold, next to the gateway's porch, facing the house, was one rod [8](he measured the gateway's porch facing the house, one rod). [9]He measured the gateway's porch: eight cubits, and its columns: two cubits; the gateway's porch was facing the house. [10]The gateway alcoves toward the east were three on one side and three on the other side, one measurement for the three of them and one measurement for the columns on each side. [11]He measured the width of the gateway opening: ten cubits; the gateway's length: thirteen cubits. [12]The barrier in front of the alcoves: one cubit, so the barrier was one cubit on each side. The alcove: six cubits on one side and six cubits on the other side. [13]He measured the gateway from the back of an alcove to the back of [an opposite] one; the width: twenty-five cubits, opening to opening. [14]He made the columns: sixty cubits, and next to the column was the gateway courtyard all the way around. [15]Starting at the front of the outer gateway to the front of the inner gateway's porch was fifty cubits. [16]There were narrow windows to the alcoves and to their columns inside the gateway all the way around, and similarly to the porches there were windows all the way around on the inside, with palms on a column.

[17]He brought me to the outer courtyard, and there—rooms, and a pavement made for the courtyard all the way around, thirty rooms to the pavement. [18]The pavement was by the side of the gateways, alongside the length of the gateways (the lower pavement). [19]He measured the width from in front of the lower gateway to the front of the outer courtyard: a hundred cubits, east and north.

[20]The gateway whose face was toward the north, belonging to the outer courtyard—he measured its length and width, [21]its three alcoves on one side and three on the other side, its columns, and its porches. Like the measurement of the first gate, its length: fifty cubits, and the width: twenty-five cubits. [22]Its windows, its porches, and its palms were like the measurement of the gateway that faced toward the east. By seven steps people would go up onto it, and its porch would be in front of them. [23]There was a gateway to the inner

courtyard facing the northern gate as well as the east; he measured from one gateway to the other gateway: a hundred cubits.

24He took me toward the south. There—a gate toward the south. He measured its columns and its porches, in accordance with these measurements. 25It and its porches had windows all the way around like these windows. The length: fifty cubits, and the width: twenty-five cubits. 26There were seven steps up to it. Its porch was in front of them. It had palms, one on one side and one on the other side, on its columns. 27The inner courtyard had a gateway toward the south. He measured from the gateway to the gateway on the south: a hundred cubits.

28He brought me to the inner courtyard through the southern gateway and measured the southern gateway in accordance with these measurements. 29Its alcoves, its columns, and its porches were in accordance with these measurements. It and its porches had windows all the way around. The length: fifty cubits, and the width: twenty-five cubits 30(the porches all the way around, the length: twenty-five cubits, the width: five cubits). 31Its porch was toward the outer courtyard. There were palms on its columns and eight steps in its staircase.

32He brought me to the inner courtyard toward the east and measured the gateway in accordance with these measurements. 33Its alcoves, its columns, and its porches were in accordance with these measurements. It and its porches had windows all the way around. The length: fifty cubits, and the width: twenty-five cubits. 34Its porch was toward the outer courtyard. There were palms on its columns, on one side and on the other side, and eight steps in its staircase.

35He brought me to the northern gateway and measured it in accordance with these measurements—36its alcoves, its columns, and its porches, and its windows all the way around. The length: fifty cubits, and the width: twenty-five cubits. 37Its columns were toward the outer courtyard. There were palms on its columns, on one side and on the other side, and eight steps in its staircase.

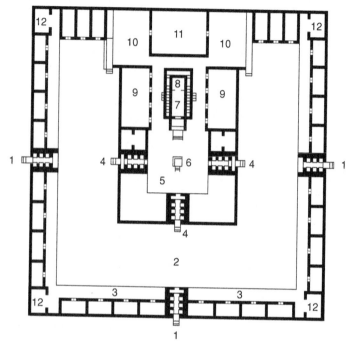

Start: Eastern gateway

The list approximately follows Ezekiel's walk through the temple
1 Outer gateways
2 Outer courtyard
3 Lower pavement
4 Inner gateways
5 Inner courtyard
6 Altar
7 Sanctuary
8 Most sacred place
9 Rooms for ministers
10 Separate place
11 Building (storage?)
12 Kitchens

The Temple in Ezekiel's Vision

I've mentioned a weird experience I had the last time I entered the United States. The immigration officer asked how long I'd been living here, and I said fifteen years. "So why aren't you a citizen? Are you just using America?" I responded that I'm here by invitation; if anything, America is using me. "Are you afraid of blood?" he asked. I wondered whether he was implying that I was afraid to fight in the army. But in principle, no, I'm not afraid of blood. "You must be a son of Cain, then," he responded. I didn't quite get this, but I was content that he then decided that I was saved, stamped my passport, and granted me entry.

The beginning of Ezekiel's last vision is about passport control. Its opening date is the first since he reported the arrival of news concerning Jerusalem's fall (chapter 33). It marks the distinctive importance of this section of the book. The date also indicates that time is dragging on; the vision promises that it won't drag on forever. Temple, city, and land won't stay in their desolate state forever. The vision comes at the new year, and speaks of a new future. On the other hand, twenty-five years is only halfway to a Jubilee. Restoration and renewal are certain; Ezekiel's seen them. But there's a long haul ahead. It will be more than thirty years before **Judahites** can start restoring the temple.

This section will turn out to be the last. The book's closing nine chapters form one vision, by far the most substantial in the book, a vision of a new temple, a new city, and a new land. It's explained to the prophet by a supernatural architect or project manager, who gives all the measurements in terms of long cubits. A regular cubit was about half a yard; a long cubit was about half a meter (**Israel** wasn't the only people that had more than one measuring standard; we don't know why Ezekiel uses the long cubit standard). Either way, you'll get an idea of the measurements by halving the cubit statistics and thinking of the numbers in terms of yards or meters.

Like preceding visions, it's not a preview of what the renewed city and temple will literally be like, any more than the dry bones vision (for instance) is a preview of a literal coming together of bones and revivification of corpses. The point is already indicated by locating the city on a high mountain; Jerusalem is lower than other mountains in the area. Many subsequent elements in the vision will make all the clearer that it's not speaking in the terms of literal geography. Yet the detail with all the specific measurements brings home how this isn't just a vague promise about what God intends. It's concrete and specific. It's down-to-earth reality.

The supernatural figure is a tour guide as well as a project manager, taking Ezekiel on a journey, through something that's a bit like a maze. At first it's described as a city, and the stress on the gateways makes one think of a city. But then it's described as a house, though evidently a huge house—more like a palace. It will eventually become clear that it's the house or palace of the divine King, his temple. But it's not operating at the moment; there's no one there.

The journey begins at the wall that separates off the temple area from the world outside and protects it, like a city's wall. When the Old Testament refers to the temple, it commonly denotes not merely the building, which was small, but the building plus the surrounding courtyards. The courtyard is where people gathered, as they'd gather in the yard of a house in California when they came for a barbecue. If you've seen pictures of the temple mount in Jerusalem as it now is, you'll get the idea.

This first chapter is dominated by an account of the gateways to the temple area. Don't fret at not being able to understand the details; many of them are hard to understand. When you approach the temple, it's foursquare, with that surrounding wall. You gain access by climbing steps leading to an opening in the broad wall. The opening is the temple's outer threshold, six cubits square. This outer threshold leads into a walkway. In the structure either side of the walkway are three alcoves, each with a barrier at the front. The alcoves are guard rooms, where temple guards keep an eye on people coming to the temple area. If you pass their inspection, you come to another threshold leading to another porch, this one belonging to the outer courtyard of the temple itself, one hundred cubits square. It's the lower courtyard; the inner temple courtyard is raised higher. This second threshold has columns decorated with palm trees. Around the paved courtyard to which it leads are thirty rooms. You can imagine these being used by **Levites** and/or by families who come to worship.

Why does the temple have this gateway system, and even more, why are we given this long and complicated account of it? The gateways are designed both to facilitate and control entry to the temple, like a city's gateways, or like passport control at an airport. They let in the people who should enter but keep out people who might (for instance) be a danger. The temple is a "house," **Yahweh**'s house—Yahweh lives there. Ezekiel has already described it as a "sanctuary," a place belonging to Yahweh and sharing in his holiness. People who come into your house need to be people who won't ruin it. Earlier parts of Ezekiel have made clear many ways in which Judah has been ruining Yahweh's house. Among other things, they've been entering with blood on their hands, in more than one way. They've been ignoring the rules about not rushing into Yahweh's presence when you've been in contact with blood (for instance, through menstruation) or with death in other ways (for instance, through having to bury someone), because death and Yahweh are incompatible. They've been shedding blood, in sacrificing children to Yahweh or to other gods or in more "**ordinary**" ways. They haven't been people who can come into Yahweh's presence without being **purified**. The new temple needs to be safeguarded from being ruined by such people. The guards are there to protect it by keeping their eyes peeled and asking sharp questions. The new temple must not go the way of the old.

EZEKIEL 40:38–41:12

Giving, Cleansing, Celebrating

[38]There was a room and its doorway in the porch at the gateways, where they'd wash the burnt offering. [39]In the gateway porch were two tables on one side and two tables on the other side for slaughtering the burnt offering, the purification offering, and the restitution offering on them. [40]On the outer sidewall for someone going up to the doorway of the northern gateway were two tables and on the other sidewall in relation to the gateway's porch were two tables, [41]four tables on one side and four tables on the other side at the sidewall of the gateway, eight tables on which they'd slaughter things. [42]The four tables for the burnt offering were of hewn stone. The length was a cubit and a half, the width was a cubit and a half, and the height was one cubit. On them they'd laid down the things with which they'd slaughter the burnt offering and the sacrifice. [43]There were ledges, one handbreadth, fixed inside all the way around. The flesh of the offering was on the tables.

[44]Outside the inner gateway were the singers' rooms in the inner courtyard, one that was on the sidewall of the northern gateway with their face toward the south, one on the sidewall of the eastern gateway facing toward the north. [45]He explained to me: "This, the room that faces toward the south, is for the priests having charge of the house. [46]The room that faces toward the north is for the priests having charge of the altar. They're the Zadoqites, who of the Levites approach Yahweh to minister to him."

[47]He measured the courtyard. The length: a hundred cubits, its width: a hundred cubits, foursquare. The altar was in front of the house. [48]He brought me to the porch of the house and measured a porch column: five cubits on one side, and five cubits on the other side. The width of the gateway: three cubits on one side and three cubits on the other side. [49]The length of the porch: twenty cubits, and the width: eleven cubits. It was by steps that people would go up to it. There were pillars by the columns, one on one side, one on the other side.

⁴¹:¹He brought me into the palace and measured the columns: six cubits the width on one side, six cubits the width on the other side (the width of the tent). ²The width of the doorway: ten cubits, and the sidewalls of the doorway: five cubits on one side and five cubits on the other side. He measured its length: forty cubits, and the width: twenty cubits. ³He came inside and measured a doorway column: two cubits, the doorway: six cubits, and the doorway's width: seven cubits. ⁴He measured its length: twenty cubits, and the width: twenty cubits, in front of the palace. He said to me, "This is the most sacred place."

⁵He measured the wall of the house: six cubits, and the width of a side room: four cubits, around the house, all the way around. ⁶The side rooms were three [stories], one side room above another side room, thirtyfold. There were insets in the wall that belonged to the house for the side rooms all the way around, to be supports but so that they wouldn't be supports in the wall of the house. ⁷[A way up] widened as it went around higher and higher to the side rooms. Because the house's surrounding went higher and higher all the way around the house, consequently the width of the house went higher, and one goes up from the lowest to the highest via the middle. ⁸I saw belonging to the house a raised area all the way around, the foundations of the side rooms. Its height: the full length of a rod. ⁹The width of the wall of a side room on the outside: five cubits. What was left clear between the side rooms of the house ¹⁰and between the rooms, the width: twenty cubits around the house, all the way around. ¹¹The doorway of a side room toward what was left clear, one doorway toward the north, one doorway to the south, and the width of the place that was left clear: five cubits all the way around. ¹²The building that was toward the front of the separate place at the corner toward the west—the width: seventy cubits. The wall of the building—the width: five cubits all the way around, and its length: ninety cubits.

In the middle of our communion service each week, we pray and give thanks, then we confess our sins and receive God's forgiveness, then we share the peace with one another, then we make our offerings to God. We pray some regular prayers for the Church and the world and for needs people share, and hear of the blessings that people also have to share such as birthdays, anniversaries, and recovery from sickness. We acknowledge the way we've failed God and our neighbor. We greet each other in God's name. And we bring bread and wine to the altar for communion and gather our monetary offerings and present them.

These aspects of our worship make for an interesting comparison with the aspects of worship in the temple of which Ezekiel speaks when referring to the burnt offering, the **purification offering**, the restitution offering, and simply "the sacrifice." A burnt offering involved slaughtering an animal and burning the whole of it. You could say it was a total waste. The animal in its entirety was given over to God as a sign of people's **commitment** of themselves to God. Sometimes the offering might accompany a prayer for something, but sometimes people made burnt offerings without expecting to get anything out of it. So there's an overlap with our monetary offerings, but we benefit from those. They pay the pastor's salary so we can receive his or her services, and they keep the church building warm or cool. **Israelites** didn't benefit from these offerings, as they did from some other types of offering. The question Ezekiel raises is, when do we give something from which we get no benefit?

The purification offering recognizes that we need cleansing from stain. We noted in connection with Ezekiel 39 that thinking about events such as the marines' unintended killing of Armenian Christians or the slaughter in a Connecticut school makes one realize that we lack ways of finding cleansing. The restitution offering belongs in a context where it's recognized that wrongdoing needs the response not merely of punishment nor merely of confession but of restoration toward God and toward other people.

The word *sacrifice* applies especially to the kind of offering you make when you're expressing gratitude to God for some blessing, maybe an answer to prayer, but a distinctive feature is that you and your family share in eating some of it. Such a sacrifice is a fellowship meal that you, your family, and God take part in together.

The gateways Ezekiel speaks of aren't the ones leading from right outside into the outer courtyard, but gateways leading from there into the inner courtyard where the **altar** is. At the western end of this inner courtyard is the actual temple building. Hebrew doesn't have a special word for *temple*, so it uses the **ordinary** words for a house and for a palace—a house as a dwelling, and a palace as a house fit for a king. Ezekiel uses *house* for the structure as a whole and also for the actual temple building; he also uses the word *palace* for the temple building. Laypeople could come into the two courtyards and thus be in God's presence and take part in worship and in the sacrifices, being present for the slaughter of animals and for their burning on the altar. That applies to both men and women in the Old Testament (a restriction came in later). In addition, the outer court was a place where a prophet such as Jeremiah (or Ezekiel, if he hadn't been in **exile**) or a preacher such as Jesus might address the people who came there. The palace was the King's private rooms. It was divided into two, the inmost room being the most **sacred** place. Even priests didn't normally go there. The Zadoqites are a subgroup within the line of Aaron, itself a subgroup of the line of Levi; they're the descendants of Zadoq, one of the senior priests in David's day.

The thirty side rooms in three stories surround the temple building on three sides. One might guess that they're store rooms for tithes and offerings, equipment, and so on. The temple walls get thinner as they get higher, which also means that the side rooms get wider the higher they go, up the three stories.

EZEKIEL 41:13–42:20

The Sacred and the Ordinary

[13]He measured the house. The length: a hundred cubits. The separate place, the building, and its walls—the length: a hundred cubits. [14]The width of the front of the house and the separate place on the east: a hundred cubits. [15]He measured the length of the building facing the separate place that was at the back, and the galleries on one side and on the other side: a hundred cubits. The palace inside, the courtyard porches [16](the thresholds), the narrow windows, and the galleries around the three of them by the threshold, were paneled with wood all the way around. From the ground up to the windows, and the windows, they were covered, [17]above the doorway and as far as the house, inside and outside.

On the entire wall, all the way around, inside and outside, was a measured area. [18]Cherubs and palms were made, a palm between cherub and cherub. A cherub had two faces, [19]a human face toward the palm on one side and a lion face toward the palm on the other side. It was made on the entire house all the way around. [20]From the ground to above the doorway the cherubs and the palms were made, and the palace wall. [21]The palace: there was a square doorframe, and facing the sanctuary something with an appearance like the appearance of [22]a wood altar. The height: three cubits, its length: two cubits. It had corners, and its length and its walls were wood. He spoke to me: "This is the table that's before Yahweh." [23]The palace had double doorways, and the sanctuary [24]had double doorways, and the double doorways had double doors that could be turned, two doors for one and two doors for the other. [25]Cherubs and palms were made for them (for the palace doors) as they were made for the walls. There was a wood canopy in front of the porch, on the outside. [26]There were narrow windows and palms on one side and on the other, on the porch's sidewalls and the side rooms of the house and the canopies.

[42:1]He took me out into the outer courtyard by the way toward the north and brought me into the room that was opposite the separate place and opposite the northern building. [2]Facing the length, a hundred cubits, was the northern doorway. The width was fifty cubits. [3]Opposite the twenty [cubits] of the inner courtyard, and opposite the pavement of the outer courtyard, one gallery was facing another gallery in threes. [4]Facing the rooms was a walkway (the width: ten cubits, on the inside; a path: one cubit), with its doorways to the north. [5]The upper rooms were cut back, because galleries had an effect on them, more than the lowest and the middle ones in the building, [6]because they were divided into three, and they had no pillars like the pillars in the courtyards. Therefore it got narrower from the lowest and from the middle, from the ground. [7]There was a wall outside, alongside the rooms, toward the outer courtyard facing the rooms. Its length: fifty cubits, [8]because the length of the rooms belonging to the outer court was fifty cubits. So there, in front of the palace, it was a hundred cubits. [9]From below these rooms was the passageway from the east when someone comes here from the outer courtyard. [10]In the width of the wall toward the east, facing the separate place and facing the building, there were rooms. [11]Toward the front of them was a similar appearance of rooms that were toward the north. Corresponding to their length, so was their width. All their exits were in accordance with the prescriptions for them and in accordance with their doorways. [12]Like the rooms' doorways that were toward the south was the doorway at the head of the path, the path in front of the wall going toward the east, as one comes into them.

[13]He said to me, "The northern rooms, the southern rooms, that are facing the separate place, are the sacred rooms where the priests who come near Yahweh will eat the most sacred things. They'll lay down the most sacred things there (the grain offering, the purification offering, and the restitution offering), because the place is sacred. [14]When the priests come in, they won't go out from the sanctuary to the outer courtyard. They'll lay down their garments in which they minister there, and put on other garments and go near the people's area."

[15]He finished measuring the inner house and took me out toward the gateway that faces toward the east, and measured

all the way around. [16]He measured the eastern side with the measuring rod: 500 (in rods) with the measuring rod. He turned [17]and measured the northern side: 500 (in rods) with the measuring rod. He turned [18]to the southern side and measured: 500 (in rods) with the measuring rod. [19]He turned to the western side and measured: 500 (in rods) with the measuring rod. [20]Four sides he measured it. It had a wall all the way around (the length: 500, the width: 500) to separate between the sacred and the ordinary.

I've just come back from church, but it's Wednesday, and we were receiving back our pews from a company that has been refurbishing them, along with the rest of the church's furnishings. We were able to try out a new configuration of them as we arranged them on the beautiful new floor that has been laid in their absence. One of our laypeople has painted the inside walls. On Sunday we shall worship in a wondrously refurbished sanctuary, and we shall begin the service by dedicating the refurbished building to God. American English calls a church building a *sanctuary*; British English uses that word only to refer to the especially sacred segment of the building at the eastern end. Many laypeople hesitate to set foot there.

In distinguishing in this way between the **sacred** or holy and the **ordinary**, Christians follow **Israel**'s practice, assumed here by Ezekiel. It's a common human instinct. The antithesis can be formulated as one between the sacred and the profane, but the trouble with that antithesis is that profanity has now come to suggest something irreligious or anti-religious, as when people "take the Lord's **name** in vain." But Ezekiel's distinction doesn't mean that the sacred is good and the ordinary is bad. The first six days of the week are just as good as the seventh day, but only the seventh is sacred. The space outside church is good, but the space inside church is a sanctuary in the sense that it's set aside. We don't do everyday things

there, if the church is a sanctuary. In our seminary chapel in England we also had lectures and dances, which safeguarded against a wrong idea of the holy or the sacred. In contrast, at the back of our church we have a framed document, signed by the bishop in 1933 when he dedicated the church, which declares that as a result of its dedication the building isn't to be used for such ordinary or "unhallowed" purposes. Having places, times, people, and acts that are sacred makes its own point. God is a different person from us, and we need to be reminded. It's been said that the difference between God and us is that God doesn't think he's us.

The whole temple complex, 250 meters square, is a sacred space, with a wall to distinguish between the sacred or holy and the common or everyday. Israel lives its regular life in the context of the common or the everyday, and God is involved with people there. But it does so knowing that it lives this life with the sacred at the center of it, and from time to time for different reasons people go through those gateways and stay for a while in the context of the sacred. The move between the two corresponds to the rhythm between the six working days of the week, the ordinary days, and the rest day, the sacred day. All seven days are good days and days of blessing, but they're not the same.

Within the holy area, the temple itself is even more sacred, and its innermost room is yet more so. The separate place is a kind of safety zone between the "regular" sacred area and the house. Related to that provision is the provision of places for the priests where the priests take off the robes they wore in the sanctuary and put their ordinary clothes back on. There were some elements in the offerings that were offered to God yet were to be eaten by the priests, and these rooms were also the place where the priests ate them. Such sacred food was not taken outside. The **cherubs** and the palm trees that decorate the temple are motifs from Solomon's temple. The cherubs are impressive supernatural figures that suggest God's majesty because they're his attendants. The palm tree was a sacred symbol in the Middle East, and specifically suggested the tree of life.

In the outer room of the temple is a table that's like an **altar** but isn't a place for sacrifices but rather a place where bread was placed each Sabbath (the Old Testament never explains the practice).

EZEKIEL 43:1–44:3

The Glory Returns

¹He took me to a gateway, the gateway that faces toward the east. ²There—the splendor of Israel's God was coming from the eastern direction, its sound like the sound of many waters. The earth was lit up by his splendor. ³The appearance was like the appearance that I saw, like the appearance that I saw when I came to destroy the city, and the appearance was like the appearance that I saw at the river Kebar. I fell on my face. ⁴Yahweh's splendor came into the house by way of the gateway whose face is toward the east. ⁵A spirit lifted me up and brought me to the inner courtyard. There, Yahweh's splendor was filling the house. ⁶I heard speaking addressed to me from the house, while the man was standing next to me. ⁷[Yahweh] said to me, Young man: the place for my throne and the place for the soles of my feet, where I shall dwell among the Israelites forever—Israel's household shall not defile my sacred name anymore, they and their kings by their immorality and by their kings' corpses, their funeral mounds. ⁸When they put their threshold with my threshold and their doorframe next to my doorframe with a wall between me and them, they'd defile my sacred name with their outrages that they committed, and I consumed them in my anger. ⁹Now they're to put their immorality and their kings' corpses far away from me, and I shall dwell among them forever.

¹⁰You, young man, tell Israel's household about the house. They're to be ashamed of their acts of waywardness, but

they're to measure out the plan. [11]When they're ashamed of all that they did, make known the house's form, its plan, its exits, its entrances, all its forms, all its laws, all its forms, and all its instructions. Write it down before their eyes so they may keep its entire form and all its laws and do them. [12]This is the instruction for the house on the mountain top. Its entire boundary all the way around is most sacred. There: this is the instruction for the house.

[13]These are the measurements of the altar in cubits (a "cubit" is a cubit plus a handbreadth). The base: a cubit, and the width: a cubit. Its rim at its lip all around: one hand span. This is the altar's mound. [14]From the base in the ground to the lower ledge: two cubits, and the width: one cubit. From the small ledge to the big ledge: four cubits, and the width: a cubit. [15]The hearth: four cubits, and from the hearth upward, four horns. [16]The hearth—the length twelve cubits, the width: twelve cubits, made square on its four square sides. [17]The ledge—the length: fourteen cubits, with the width: fourteen, on its four sides. The rim around it: half a cubit. The base to it: one [cubit] around it, with its steps facing east.

[18]He said to me, Young man, the Lord Yahweh has said this: These are the laws for the altar on the day it's built, for offering the burnt offering on it and tossing blood on it. [19]You're to give to the Levitical priests who are of the offspring of Zadoq, who come near to me (a declaration of the Lord Yahweh) to minister to me, a bullock from the herd as a purification offering. [20]You're to take some of its blood and put it on its four horns and to the four corners of the ledge and to the rim around, and purge it and expiate it, [21]and take the bullock of the purification offering and burn it in the appointed place in the house, outside the sanctuary. [22]On the second day you're to present a male goat, whole, as a purification offering. They're to purge the altar as they purged it with the bull. [23]When you've completed the purging, you're to present a bullock from the herd, whole, and a ram from the flock, whole. [24]You're to present them before Yahweh, and the priests are to throw salt on them and offer them as a burnt offering to Yahweh. [25]For seven days you're to prepare a goat as a purification offering, daily,

and they're to prepare a bullock from the herd and a ram from the flock, whole. ²⁶For seven days they're to expiate the altar and purify it and fill its hands. ²⁷They're to complete these days, and on the eighth day and onward the priests are to make on the altar your burnt offerings and your fellowship sacrifices. And I shall favor you (a declaration of the Lord Yahweh).

⁴⁴:¹He took me back toward the sanctuary's outer gateway that faces east. It was shut. ²Yahweh said to me, This gateway is to be shut. It's not to be opened. No one is to come through it, because Yahweh, Israel's God, came through it. It's to be shut. ³As for the ruler, the ruler himself will sit in it to eat bread before Yahweh. By way of the gateway's threshold he may come in and by way of it he may go out.

In a discussion with some students, we were looking at Psalm 51 with its prayer, "Don't take your Holy Spirit from me." Someone commented, "Isn't it great to know that God wouldn't now take his Spirit from us?" I can't remember what I said at the time, but I've often wondered about that comment. Then during the time we spent in Turkey this year, I became more convinced that God not only could do so, but had done so. In that area there had been so many flourishing churches, but now virtually nothing. It applies not only to places such as Ephesus or Sardis where there's no city at all but also to places such as Pergamum and Smyrna where there are huge modern cities but virtually no church.

Having lived for weeks with Ezekiel's vision of judgment on Jerusalem, and in particular with his vision of **Yahweh**'s splendor leaving the city, I practically jumped out of my seat when I read of Yahweh's splendor returning. I knew the chapter was coming, but the reality of God's leaving had been dominating my thinking. God may leave, but that doesn't stop him coming back, even when he's said he's gone forever or when you think he has or when you know you deserve him to have done so. Ezekiel makes a threefold link between the splendor of

God that used to be in the temple but left, the splendor that appeared to him in **Babylon**, and the splendor that he sees returning. The departure is devastating. The appearance in Babylon is comforting and encouraging; you might wonder whether God has indeed finally abandoned Jerusalem and is simply going to live among the exiles. Over future centuries, and until our own day, the descendants of **Israel** have lived all over the world, and for the past two millennia there have always been more spread around the world than living in the land. God has been among them there. If you're living in Ezekiel's day, you might wonder whether being scattered through the whole world is the regular situation for them. In a sense it was, and it facilitated their being the people of Yahweh as it brought about a spread of the acknowledgment of Yahweh to which Ezekiel keeps referring. But Yahweh's commitment to this land and city and temple made it impossible simply to abandon it. Such abandonment would leave a hole at the center of the story.

So Ezekiel sees Yahweh's splendor return there. The story of the temple's restoration in Ezra-Nehemiah makes no reference to Yahweh's splendor filling the temple, as it did when Solomon's temple was built. Later Jewish teaching notes ways in which the rebuilt temple fell short of Solomon's temple, and one is the absence of the "Dwelling" (a way of referring to God's splendor). There was surely a sense in which God fulfilled his promises of his presence given through Ezekiel and other prophets, yet the pattern that appears in other promises reappears here. God did something, yet not everything.

Whether God does everything or just something, there needs to be a response from people, and the nature of the response plays a part in determining what kind of fulfillment they receive. Ezekiel emphasizes that it's no use simply going back to their old ways. There needs to be no more immorality—that is, unfaithfulness to Yahweh in having "affairs" with other gods. That requirement overlaps with the comments about the kings. The king's palace in Jerusalem had adjoined Yahweh's palace, which easily became an adjunct to it, like a royal chapel. In keeping with the stress on **sacredness** over against ordinariness, the distinctive sacredness of Yahweh's palace needs to be safeguarded, as is suggested by the shutting of gateways (not to keep Yahweh in but to keep alien elements out).

That need is underscored by the fact that kings were commonly buried near the palace, and therefore near the temple. The fact that death and Yahweh have to be kept separate made that practice another infringement of the principle of separating the sacred and the **ordinary**. Yet further, one of the expressions of religious "immorality" in Jerusalem was the making of offerings in honor of dead people, which was associated with seeking their guidance and seeking the help of other deities. The community needs a proper sense of shame at those features of its past life so it can be the proper recipient of Yahweh's **teaching** about his house.

The instructions about the construction of the **altar** are again difficult to follow in detail. In thinking about the altar in the Old Testament, we have to put out of our mind the altar in a church, which a priest stands behind. The priest stands upon this altar. It's a four-story structure, five meters high, ten meters wide at the bottom, and narrowing to six meters wide at the top. The top platform is the "hearth," where the priest would burn the animal (which had been slaughtered on one of the tables mentioned earlier in the vision). The hearth has horns at the corners. It would be inevitable that the altar's constituent parts had been in contact with things that were defiled, so Yahweh goes on to prescribe the ritual for **purifying** it so it may be properly set apart for its role in temple worship. The altar is cleansed by the application of the blood from an animal that has been used in a purification sacrifice. Prescribing the animals for the ritual as "whole" means not being able to offer an animal that has something wrong with it.

EZEKIEL 44:4–27

Who Can Properly Minister?

⁴He brought me by way of the northern gateway to the front of the house. I looked, and there—Yahweh's splendor was filling Yahweh's house. I fell on my face. ⁵Yahweh said to me, Young man, give your mind, look with your eyes, listen with your ears to all that I'm going to speak with you regarding all the laws for Yahweh's house and all the instructions for it. Give your attention to the entrance into the house with all the exits from the sanctuary. ⁶You're to say to the rebellious, to Israel's household: The Lord Yahweh has said this: You have plenty of all your outrages, Israel's household, ⁷in your bringing foreigners, uncircumcised in spirit and uncircumcised in flesh, to be in my sanctuary, to make my house ordinary when you present my food, the fat and blood. You've contravened my covenant with all your outrages. ⁸You haven't kept the charge of my sacred things; you've appointed them as people to keep my charge in my sanctuary for you.

⁹The Lord Yahweh has said this: No foreigner, uncircumcised in spirit and uncircumcised in flesh, is to come into my sanctuary, of any foreigner who's among the Israelites. ¹⁰Rather, the Levites who went far from me when Israel went astray (when they went astray from me, following their lumps) will carry their waywardness. ¹¹In my sanctuary they'll be ministering with oversight at the gateways of the house and ministering to the house. They'll slaughter the burnt offering and the sacrifice for the people. They'll stand before them to minister to them. ¹²Because they used to minister to them before their lumps, and to Israel's household they were obstacles that tripped them into waywardness, therefore I've raised my hand [to swear] concerning them (a declaration of the Lord Almighty) that they'll carry their waywardness. ¹³They're not to come near me to act as priests to me or to come near to any of my sacred things, to the most sacred things. They're to carry their shame, the outrages that they performed. ¹⁴I shall make them guards in charge of the house, for all its service and for all that's done in it.

¹⁵But the Levitical priests who are descendants of Zadoq, who kept the charge of my sanctuary when Israel's household went astray from me, they may draw near to me to minister to me. They may stand before me to present the fat and blood to me (a declaration of the Lord Yahweh). ¹⁶They're the ones to come into my sanctuary. They're the ones to draw near to my table to minister to me, and they'll keep my charge. ¹⁷When they come to the gateways of the inner courtyard they're to wear linen garments. They're not to put wool on themselves when they minister in the gateways of the inner courtyard and inside. ¹⁸Linen attire is to be on their head and linen pants around their waist, but they're not to put on anything sweaty. ¹⁹When they go out to the outer courtyard (to the outer courtyard to the people) they're to take off their garments in which they were ministering, lay them down in the sacred rooms, and put on other garments, and not make the people sacred by their garments. ²⁰They're not to shave their head or grow long hair, but definitely to trim their heads. ²¹No priest is to drink wine when he goes into the inner courtyard. ²²They're not to take a widow or a divorcée for themselves as wives, but rather to take a girl from the offspring of Israel's household or a widow who's a priest's widow.

²³They're to teach my people [the difference] between the sacred and the ordinary and enable them to know [the difference] between the clean and the defiled. ²⁴In connection with a dispute, they're the ones to stand to make a decision; they're to decide by my decisions. They're to guard my instructions and my laws regarding all set occasions, and to keep my Sabbaths sacred. ²⁵A person isn't to go in to someone dead, except that he may defile himself for father or mother, son or daughter, brother or sister (who hasn't come to belong to a man). ²⁶After his cleansing they're to count seven days for him, ²⁷and on the day he comes into the sanctuary, into the inner courtyard, to minister in the sanctuary, he's to present his purification offering (a declaration of the Lord Yahweh).

I read that a Baptist seminary in the South ran degree programs for inmates in state prisons, some incarcerated for very serious charges, and that twenty-eight inmates had been ordained. Can one imagine them having a ministry "outside"? A friend of mine left the ministry after acknowledging that he was addicted to porn. Can one imagine a church calling him to be its pastor? In 1985, a Santa Barbara teenager was involved in a murder. In prison he studied for ordained ministry and was ordained as an Episcopalian priest. The victim's father thought he should remain in prison; he could preach to people inside. After twenty years he was released and became rector of a San Francisco church, where he was subsequently suspended from the ministry for sexual abuse and committing adultery with a parishioner.

Ezekiel is concerned about the role in the temple that's open to ministers who've been unfaithful in the past, though he's concerned not with individuals but with the **Levites** as a group. Attempting to trace the history of the priests and the Levites involves connecting a number of widely spaced dots. The Old Testament gives the impression that worship in the various sanctuaries spread throughout the country involved even more unfaithfulness to Yahweh than worship in Jerusalem. It also associates the Levites' ministry with those various sanctuaries. So Yahweh rules out the Levites' involvement in priestly ministry (in the narrow sense) in the temple. It's partly a safeguard against unfaithfulness recurring. It's partly a disciplinary move, to avoid treating a group that had been defiled in a way that suggested that its actions didn't matter.

It's also a practical measure. In these chapters Ezekiel combines visionary and metaphorical material with material that looks more like instructions for straightforward implementation, and it's difficult to be sure in distinguishing between these. It doesn't make much difference for us; even where he intended straightforward implementation, its significance for us is what it indicates about how God looks at topics such as ministry. Ezekiel doesn't mention the problem of having too many people of priestly status to use in the technical priestly

work of the temple. He does mention another problem. Foreigners used to have jobs in the temple, fulfilling positions
such as guards and other menial tasks. Ezekiel doesn't say that
the only people who can be involved in the temple's work are
native-born **Israelites**. He does say that people who are physically and spiritually uncircumcised shouldn't be involved. The
temple must give up hiring such foreigners just to meet its
practical needs. Those are the roles that Levites can fulfill. The
Levites might not have been too thrilled with this information; when Ezra took his party to Jerusalem, no Levites wanted
to come (see Ezra 8).

Priestly work proper (offering sacrifices) is to be confined
to Levites descended from Zadoq, one of the leading priests in
David's day. The surprise about the chapter is the declaration
that they'd "kept the charge of my sanctuary" when other Israelites were unfaithful. Ezekiel has described how the temple has
been as apostate as those other sanctuaries. One would have
assumed the Zadoqites were involved in that apostasy. Ezekiel
is implying that it was not so, and it seems unlikely that he
didn't know the real truth or that he's telling us a deliberate
lie (even if he was a Zadoqite himself and was building up the
position of his family by means of this vision). The Zadoqites
evidently failed to keep the temple on the right track; but
maybe they lacked the **authority** to take the action that would
do so, particularly in a context where in practice the king
exercised considerable authority there.

Not surprisingly, some of the requirements of the priests
overlap with instructions in the **Torah**. Their vestments are
to be linen, not woolen, which would be sweaty—apparently
sweat would be regarded as unclean. These vestments come
to share in the **sacredness** of being in Yahweh's presence, so
they're to be left in the immediate temple area, not brought
outside, like the food from sacrifices that priests were to eat.
Priests have to avoid as far as is reasonable the defilement that
comes from contact with death, which other people didn't

have to be too concerned about. The rules about hair may also link with mourning and related pagan rites.

EZEKIEL 44:28–45:17

Supporting the Ministry

[The priests]²⁸ are to have as their own property: I'm their own property. You're to give them no allotment in Israel. I'm their allotment. ²⁹The grain offering, the purification offering, and the restitution offering—they're the ones to eat them. Everything devoted in Israel will be theirs. ³⁰The first of all the firstfruits of everything and every donation of anything, of all your donations, will be the priests'. The first of your dough you're to give to the priest, for a blessing to rest on your house. ³¹The priests aren't to eat anything that's died naturally or any prey, bird or animal.

⁴⁵:¹When you allot the country as a possession, you're to raise a donation to Yahweh, a sacred area of the country. The length: 25,000 [cubits] in length; the width: 10,000. It's to be a sacred area in its entire border, all around. ²Of this, there's to be 500 by 500 squared all around for the sanctuary, and 50 cubits as an open space all around. ³From this measurement you're to measure 25,000 in length and 10,000 in width; in it is to be the sanctuary, the most sacred place. ⁴It will be the sacred area of the country, for the priests, the sanctuary ministers, who draw near to minister to Yahweh. It will be a place for homes for them, and a sanctuary for the sanctuary. ⁵25,000 in length and 10,000 in width will be for the Levites, the ministers of the house, for them as an allotment, twenty rooms. ⁶The city's allocation: you're to give 25,000 in width, and in length 5,000, alongside the sacred donation. It will belong to Israel's entire household. ⁷To the ruler there'll belong on one side and on the other side of the sacred donation and of the city's allocation, in front of the sacred donation and in front of the city's allocation, on the west westward and on the east eastward, a length alongside one of the shares [of the clans], from the western border to the eastern border ⁸of the

country. It will be an allotment for him in Israel. My rulers are no more to wrong my people. They'll give the country to Israel's household, to their clans.

⁹The Lord Yahweh has said this: There's been plenty for you, Israel's rulers. Remove violence and destruction. Implement authority with faithfulness. Lift your expulsions of my people (a declaration of the Lord Yahweh). ¹⁰You're to have faithful balances, a faithful *ephah* [a dry measure], a faithful *bat* [a liquid measure]. ¹¹The *ephah* and the *bat* are to be one size. The *bat* is to contain a tenth of a *homer*, the *ephah* a tenth of a *homer*. The size will be based on the *homer*. ¹²The *shekel* [a measure for silver and gold] is twenty *gerahs*. Twenty *shekels* plus twenty-five *shekels* plus fifteen *shekels* are a *mina* for you.

¹³This is the donation that you're to raise: a sixth of an *ephah* from a *homer* of wheat. Give a sixth of an *ephah* from a *homer* of barley. ¹⁴The law for oil—oil [being measured by] the *bat*: one tenth of a *bat* from a *kor* (ten *bats*, a *homer*, because ten *bats* make a *homer*). ¹⁵One sheep from the flock, out of 200. [These are] from Israel's pastureland for the grain offering, the burnt offering, and the fellowship sacrifice, to make expiation for them (a declaration of the Lord Yahweh). ¹⁶The entire people of the country are to be involved in this donation to the ruler in Israel, ¹⁷but the burnt offering, the grain offering, the libation, at festivals and on Sabbaths, on all set occasions for Israel's household, are incumbent on the ruler. He's to provide the purification offering, the grain offering, the burnt offering, and the fellowship sacrifice to make expiation for Israel's household.

Our church treasurer has been urging people to make their pledges for the coming year so he can draw up a budget, and they've been slow to do so. It was the same last year, but eventually they came through. The odd thing was, through the current year the giving has been way above what people pledged. It's one reason why we've been able to have a new floor laid in our church building and have the pews refurbished (I must go now because the last set is due to arrive in ten minutes).

But our inability to raise enough in a small congregation is the reason why we had to let go of our rector.

There are some overlaps between modern Christian approaches to church finance and Israel's approach, and some differences. Ezekiel's account begins dramatically. Priests don't own land. It puts them and their families in a vulnerable position. Only if you own land can you grow food. No land, no food; you're dependent on people's charity—hence the Torah's bidding people to contribute to the needs of Levites alongside widows and orphans. These are all groups without land. It's in this sense (Ezekiel begins) that priests have no property of their own, no allotment. When the land was allocated by lot to the clans and then to the families within the clans, the priests weren't part of the distribution.

The good news is that they have God as their "property" or "allocation." It doesn't mean they "own" God—Israelites didn't exactly "own" their land. They were more like God's tenants. As they could be sure of their land, however, because no one had the right to take it from them, the priests can be sure of God and of God's provision. God ensured that provision by redirecting to the priests part of the tithes and offerings that come to him. They must resist the temptation to cook and eat an animal that has died of natural causes or been killed by another animal, when they're afraid they won't have enough to eat. The Torah's regulations lay down which parts of offerings are given to God by being burned, which parts are shared by the worshipers in an act of fellowship, and which parts are given to God but passed on to the priests as God's representatives. Things that are "devoted" are things such as a field or a donkey (the equivalent of a truck).

In this vision of the new age that's coming, the land is allocated in an artificial fashion in strips stretching from the Mediterranean to the Jordan. The central strip is a "donation" to Yahweh, an area given over to him. Within this strip, the middle part centers on the sanctuary, surrounded by an area where the priests can live, and then on one side by an area where the Levites can live, and on the other side by the city and its land. The extremes of this central strip, the land on the coast and by the Jordan, are allocated to the head of state. Ezekiel doesn't always avoid calling him a king, but often does so; the king and his people might thereby be reminded that Yahweh alone is King and/or that an Israelite ruler is to be different from a **Babylonian** king and/or that the notion of Israelite kingship has been discredited by many of the people who've occupied the position. Such implications link with the declaration that Yahweh's rulers aren't to "wrong" his people. The Hebrew verb suggests extortion and defrauding people of their property. Although it was theoretically impossible to sell your land, desperate circumstances on the part of people down on their luck, and greed on the part of powerful people, meant that Israel found ways of transferring control of land and avoiding the thrust of Yahweh's vision.

There was no allocation of land to the king under the old arrangement, which went back to the time before there were kings. Ezekiel doesn't seek to go back to those days, but providing the ruler with land removes the excuse for appropriating ordinary people's land. The land belongs to Israel's household, to its clans. As well as not dispossessing people, the ruler has the job of making sure that economic affairs are conducted fairly. He is also allocated donations from the people (we'd call them taxes), which might further leave him without excuse, and out of those donations he's also expected to underwrite the cost of many of the regular sacrifices in the temple.

EZEKIEL 45:18–46:24

Daily, Weekly, Monthly, Annually, and Spontaneously

[18]The Lord Yahweh has said this: On the first of the first month, you're to take a bullock from the herd, whole, and purify the sanctuary. [19]The priest is to take some of the blood of the

purification offering and put it on the doorframe of the house, on the four corners of the altar's ledge, and on the doorframe of the gateway to the inner courtyard. [20]So you're to do on the seventh of the month because of someone making a mistake or being ignorant. You're to expiate the house.

[21]In the first [month], on the fourteenth day of the month, it's to be Passover for you. For the seven-day festival, flat bread is to be eaten. [22]On that day the ruler is to provide on his behalf and on behalf of the entire people a bull as a purification offering. [23]For the seven days of the festival he's to provide a burnt offering to Yahweh, seven bullocks and seven rams, whole, daily for the seven days, and as a purification offering a male goat, daily. [24]He's to provide as a grain offering an *ephah* for the bullock, an *ephah* for the ram, and oil: a *hin* for the *ephah*. [25]In the seventh [month], on the fifteenth day of the month, during the festival, he's to provide in accordance with these for seven days, in accordance with the purification offering, the burnt offering, the grain offering, and the oil.

[46:1]The Lord Yahweh said this: The gateway of the inner court facing east is to be shut for the six days of work, but on the seventh day it's to be open, and on the new moon day it's to be open. [2]The ruler is to come in by way of the outer gateway's threshold and to stand at the doorframe, and the priests are to make his burnt offering and his fellowship sacrifices. He's to bow low at the gateway's terrace and go out, but the gateway isn't to be shut until evening. [3]The country's people are to bow low at that gateway door on Sabbaths and new moons, before Yahweh. [4]The burnt offering that the ruler presents to Yahweh on the Sabbath day: six lambs, whole, and a ram, whole, [5]and a grain offering: an *ephah* for the ram, and for the lambs as a grain offering a gift from his hand, and oil: a *hin* for the *ephah*. [6]On the day of the new moon: a bullock from the herd, whole, and six lambs, and a ram; they're to be whole. [7]He's to provide an *ephah* for the bullock, an *ephah* for the ram as a grain offering, and for the lambs as his hand attains to, and oil: a *hin* for the *ephah*.

[8]When the ruler comes in, he's to come in by way of the gateway's threshold, and go out the same way. [9]But when the

country's people come in before Yahweh on the set occasions, someone who comes in by way of the northern gateway to bow low is to go out by way of the southern gateway, and someone who comes in by way of the southern gateway is to go out by way of the northern gateway. He isn't to return by way of the gateway by which he came in but go out by the one opposite it. ¹⁰The ruler will come in among them when they come in, and go out when they go out. ¹¹On festivals and set occasions the grain offering is to be an *ephah* for the bullock, an *ephah* for the ram, for the lambs a gift from his hand, and oil: a *hin* for the *ephah*. ¹²When the ruler prepares a burnt offering as a voluntary offering or fellowship sacrifices as a voluntary offering to Yahweh, someone is to open the gateway facing east for him and he's to provide his burnt offering and his fellowship sacrifices as he does on the Sabbath day, and he's to go out. Someone is to shut the gateway after he goes out.

¹³With a lamb of the first year, whole, you're to prepare an offering for the day to Yahweh; morning by morning you're to prepare it. ¹⁴You're to prepare a grain offering with it morning by morning: a sixth of an *ephah* and a third of a *hin* of oil to moisten the fine flour as a grain offering to Yahweh—permanent laws, regularly. ¹⁵They're to prepare the lamb, the grain offering, and the oil morning by morning, a regular burnt offering.

¹⁶The Lord Yahweh said this: When the ruler gives a gift to one of his sons, it will be his property; it will belong to his sons. It will be their allotment as personal property. ¹⁷But when he gives a gift out of his property to one of his staff, it will belong to him until the year of release, and return to the ruler. After all, his sons—his property is to belong to them. ¹⁸But the ruler isn't to take from the people's property, defrauding them of their allotment. From his own allotment he may bestow upon his sons, so that my people may not be scattered, each person from his allocation.

¹⁹He brought me by the entrance that's by the side of the gateway to the sacred rooms belonging to the priests, facing north. There: in the far parts to the west, a place was there. ²⁰He said to me, "This is the place where the priests are to cook

226

the restitution offering and the purification offering, where they're to bake the grain offering, so as not to have them go out into the outer courtyard and make the people sacred." [21]He took me out into the outer courtyard and got me to pass the courtyard's four corners. There, a courtyard in the courtyard corner, a courtyard in the courtyard corner. [22]In the four corners of the courtyard were enclosed courtyards—length: forty; width: thirty; one measurement for the four of them set in corners, [23]with a ledge all around them (all around the four of them), and cooking places made underneath the ledges all around. [24]He said to me, "These are the kitchens where the ministers in the house will cook the people's fellowship sacrifice."

It's the day before Christmas Eve, a confusing Sunday where we live. Outside our house, contractors have been erecting grandstands for a New Year Parade. Inside our house, we've been thinking about menus for various celebrations over the next ten days. But we've also just begun the day by praying our morning prayers. In our church building, we expected to have the refurbishing well-finished for today, but it's not quite done and we have to adapt a bit. One of our laypeople called because he wasn't sure whether we count today's services as the beginning of Christmas or whether they're still part of Advent (they're still part of Advent even though we're having a Sunday school presentation of the Christmas story).

Ezekiel's chapter is a mélange, with overlapping features. It does let us see something of the equivalent dynamic of Old Testament spirituality, in terms of a daily, weekly, monthly, and annual cycle, and also occasions when people came to the temple because of something God had especially done for them. Much of the section reformulates instructions that also come in the **Torah**.

Some offerings are made in the temple "regularly," the word used to denote sacrifices made every day. By means of the priests' ministry, as morning dawned **Israel** began the day by making a burnt offering as an act of worship and commitment; the Torah speaks of a parallel offering when night falls. **Ordinary** people wouldn't usually go to the temple on these occasions (for one thing, most people lived too far away), but they'd know the offerings were being made and they could join in from a distance.

Then there are special offerings made on the Sabbath. The basic thing about the Sabbath was not worship but sanctifying the day by not trespassing on it, and keeping off it, and thus not working, but this vision of Ezekiel's is one of the few places mentioning special offerings for the Sabbath. It would be more practical for people in Jerusalem to go to the temple on the Sabbath than on other days.

There are special offerings for the "new moon," the beginning of each month, as there are for the beginning of each day. It's a reminder of **Yahweh**'s involvement with the cycle of creation. Then there's the round of annual festivals. At the new year Israel is to **purify** the sanctuary, apparently twice to make sure. For all the attentiveness of the guards in those gateways, some defilement will get into the sanctuary. Maybe someone has come to the temple after being in contact with death without knowing, or without knowing the proper way to get purified before coming. Or it might happen through the defiling effect of worshiping other gods or neglecting the needs of poor people. The provision for purification overlaps with the significance of the Expiation Day (the Day of Atonement) in the Torah. Ezekiel doesn't mention this day; he envisages a different way of achieving the same end.

On the fourteenth of the first month, March–April, there comes Passover, which leads into the Flat Bread Festival, commemorating Israel's making do with flat bread at the exodus when they had no time to let their bread rise. On this occasion, too, there are purification offerings and burnt offerings; there's also mention of the grain offering and the oil needed to mix with the grain to make the bread.

While the religious calendar thus begins with the month of Passover in spring, the agricultural year begins in the fall, when the rains come. The seventh month is thus the end of the old agricultural year and the beginning of the new year, marked by the feast of Sukkot or Shelters, which also reminded Israel of the makeshift homes they had on the way from Egypt to Canaan.

Ezekiel specifies what was needed for these festivals because one of the passage's points is to give more detail on what the ruler is expected to supply. Among other peoples the king could also be a priest, and in Israel kings often took too big a role in worship, encouraging worship that was unfaithful to **Yahweh**. These instructions concerning the ruler's involvement in worship both safeguard and contain his position. There's parallel safeguarding and containing in the rules about gifts to other people, which mustn't compromise the position of the holdings that God gives to the ruler for the benefit of the whole people. The note about worshipers leaving by the gateway opposite to the one by which they enter safeguards order in the temple area on festival occasions when very many people did come to the temple at the same time.

We've noted that fellowship sacrifices are the kind that can't be scheduled, like burnt offerings and purification offerings. People make fellowship sacrifices because they've received a special blessing or an answer to prayer and they come to celebrate in fellowship with God and with one another. These family and community celebrations (who would think of thanking God for an answer to prayer on one's own?) therefore required kitchens separate from the places that served the other sacrifices. The last paragraph realistically provides these. The flexibility that belongs to the fellowship sacrifice extends to some other aspects of the sacrifices. Ezekiel refers to "a gift from his hand" and to what his hand attains to, phrasing that suggests what a person is willing and able to give in a particular context.

EZEKIEL 47:1–23

Life-giving Waters

[1]He took me back to the doorway of the house. There, water was going out from under the house's terrace, eastward, because the front of the house was to the east. The water was going down from under the right side of the house, south of the altar. [2]He took me out by way of the northern gateway and took me around by way of the outside to the outer gateway, the way facing east. There, the water was flowing from the right side. [3]As the man went out eastward with a line in his hand, he measured a thousand cubits and got me to pass through the water, water ankle-deep. [4]He measured a thousand and got me to pass through the water, the water being knee-deep. He measured a thousand and got me to pass through the waist-deep water. [5]He measured a thousand, a wash that I couldn't pass through because the water had risen, swimming water, a wash that couldn't be passed through. [6]He said to me, "Have you seen, young man?" and got me to go and return to the wash's bank. [7]As I returned, there—on the wash's bank, very many trees, this side and the other side. [8]He said to me, "This water's going out toward the eastern region and going down to the Steppe and coming to the sea, to the sea of polluted water. The water will become healthy. [9]Any living being that moves will live wherever the wash goes, and the fish will be very abundant because this water comes there. It will be healthy, and anything will live where the wash comes. [10]Fishermen will stand by it. From En-gedi to En-eglaim they'll be a place for spreading nets. In kind their fish will be like the fish of the [Mediterranean] Sea, very abundantly great. [11]But its swamps and marshes won't become healthy; they're given over to salt. [12]By the wash there'll grow, on its bank this side and the other side, every tree for food. Their foliage won't wither, their fruit won't come to an end. By their months they'll produce, because their water is going out from the sanctuary. Their fruit will be for food and their foliage for medicine."

[13]The Lord Yahweh said this: This is the border by which you're to give out the country to Israel's twelve clans (Joseph:

[two] allocations). ¹⁴You're to share it out (each the same as his brother), that which I raised my hand [to swear] to give your ancestors. This country will fall to you as your own. ¹⁵This is the border of the country. On the northern side: from the Great Sea by way of Hethlon, Lebo, to Sedad, ¹⁶Hamat, Berotah, Sibraim (which is between the border of Damascus and the border of Hamat), Hazer-hattikon (which is on the border of Hauran). ¹⁷The border will be from the Sea to Hazer-enon, the border of Damascus and north, northward, and the border of Hamat, with regard to the north side. ¹⁸The east side: from between Hauran and Damascus and Gilead and Israel's country, the Jordan, you're to measure from the border to the Eastern Sea, regarding the eastern side. ¹⁹The southern side: to the south from Tamar to the waters at Meribot-qadesh, the Wash, to the Great Sea, regarding the southern side, to the south. ²⁰The western side: the Great Sea from the [southern] border to opposite Lebo-hamat. This is the western side. ²¹You're to divide up this country for yourselves among Israel's clans. ²²You're to allot it as personal property for yourselves and for the aliens residing among you who've had children among you. They're to be like natives among the Israelites. With you they'll receive lots in the property amid Israel's clans. ²³In the clan with which the alien resides, there you're to give his property (a declaration of the Lord Yahweh).

There was water flowing from under the terrace of our building yesterday, forming a river in the garage. It was not life-giving water and it was not good news. The building is forty years old and nowadays that's apparently longer than you expect plumbing to last. We're also being urged to reduce our water consumption, because our area would be desert if we didn't import water from elsewhere, and we import it not only to take long showers but also to sprinkle it on lawns to make them look like England.

Jerusalem gets enough rain but the clouds from the west empty themselves on its mountain chain. East of the city, it's desert. You plunge from Jerusalem 4,000 feet in fifteen miles until you're way below sea level at the Dead Sea. The Jordan waters flow into this sea and depart only by evaporation, leaving their chemicals behind so that the water smells unpleasant, tastes worse, feels painful on any broken skin, but can also be healing and make it impossible to sink. Nothing grows except at one or two oases. En-gedi is halfway down the Dead Sea. En-eglaim is perhaps the other oasis by the sea, En-feshka, near Qumran.

Ezekiel's vision portrays a transformation of a desert landscape. His visions have incorporated a set of practical, down-to-earth instructions that could be implemented in a rebuilt temple and a restored city, but the closing chapters remind us that they are indeed visions, like the earlier chapters. They're designed to communicate **Yahweh**'s purpose and Yahweh's expectations, but they aren't a program for human implementing or an announcement of what Yahweh literally intends to do.

This chapter's implication is that the temple as the special location of Yahweh's presence is the source of new life for the entire country, and specifically for areas that seem dead. Its promise is thus parallel to that of the valley of dry bones. Yahweh can bring the dead back to life, and can do it to the land as well as the people, though it's typically down-to-earth of Ezekiel to recognize that the Dead Sea isn't all bad. While there'll be an implication that the people will need to give themselves to the rebuilding of the temple, the vision is more a promise that the return of Yahweh's splendor there will make the temple the source of life again for the land and the people. The talk of trees and fruit (and of rivers of water flowing) reminds one of the creation story and suggests that God is renewing the land in such a way as to fulfill his original creation purpose.

On the west and east, the borders of the country are the obvious ones, the Mediterranean and the Jordan. On the north, the border runs approximately from Tyre to the sources of the Jordan. On the south, it runs westward from the bottom of the Dead Sea. The specification thus compares and contrasts with other Old Testament accounts of the country's borders, and with the situation today. It excludes the area east of the Jordan once allocated to Gad, Reuben, and part of Manasseh, which will receive allocations west of the Jordan. It covers the modern boundaries of Israel and Palestine, plus a corner of Lebanon at the northwest and a corner of Egypt at the southwest. The variation within the Old Testament shows that there was nothing eternally fixed about the boundaries of the country, though the idea that there was a country in this region that Yahweh had promised to Abraham and given to **Israel** was all-important.

The chapter's final note affirms that membership of Israel's clans isn't purely ethnically based. While Ezekiel's vision bans the employment of foreigners in the temple, it refers to people uncircumcised in spirit and flesh, employed to do jobs that Israelites might not want to do. What of foreigners who've shown they want to associate themselves with Israel on a permanent basis by having resided in Israel long enough to have children? They're a different matter. In connection with the allocation of the land, they're on equal terms with native-born Israelites.

EZEKIEL 48:1–35

Yahweh-Is-There

[1]These are the names of the clans. At the northern end, by the side of the Hethlon road to Lebo-hamat, Hazar-enan, the border of Damascus to the north by the side of Hamat, from the eastern side to the Sea will belong to it: one, Dan. [2]At Dan's border, from the eastern side to the western side: one, Asher. [3]At Asher's border, from the eastern side to the western side: one, Naphtali. [4]At Naphtali's border, from the eastern side

to the western side: one, Manasseh. ⁵At Manasseh's border, from the eastern side to the western side: one, Ephraim. ⁶At Ephraim's border, from the eastern side to the western side: one, Reuben. ⁷At Reuben's border, from the eastern side to the western side: one, Judah.

⁸At Judah's border, from the eastern side to the western side, will be the donation that you raise, width and length: 25,000 [cubits], like one of the allocations from the eastern side to the western side. The sanctuary will be in the middle of it. ⁹The donation that you raise for Yahweh—length: 25,000, width: 10,000. ¹⁰It will belong to these: the sacred donation to the priests, on the north: 25,000, on the west the width: 10,000, on the east the width: 10,000, and on the south the length: 25,000. Yahweh's sanctuary will be in the middle of it. ¹¹What's sanctified will belong to the Zadoqite priests, who kept my charge, who didn't go astray when the Israelites went astray, as the Levites went astray. ¹²It will belong to them as a donation out of the donation from the country, most sacred, at the Levites' border. ¹³The Levites, alongside the priests' border—length: 25,000, and width: 10,000 (the entire length: 25,000, and the width: 10,000). ¹⁴They're not to sell any of it. A person isn't to exchange or transfer the firstfruits of the country, because it's sacred to Yahweh.

¹⁵The remaining 5,000 in width by 25,000 in length: it's ordinary [land] for the city, for dwellings and for pasture. The city will be in the middle of it. ¹⁶These are its measurements: the northern side: 4,500; the southern side: 4,500; the eastern side: 4,500; and the western side: 4,500. ¹⁷The pasture will belong to the city, northward: 250, southward: 250, eastward: 250, and westward: 250. ¹⁸What remains in the country alongside the sacred donation will be 10,000 eastward and 10,000 westward. It will be alongside the sacred donation, and its produce will be for food for the city's servants. ¹⁹The person who serves the city—from all Israel's clans they'll serve it. ²⁰The entire donation, 25,000 by 25,000 square, you're to raise, the sacred donation together with the city's allocation. ²¹What remains will belong to the ruler, on this side and on the other side of the sacred donation and the city's allocation. From in front

of the 25,000 of the donation to the eastern border, and on the west from in front of the 25,000 to the western border, alongside the allocations, will belong to the ruler. The sacred donation and the sanctuary belonging to the house in the middle of it, ²²and apart from the Levites' allocation and the city's allocation amid what belongs to the ruler, between Judah's border and Benjamin's border will belong to the ruler.

²³The rest of the clans, from the eastern side to the western side: one, Benjamin. ²⁴At Benjamin's border, from the eastern side to the western side: one, Simeon. ²⁵At Simeon's border, from the eastern side to the western side: one, Issachar. ²⁶At Issachar's border, from the eastern side to the western side: one, Zebulun. ²⁷At Zebulun's border, from the eastern side to the western side: one, Gad. ²⁸At Gad's border, to the southern side, southward: the border will be from Tamar to the waters at Meribat-qadesh, the Wash, to the Great Sea. ²⁹This is the country that you're to allot as property to Israel's clans. These will be the shares (a declaration of the Lord Yahweh).

³⁰These are the city's exits. On the northern side, the measurement is 4,500 [cubits] ³¹(the city's gateways will be by the names of Israel's clans), three northern gateways: one the Reuben gateway, one the Judah gateway, one the Levi gateway. ³²On the eastern side, 4,500, and three gateways: one the Joseph gateway, one the Benjamin gateway, one the Dan gateway. ³³On the southern side, the measure is 4,500, and three gateways: one the Simeon gateway, one the Issachar gateway, one the Zebulun gateway. ³⁴On the western side, 4,500, their three gateways: one the Gad gateway, one the Asher gateway, one the Naphtali gateway. ³⁵All around is 18,000. The city's name from now on will be Yahweh-Is-There.

I've just read a Christmas letter from two friends who've moved with their two children from a city near ours to a seven-acre farm 700 miles away, where they rely on solar power and an emergency generator, and their water comes from a well. I'm a city boy, myself, and I love the opportunity and the excitement. Yet I know that God started things off in a garden (it would be better to call it a farm, though). And I know that the city is a place of poverty, inequality, crime, and loneliness. Just last week we visited a juvenile detention center to help run a Christmas party; our section were all city teenagers about to be sentenced to years in prison for murder. It happens in the country, but one suspects it happens more in the city.

I'm therefore as excited by the closing sentence of Ezekiel as I am about the paragraph in chapter 43 that describes **Yahweh**'s splendor returning. The city's name will be Yahweh-Is-There. Ezekiel doesn't mean the road signs will be changed, any more than Matthew 1 means Jesus will be "called" Immanuel as his personal name. The **name** refers to the reality, not merely the label. The city will be the place where God is. It will be such a contrast with the city Ezekiel has known. Its rebellious and oppressive nature didn't make it look like one where Yahweh lived. Its destruction reflected God's departure and its loss of the protection that came from his presence. But Yahweh is committed to being there again.

The first and third paragraphs in this closing chapter simply list the clans according to their land allocation. The allocations come in strips from the Mediterranean to the Jordan, listed from north to south. Whereas originally Levi had counted as a regular clan, it had become the priestly clan, but people who traced their descent back to Joseph could be linked with his two sons; **Ephraim** and Manasseh both became clans, which preserved twelve as the total number. The division into strips—ignoring the physical nature of the country—again makes clear that Ezekiel isn't talking literal geography. The point is that the land is allocated and that every clan gets its fair share, if one ignores the different sizes of the clans. The division by clans makes another point. In Ezekiel's day, nearly all the clans don't exist. **Judah** and Benjamin exist, and a few people could trace their origin to one of the other clans, but as entities they went out of existence decades or centuries ago. Allocating the country to the twelve clans is an extraordinary act of hope. Or rather—as it's Yahweh who speaks—it's an extraordinary promise and invitation to hope. Yahweh really is committed to **Israel** as a people. Given that the nature of the allocation suggests it's inherently figurative, it helps us hold onto this promise as a commitment to the people of God in its various parts.

Between the listing of the six northern and the six southern clans comes another description of the central strip (the "donation" or reservation) occupied by the sanctuary, the priests' and **Levites'** areas, the city, and the ruler's allocation. There's an order about this new land, with the sanctuary at the center.

GLOSSARY

altar

An altar is a structure for offering a sacrifice (the Hebrew word comes from the word for sacrifice), made of earth or stone. It might be relatively small, like a table, and the person making the offering would stand in front of it. Or it might be higher and larger, like a platform, and the person making the offering would climb onto it.

Assyria, Assyrians

The first great Middle Eastern superpower, the Assyrians spread their empire westward into Syria-Palestine in the eighth century, the time of Amos and Isaiah. They made **Ephraim** part of their empire; then when Ephraim kept trying to assert independence, they invaded Ephraim, destroyed its capital at Samaria, transported its people, and settled people from other parts of their empire in their place. They also invaded **Judah** and devastated much of the country, but they didn't take Jerusalem. Prophets such as Amos and Isaiah describe how **Yahweh** was thus using Assyria as a means of disciplining **Israel**.

authority, authoritative

English translations commonly translate the Hebrew *mishpat* with words such as *judgment* or *justice*, but the word suggests exercising authority and making **decisions** in a broader sense. It's a word for *government*. In principle, then, the word has positive implications, though it is quite possible for people in authority to make decisions in an unjust way. It's a king's job to exercise authority in accordance with **faithfulness** to God and people and in a way that brings deliverance. Exercising authority means making decisions and acting decisively on behalf of people in need and of people wronged by others. Thus speaking of God as judge implies good news (unless you are a major wrongdoer). God's "decisions" can also denote God's authoritative declarations concerning human behavior and about what he intends to do.

Babylon, Babylonians

Previously a minor power, in Ezekiel's youth Babylon took over as the regional superpower from **Assyria** and kept that position for nearly a century until conquered by **Persia**. Prophets such as Ezekiel describe how **Yahweh** was using the Babylonians as a means of disciplining **Judah**. Their creation stories, law codes, and more philosophical writings help us understand aspects of the Old Testament's equivalent writings while their astrological religion also forms background to aspects of polemic in the Prophets.

cherubs

Cherubs were not cute baby angelic figures (as that word suggests in modern usage) but awe-inspiring winged creatures that transported **Yahweh**. There were statues of them in the temple; they thus pointed to the presence of Yahweh there, enthroned invisibly above them.

commitment

The word *commitment* corresponds to the Hebrew word *hesed*, which translations render by means of expressions such as "steadfast love" or "loving-kindness" or "goodness." It's the Old Testament equivalent to the special word for love in the New Testament, the word *agapē*. The Old Testament uses this word to refer to an extraordinary act whereby a person pledges himself or herself to someone else in some act of generosity, allegiance, or grace when there is no prior relationship between them and therefore no obligation to do so. It can also refer to a similar extraordinary act that takes place when there is a relationship between people but one party has let the other party down and therefore has no right to expect any continuing **faithfulness**. If the party that has been let down continues being faithful, they are showing this kind of commitment.

decision, see authority

Ephraim, Ephraimites

After the reign of David and Solomon, the nation of **Israel** split into two. Most of the twelve Israelite clans set up an independent state in the north, separate from **Judah** and Jerusalem and from the line of David. Because it was the bigger of the two states, politically it kept the name Israel, which is confusing because Israel is still the name of the whole people of God. In the Prophets, it is sometimes difficult to tell whether "Israel" refers to the people of God as a whole or just to the northern state. Sometimes the state is referred to by the name of Ephraim, one of its dominant clans, so I use this term to refer to that northern state to try to reduce the confusion.

evil

The Old Testament uses this word in a similar fashion to the way English uses the word *bad*—it can refer both to the bad things that people do and the bad things that happen to them, both to morally bad actions and to bad experiences. Prophets can thus speak of God doing evil in the sense of bringing calamity to people. They sometimes use the word with both connotations in the same context, pointing toward the fact that bad things often happen because people do bad things—though they know that this is not invariably so.

exile

During Ezekiel's youth **Babylon** became the major power in **Judah**'s world, but Judah was inclined to rebel against its **authority**. As part of a campaign to get Judah to submit properly to its authority, in 597 and in 587 BC the Babylonians transported many people from Jerusalem to Babylon. They made a special point of transporting people in leadership positions, such as members of the royal family and the court, priests, and prophets (including Ezekiel). These people were thus compelled to live in Babylonia for the next fifty years or so. Through the same period, people back in Judah were also under Babylonian authority. They were not physically in exile, but they were also living *in* the exile as a period of time.

faithfulness

In English Bibles this Hebrew word (*sedaqah*) is usually translated "righteousness," but it denotes a particular slant on what we might mean by righteousness. It means doing the right thing by the people with whom one is in a relationship, the members of one's community. Thus it is really closer to "faithfulness" than "righteousness."

faithlessness

A word for sin that suggests the opposite of **faithfulness**, an attitude to God and to other people that expresses contempt for what right relationships deserve.

Greece, Greek

In 336 BC Greek forces under Alexander the Great took control of the **Persian** Empire, but after Alexander's death in 333 his empire split up. The largest part, to the north and east of Palestine, was ruled by one of his generals, Seleucus, and his successors. **Judah** was under its control for much of the next two centuries, though it was at the extreme southwestern border of this empire and sometimes came under the control of the Ptolemaic Empire in Egypt (ruled by successors of another of Alexander's officers). In 167 the Seleucid ruler Antiochus Epiphanes attempted to ban observance of the **Torah** and persecuted the faithful community in Jerusalem, but they rebelled and experienced a great deliverance.

Israel, Israelites

Originally, Israel was the new name God gave Abraham's grandson, Jacob. His twelve sons were then forefathers of the twelve clans that comprise the people Israel. In the time of Saul and David these twelve clans became more of a political entity. So Israel was both the people of God and a nation or state like other nations or states. After Solomon's day, this state split into two separate states, **Ephraim** and **Judah**. Because Ephraim was far the bigger, it often continued to be referred to as Israel. So if one is thinking of the people of God, Judah is part of Israel. If one is thinking politically, Judah isn't part of Israel. Once Ephraim has gone out of existence, then for practical purposes Judah *is* Israel, as the people of God.

Judah, Judahites

One of the twelve sons of Jacob and the clan that traces its ancestry to him, then the dominant clan in the southern of the two states after the time of Solomon. Effectively Judah *was* Israel after the fall of Ephraim.

Kaldeans

Kaldea was an area southeast of Babylon from which the kings who ruled Babylonia came in the time Babylonia ruled Judah. Thus the Old Testament refers to the Babylonians as the Kaldeans.

Levites

Within the clan of Levi, the descendants of Aaron are the priests, the people who have specific responsibilities in connection with offering the community's sacrifices and helping individuals to offer their sacrifices by performing some aspects of the offering such as the sprinkling of the animal's blood. The other Levites fulfill a support and administrative role in the temple and are also involved in teaching the people and in other aspects of leading worship. In his vision of a new temple, Ezekiel gives the position of priests in the narrow sense to the descendants of Zadoq within the line of Aaron.

lumps

This is a favorite word in Ezekiel for images. These are sometimes explicitly images of gods other than Yahweh, but the word may sometimes refer to images of Yahweh. Ezekiel might see little difference between these two meanings, because making images of Yahweh is an impossible idea. Something that purports to be an image of Yahweh must in reality be an image of a different god. Whereas "image" isn't such a pejorative word, "lumps" is an insult. At best it suggests that these divine images, precious to their makers, are really blocks of wood or stone. At worst, it suggests they are lumps of excrement (the word for excrement in chapter 4 is almost the same as this word for lumps).

name

The name of someone stands for the person. The Old Testament talks of the temple as a place where God's name dwells. It is one of the ways it handles the paradox involved in speaking of the temple as a place where God lives. It knows this idea is a nonsense: how could a building contain the God who could not be contained by the entire heavens, no matter how far you could travel across them? Yet **Israel** also knows that God does in some sense dwell in the temple and that people can talk with God when they go there. They are aware that they can talk with God anywhere, but there is a special guarantee of this possibility in the temple. They know they can make offerings there and that God will receive them (supposing they are made in good faith). One way they try to square the circle in speaking of the presence of God in the temple is therefore to speak of God's name being present there, because the name sums up the person. Uttering the name of someone you know brings home his or her reality to you; it's almost as if the person is there. When you say someone's name, there is a sense in which you conjure up the person. When people murmur "Jesus, Jesus" in their prayer, it brings home the reality of Jesus' presence. Likewise, when Israel proclaimed the name **Yahweh** in worship, it brought home the reality of Yahweh's presence.

ordinary, see the comments on 41:13–42:20

Persia

Persia was the third Middle Eastern superpower. Under the leadership of Cyrus the Great, the Persians took control of the **Babylonian** Empire in 539 BC. Ezra 1 sees **Yahweh** fulfill his promises in the Prophets by raising up Cyrus as the means of restoring **Judah** after the **exile.** Judah and surrounding peoples such as Samaria, Ammon, and Ashdod were then Persian provinces or colonies. The Persians stayed in power for two centuries until defeated by **Greece.**

Philistia, Philistines

The Philistines were people who came from across the Mediterranean to settle in Canaan at the same time as the **Israelites** were establishing themselves in Canaan, so that the two peoples formed an accidental pincer movement on the existing inhabitants of the country and became each other's rivals for control of the area. By Ezekiel's day, like **Judah** they are a minor power.

purification, purify, purification offering

A major concern of the **Torah** is dealing with the **taboo** that can come on people and places. There is nothing wrong with being involved in burying someone, for instance, but you have to give the taint of death time to dissipate or have it removed before coming into God's presence. A purification rite can bring that about.

sacred, see the comments on 41:13–42:20

taboo

I use the word *taboo* to render the Hebrew word often translated "impure" or "unclean," because the Hebrew word suggests a particular quality rather than the absence of something. There are certain things that can seem mysterious, extraordinary, perplexing, and worrying. Among these are menstruation and childbirth, because they suggest both death and life. These are opposites, and God is the God of life and not of death, yet menstruation (with its association of blood and life) and giving birth (which is both life-giving and dangerous) bring them into close connection. So contact with them makes people taboo; they cannot go into God's presence until they are **purified**. Taboo also arises in other connections such as sex and worship of other deities.

Teaching, see Torah

Torah

This Hebrew word is traditionally translated "law," but this gives the wrong impression, as the word covers instruction in a broader sense. The framework of "the Torah" (the books from Genesis to Deuteronomy) is the story of **Yahweh**'s relationship with the world and with **Israel**, though the Torah is dominated by instructions. "Teaching" is the nearest English word. The Hebrew word can thus apply to the teaching of people such as prophets as well as to the instructions in Genesis to Deuteronomy. It is sometimes not clear whether it refers to the Torah or to teaching in that wider sense.

well-being

The Hebrew word *shalom* can suggest peace after there has been conflict, but it often points to a richer notion of fullness of life. The KJV sometimes translates it "welfare," and modern translations use words such as "well-being" or "prosperity." It suggests that everything is going well for you.

Yahweh

In most English Bibles, the word "LORD" often comes in all capitals as does sometimes the word "GOD." These actually represent the name of God, Yahweh. In later Old Testament times, Israelites stopped using the name and started referring to Yahweh as "the Lord." There may be two reasons. They wanted other people to recognize that Yahweh was the one true God, but this strange foreign-sounding name could give the impression that Yahweh was just Israel's tribal god. A term such as "the Lord" was one anyone could recognize. In addition, they didn't want to fall foul of the warning in the Ten Commandments about misusing Yahweh's name. Translations into other languages then followed suit and substituted an expression such as "the Lord" for the name Yahweh. The downsides are that often the text refers to Yahweh and not some other (so-called) god or lord and that the practice obscures the fact that God wanted to be known by name and instead gives the impression that God is much more "lordly" and patriarchal than actually God is. (The form "Jehovah" isn't a real word but a mixture of the consonants of Yahweh and the vowels of that word for "Lord," to remind people in reading Scripture that they should say "the Lord" and not the actual name.)

Zion

The word is an alternative name for the city of Jerusalem. Jerusalem is more a political name; other peoples would refer to the city as "Jerusalem." Zion is more a religious name, a designation of the city that focuses on its being the place where Yahweh dwells and is worshiped.